HIS-STORY OF GOOD COOKING

by

FRANCOIS BOERES,
Chef de Cuisine

© 2004 by Francois Boeres, Chef de Cuisine. All rights reserved.

No part of this book may be reproduced, stored in a retrieval system, or transmitted by any means, electronic, mechanical, photocopying, recording, or otherwise, without written permission from the author.

First published by AuthorHouse 05/26/04

ISBN: 1-4184-5960-7 (e-book)
ISBN: 1-4184-4984-9 (Paperback)

Printed in the United States of America
Bloomington, IN

This book is printed on acid free paper.

On the Cover

Vegetable aspic in wine / New York State Champagne / Assortment of vegetables with Belgian endives and 'spiral' Mushroom caps / Shish Kebab and Attelets /
Old 18th. Century pewter on fine linen from Bruge.

About the Book

Just another cookbook? No way! This. "His-Story of Real Good Cooking" by Francois... is great. One can't wait to turn over to the next page... 'peppered' with plenty of food related history, anecdotes, reflections and quotes with over 300 selected recipes, but this is only the beginning. To arouse the interest of great dishes and the one that had been overlooked by years gone by, I felt compelled to capture my 54 years of cooking into this book. All recipes are explained in an easy, leisurely, salutary and rewarding manner to the gourmet and novice alike.

I believe this book is very special and stands out by traveling through time and antiquity, passing through deMedici's kitchens, cooking up a storm in our young Republic and complete the culinary excursion through the kitchens I had worked in as a Chef and Restauranteur.

The second and last chapter describes the days of the "Great War," the years of apprenticeship, the way of life in the past... cooking in Europe and in America. The over 230 pages of 'tasty' adventures and interesting recipes from a seasoned chef should be of great value.

There is no magic about originality.
You simply take what you have seen,
read, heard, and then add Yourself.
                              Stebbins

Dedication

To my wife
Friederun
Who has endured with
great patience and
perseverance living
with a sedulous
inattentive
husband
trying to put his thoughts
into words.

Contents

About the Book iii

Dedication vii

Preface xiii

PART ONE

CHAPTER 1 ... ANCIENT FARES 1

History of Cookery 1
The Legacy of the Medici (1562-1610) 3
Henry IV and the Court of Frederick the Great 4

CHAPTER 2 ... THE AMERICAN EXPERIENCE 19

The New Englanders and an old Virginian Story 19
The Oyster Cult and the Preparation of Fish 22
The Cause of our Revolution 29

CHAPTER 3 ... THE LOST ART OF HOMESTEADING and DRINKING IN THE OLD DAYS 35

Ooh...The Farm! 35
The Way People Used to Drink 49
And Give Us Our Daily Bread 57

CHAPTER 4 ... THE AMERICAN CHRONICLES 61

George Washington 61
Jawing with George! 63
Benjamin Franklin and Philadelphia 70
Thomas Jefferson, the Planter 76
Desserts 79

CHAPTER 5. ...ABOUT VEGETABLES AND SAUCES 88

Basic White And Brown Sauces 99
Making White Sauces 102
Butter Sauces 105

PART TWO

CHAPTER 6... THE LEAN AND LOST YEARS 107

The Great War and its Consequences 107
Cheese, Dumplings, Pasta And Soup.................................109
The Evacuation and Uncle Yves 120
Living in Occupied France...122
Our Canoe Club 127
My First Paying Job...132

CHAPTER 7 ... FIRE IN THE KITCHEN.............................141

What do I want to be?..141
How I Got Myself Into the Soup..143
Serving Uncooked (Raw) Meats and Fish 161

CHAPTER 8.....GOING TO AMERICA 168

Taking the Big Boat 168
Cooking at the Pickwick Arms 171
Main Street USA...193
An Encounter 201
The Chef..201
Our Own Restaurant 203
Chef Cheng 207
Venison And All Kinds Of Birds......................................211

CHAPTER 9 .... DEVILED FARE, SUCCULENT INNARDS PLUS INDIAN AND SAFFRON DISHES.................................224

Meet Some Deviled Fare 224
Serving Innards, Respectfully 230
The Other Kitchen..234
Economics and Unexpected Guests.................................249
Preparing Quick Finger Food..251

APPENDIX..258

CONSPIRACY AND INCREDULOUS SORCERY: THE GREAT CONSPIRACY AND ASSAULT ON OUR FOOD........................258

BIBLIOGRAPHY 269

INDEX 271

Preface

Oh, your grand academic halls of gastronomy , sacred culinary temples, palatal Institutions of the past, dedicated to all ceremonial offerings of wholesome good food. My love and lure to good cooking inspired me to write stories of this memorable kitchens,...adorned with rows of shiny copper pots, pans and casseroles dangling from racks above, engulfed in steam from array's of aromatic sauces, soups of bubbling meats and fish stock cooking on the huge coal-fired stove, ready to prepare all kinds of medleys to satisfy even the most 'seasoned' customer.

The old hotel kitchen with it's subdued incandescent lights still reminds me of glistening bright "gold" dancing vividly on the white kitchen wall tiles, reflected from the glare from the fiery stove. The noise of rattling pokers and oven rings, the beat of whisks, the chopping of food on long wooden tables and the ringing of calling bells...now only a symphony of sounds in my memory. Ah...this memories, desserts of life, so they say!

Over the years I have learned from great Chefs and from quite a few good, indispensable cook books. In the past, a few Southern cook books had been a selective collection of recipes generously contributed by people in their communities. A good number of fine cook books are available today to please every taste and walks of life.

An early cook book from "Orphan" Lucy Emerson's NEW ENGLAND COOKERY had been quite a success before Amelia Simmons, also an "Orphan" took over and wrote a cook book so similar to Mrs. Emerson's. I suspect this rather a bit unorthodox. Basically, we all need books, a book is a book that came out of other books that had been written in some books, as long as each book contains original and fundamental creativity. Here

I'd like to report, to the best of my knowledge, how it really was and had been done. In addition to all the recipes here, a lot of history also is to be 'digested.'

My greatest inspiration and respect for good cooking started at home. My parents' table settings, all in sterling silver and fine china, left little to be desired; special oyster plates, escargot plates with tongs to hold the shells, fish knives for fish fillets, hors d'oeuvres and cake forks. The whole setting was enhanced with center pieces, flowers and salt-cellars. The selected wine was served in appropriate crystal glasses. Guests candid conversation often lasted until midnight as coffee was finally served.

My 54 year love relationship with cooking started in European hotels and extended through my Three Star Restaurant in the United States to end "home on the range." I trust that these old and current recipes will allure the adventurous gourmet to create great and tantalizing food fares..

Francois Boeres

*"Tell me what you eat,
 And I will tell you what you are."* Brillat-Savarin

PART ONE

CHAPTER 1 ... ANCIENT FARES

History of Cookery

To us, the time of a few thousand years in the past seems worlds apart, too remote to assimilate. We, however, do value the essence of time, a matter so dear to our lives. Citizen of ancient Rome, considered modern man, used elaborate aqueducts, great roads and laws still in use today. They lived, played and loved with the same compassion and behavior familiar to us. We have a good idea of food this ancient Roman cherished, of course with the absence of items like tomatoes and potatoes, coffee, leavened bread, and most of the pastas we know of today.

In antiquity, the Mediterranean area was known as the center of the world. The bottom of the Mediterranean Sea still is scattered with earthen amphorae from ships lost at sea used in the trade. These amphorae contained wine, olive oil, olives, honey and other liquids. Other containers held salted fish, figs, dates, anchovies, sardines from Sardinia, corints from Corinth or currants from Corans. Salami, a sausage made partly from donkey meat, covered with a grayish white skin of mold and salt, from the Island of Salami... Just as today, natural casings were used to hold sausage stuffing. These dry salcicia would keep for a long time like other dried and salty meats, an ideal seafarer's staple. Stomach and other animal skins were practical for carrying all kinds of liquids and occasionally cheese was prepared in natural casings.

Francois Boeres, Chef de Cuisine

Voluminous parties were given by wealthy politicians, patricians and warriors. Lucius Lucinius (Lucullus) the great warrior and gourmet, is remembered not only for bringing the cherry tree to the Western world, but also for his lavish parties. He loved fine pickled meats and sausage made from fowl-skin from the neck stuffed with chopped meats.

This is how the great writer and satirist Petronius described a Roman Banquet given by the rich and vulgar former slave Trimalchio.

> "The extravagant, "luscious" banquet was served by slaves supplying guests with a never ending assortment of delicacies making sure the cups of wine and "medum" (wine with honey) always were replenished. The elaborate food was brought to our tables where we gathered and laid around on semicircular benches. Here we were treated to all kinds of roasted fowl and highly embellished exotic birds, pheasants, duck-salmis and a kind of European fly-catcher, seasoned with honey, cumin and saffron. Then they served cooked ostrich brains, flamingo tongues, peacock eggs, roasted goat and lamb plus all imaginable assortments of seafood, like rock lobsters, langoustines, periwinkle snails and even a roasted hare dressed with bird wings to look like Pegasus. To top this, a whole roasted wild boar was carried in and it's belly opened. Immediately, and to our astonishment, a whole flock of birds escaped, flying around us. This was followed by a pair of roasted pigs, one stuffed with Persian figs, the other pig (the appalled guests could not believe what they saw) seemed to be cooked with everything still inside.
>
> "Now, with anger aroused to a climax, all shouting 'Where is the master of the kitchen that cooked this dreadful mess? Kill that pig!' But behold! The pig was cut open and to everyone's surprise, long ropes of delicious and fragrant sausages emerged from the pig's belly. 'He is a genius!' Sounded the accolades. 'Caius, that great master of all kitchens has done it again. Bring for him silver laurels.'"

HIS-STORY of Good Cooking

What the Romans learned about cooking from the Greeks, we learned from the Romans, and eventually some of their cookery found its way into the Medici's kitchens.

Some people eat to live . . .while others live to eat.

The Legacy of the Medici (1562-1610)

The ambiance was electrifying, like a scene out of the Thousand and One Nights. Marie de Medici was giving a party, a good excuse for her husband Henry IV of France to assemble the elite so to be informed of the latest political news or form new strategies. The huge candelabras had all been lit and pulled up to the ceiling by pulleys.

The soft silvery glare of all this light was multiplied by the reflection of the great Venetian mirrors from the enormous ballroom. The master of ceremonies a Huissier, announced the entrance of formal guests by name and status. The conversational noise level was occasionally spiked with outbursts of laughter and sporadic percussion of kettledrums from a small band.

Henry himself was now talking with his close friend and finance minister Sully, as General Bassompiere and the Cardinal of Lorraine entered, followed by the Bishop of Verdun. An envoy of Rudolf II of Hapsburg was with Brantome, Duc Laurant of Urbin chatted with Antoine Bourbon and his wife. Jaques Cujas and Francois Malherbe shared a word with master painter Phobus of Flandern and Gabrielle d'Estree, as Montaigne leaned on his cane, conversing with Giovanni Palestrina, the well-known composer of Masses. Samuel Champlain had also sent an emissary from the new province of Quebec, and now stood discussing politics with Louis Crillon and two older ladies.

It was a day of great expectations, planned down to the smallest detail. Henry's biggest problem had been the insurgent Protestants, apparently the Catholics were not pleased either .As a great ruler in a bewildered time, unfortunately was assassinated. His wife, Marie de Medici did not possess the stamina of the former Catherine de Medici (wife of Henry II) but she always gave great parties to invite famous and important people for many occasions.

Francois Boeres, Chef de Cuisine

Most importantly, Marie de Medici the hostess, had brought one of the finest cuisines from Italy into the French courts; from this time on a more cultivated French cuisine would follow.

Some servants had given up their quarters to make room for new arrivals, and slept in stables, but there still was not room enough for all. With the inns all packed, some nearby burghers and farmers had accommodated their hosts with the best of quarters, now sleeping on straw-stuffed burlap bags on the kitchen floor to serve their guests a hearty breakfast in the morning. This would include smoked bacon, fried and shirred eggs, cooked ham, grits and millet-pap, buttermilk cakes, parboiled milk, foot-long slices of bread with "running" yellow cheese and apple butter.

—

The Louvre functioned like a small city, and today that city was at the service of its guests. Each department or bureau ran like the gears of a fine timepiece, ticking away to meet the guests' needs. Dressmakers, coiffeurs, tailors and doctors were at hand. They had orangeries, fisheries, botanical gardens and even a chapel complete with its own choir master. Chevaliers and noblemen were appointed to execute different offices in the court, such as the chevalier of the king's chamber, the master of ceremonies, the keeper of the house, the stables, the kitchen or the wine cellars called L'enchansonerrie. (I would loved to have that job!) There was also the king's taster, a squire, who tasted the kings food . . just in case. Every job was meticulously performed, for any blunder could bring grave consequences. These responsibilities were taken very seriously. At a dinner party in Chantilly, given for Louis the XVI by the Grande-Conde, the Maitre d'hotel Chevalier Vatel killed himself with his sword because a main entree failed to show up on time.

Henry IV and the Court of Frederick the Great

Dinner is Served

The stage was set for the traditional dinner. Guests and members of the court stood with great anticipation, waiting by the table for the King to arrive, so they could be seated. At last the royal party entered. Marie took her place at the left side of Henry, his minister to the right. As soon

HIS-STORY of Good Cooking

as the Aumonier of the court gave the benediction, the wine was poured. Especially noteworthy was the table setting; besides silver spoons and knives, a relatively new utensil was featured—the fork, which had been introduced a few years before on the table of Henry II. We may find it hard to imagine eating an elegant dinner without a fork.

The table settings of Henry IV were different from those of other royal predecessors. Here beautiful hand-blown Venetian "crested" stem-ware replaced the old beakers and goblets. Faience china plates from Faienca, Italy now topped the old pewter plates. The tables were covered with fine linen from Bruge and Flandern, and decorated with bowls of parfum and rosewater for washing fingers.

Such a dinner could easily have included ten main dishes. The feast started with soups, turtles, fricassees, wild game, stews called salm'is, salmagundi; and continued with a fish course, which could have included carp, trout, lamprey, turbot and mullet, followed by a poultry course of white hens, swans, herons, peacocks, pigeons, small capons, pheasants and guinea hens. Next a meat course which could have included young roast goats, suckling pigs, lamb, roast beef, boiled beef and roasted saddle of deer. Side dishes included little stuffed cabbages, cheese stuffed pastry called ratons, artichokes and melons. No dinner would have been complete without flummery (a sort of gelatinous "custard" made of wheat or oatmeal) cream puddings, patisseries and cakes. After a short grace and the cleaning of the tables, dinner was finely concluded with a course of sweets, candied fruits and aromatic wines similar to what we know as cordials.

Little was recorded from the Courts of Henry IV, nevertheless, game was given a lot of attention in the royal kitchens and there had been a surprising amount served. One may say that the woods and fields were the inventory and storage of food and if needed, a highly organized hunt with strict tradition was called for. Only noblemen could participate. Villagers were notified to join as "drivers" and so called "clappers", driving and flushing out the game. The big game hunt known as wood hunting was under the "Chasseurs" (Bersarii). The low hunt was divided again into the "guarde-champaitre" (Veltrarii) in the fields. The last of these "catchiatories" was the Beverarii that hunted foxes and took care of the waterfowl.

Big game like Elk, deer, wild boar and their like were commonly hunted with horses, then brought at bay and trapped by nets and packs of hounds. This was referred to as the "Chasse au Courre." Very popular was the par-force hunting where horsemen drove big game into rows of burlap cloth fences and finished them with long spears. The small field game hunt included hares, rabbits, pheasants, partridges and even waterfowl. These were hunted with nets, trapped, flushed out with dogs or hunted with Falcons. . . called "Falconry." (In Europe we occasionally hunted with ferrets to get rabbits out of their burrows.) Small birds like ortolans, larks, railbirds, etc. were the most sought after. An average daily catch could be 300 larks, mostly caught with nets or sticks made out of birch-rods dipped in glue made out of resin, oak, mistletoe glue and linseed oil. Most birds were caught at dawn. Bird catchers in Germany are called Vogelfeanger. (You meet one of them in *The Magic Flute* by Mozart.)

Dusk announced the end of the hunting day. Rows of "bagged" game were laid down in a proper manner and sequence to tally and display. The Lord of the hunt and entourage of invited guests (here King Henry) were all lined up on horseback. Other hunters and the Chasseurs of the court all stood at attention facing the rows of game.

First came a row of foxes all lined up and stretched out on their left side. Facing the line of foxes were rows of elk, big deer and other big game all neatly lined up, lying on their right side followed by rows of hares, rabbits and all kinds of birds. The last row, facing the game and Royal guests, was a line of hunters announcing the end of the hunt with horns and drums to give salute and the last respect to the animals and its creator.

The incoming darkness of the late fall evening was lit up by surrounding torch bearers that previously had been the "drivers" and "clappers." Later, they also helped to gut and clean all the game. The head and entrails called "curee" was thrown to the pack of dogs. Leftover food from the party was given to the poor (and there were many). This tradition eventually degenerated into serving the best to the "pack" and the poor hardly anything, one of the reasons that provoked the French revolution.

About this time, firearms like "Wheel locks" were used for hunting, but they were expensive to make, so, the hunting spear blade, the crossbow and the net still dominated the field until the less expensive flint-lock was invented. This brought forward a big change in warfare, hunting and bringing food to the table.

HIS-STORY of Good Cooking

"We shall nothing but eat and make good cheer..."
                                               Henry IV

Here is an old nursery rhyme from before the time of forks...

> "I eat my peas with honey,
> I've done it all my life.
> It makes the peas taste funny,
> But it keeps them on my knife."

We are now taking a quantum leap in time. The ugliness and total destruction of the Thirty-Years War had laid the greater part of Europe in ashes. Progress and civilization had been thrown back sixty years. It was absolute genocide, with the land and its people exhausted by war and plague. Now at last, people are no more a "brick in the wall" using cannons to shot down, to destroy and conquer. By now all barren and burned out land had been replanted, restored and further reconstructed by the great ruler, FREDERICK OF PRUSSIA, KNOWN AS FREDERICK THE GREAT (1712-1786).

Religion now had a different meaning. Previously it had been 'righteous', divided and gross fanatic hate. Now merely a prayer from the heart looking up to God with deep devotion for a good future to all men. Frederick's reply to religion: "Let everyone in my Kingdom be content in his soul and happy in his own way." This idea brought religious freedom into the State. Frederick also hated to see people in bondage or being suppressed. This hindered progress and economy, therefore he abolished all serfdom and bondage. He called the slave trade to America a shame and outrage and got very upset that the neighboring Frederick of Hessen sold out over 16,000 of the best able young men to George III of England, who employed them trying to subdue the American Revolution. For each man, Frederick of Hessen received 50 Thalers and an additional 50 Thalers if the man was lost

Francois Boeres, Chef de Cuisine

in battle. The payoff money was "stamped" in 1778 with a star on one side and referred to as the "Blood-Thaler."

The old Fritz (Frederick) was of medium stature, loved chamber music, played his flute and composed music for the flute. He got up early and retired late, this all by schedule. His fiery, penetrating eyes revealed a refined disposition of great discipline, polite manners connected with skillful decision of character. He was indeed a modest and modern man.

In his own words, "I know God is the light and the reason this is embedded in my heart. . . naturally the only truth and cleanliness and therefore my duties are reflected to my Christian morals and that is enough for me."

Now, why did I bridge over the epoch from Henry IV to Frederick II? I thought it to be a good jump from yesterday to a more modern time. If I had been inclined to probe into the reign of Louis the XIV in Versailles, I would not even know how to start with its grandeur and ostentatious accomplishments of this awesome "Sun King." It would be an encyclopedia all by itself.

"The whole of virtue consists in its practice."
-- Cicero

It was a time for a new class of explorers in ideas, of writing, architecture and of great composers. Spoken French and French protocols belonged to the courts. German literature was generally written in either Latin or French. Even German scholars considered the German language a kind of "wall flower" because so many different dialects of German were spoken in old Prussia. Some authors, such as Herder, were beginning to break the ice with a distinctively German literature, others, such as Leipnitz, were so disgusted by the German "mischmash" that they only wrote in French.

A new German movement was already deep in progress, people like Lessing (an admirer of Frederick), Wieland, Schiller and that "witty" giant Goethe (the other Shakespeare) now all had cleared the way to establish a distinctively German language so it could be taught proudly on the same level in accord with English. (Today, Shakespeare is the most read in Germany.)

HIS-STORY of Good Cooking

Old German . . .
ES LASST DIE BUCHSENMEISTEREY/
OB SIE ZWAR EDEL IST/ UND FREY/
NICHT VIEL MIT WOHLGEBUTSTEN WORT/
SICH BRINGEN AN EIN RICHTIGS ORT/
DIE EINFALT IST DAS MEISTERSTUCK/
UA GFERBTE WORT SEYN/ DA IST TUCK.
Josephum Furtenbach
anno 1627

Frederick was like a breath of fresh clean air after a storm on a hot sultry summer day, still walking over the same old ground as the sun emerged. Being of bold character, he still could not jump over his own shadow and was suspicious of any new German movement.

So, the old "Fritz" as the people called him, had built near Potsdam, a lovely baroque chateau he named Sanssouci, that literally means "A place without worry." Here he entertained some of his favored people like Voltaire, Racine, Diderot, Kant, Klopstock and great composers like Haydn, Johann Sebastian Bach and son Emanuel Bach, who was Frederick's court composer. Famous musicians like Amadeus Mozart played here.

As one would expect, Frederick's kitchen had the best to offer when it came to scrumptious dinners, ostentatious so called Piece-Montees and other fine trappings. Today's huge built up wedding cakes are testimonial to the once so popular Piece-Montees made out of pastry and cold aspics. By now, the kitchens of the courts became more and more logical and organized. As Frederick tried, he came to like such things as coffee, but stood by his good beer and wine and best of all, his snuff, and often asked to be served regional dishes commonly known in the Bourgeois kitchen!

Frederick had given a party in honor of his friends and Generals who helped him to win the Seven-Year Silesian War

The invited guests here were Zeithen,[1] Keith, Lehwaldt, Marwitz, Anhault von Dessau, Henry de Gatt, Prince Heinrich, Wilhelm von Seydlitz, Ferdinand vonBraunschweig and Court minister Pollnitz. The conversation

---

1. Her...Von Zeithen fell asleep at the table and his favored, the old 'Dessauer' Leopold had long "departed".

was highly "spirited" and again and again, the past came alive. The chef in charge was Monsieur Noel de Perigueux. (From Casanova's memoirs)

The fare served on this occasion ......
Turbot with capers and brown butter
Boiled beef garnie with virgin cabbage
Roulades, called lost birds (verlorene voegel)
Pheasants with quince and pomegranate
Truite (trout) au bleu with chateau potatoes
and braised leeks in drawn butter
Calf's head with vinaigrette and pickles
Smoked eels and Kassler-ripchen (smoked pork chops)

There was a lot more to follow, but it all finished with a big Yuzzahh!

The wine served: a Hungarian Tokay, a Mosel Speatauslese and a nice Moselbluemchen spiked with woodruff.
Music: sonatas by Handel and Frederick's own flute concerti.

Here we have noticed the presence of a new "vegetable"-the potato.
Frederick pressed hard to endorse this prolific and nutritious vegetable through the years of famine like the one in 1751, here he sent wagon-loads of these tubers for food and planting so to prevent further disasters, but it took some convincing.
In France, the agronomist Parmentier had been commissioned by the King to introduce the potato. He made great progress. All dishes now called Pamentier are made of potatoes.
The "Sanssouci" chateau was the place for many festivities and banquets displaying great fire and waterworks, swans and dragon-like creatures hurling sparks and fireballs that made spectacular glary reflections from the enormous spring-fountain.
Some people listened to the nearby concert, others promenaded in the Royal Gardens. A row of tree arcades and a maze of Arbor Vitae hedges revealed only the sound of amusing "coqueteries" but concealed many stolen kisses. The place was crammed, people everywhere, Frederick's wife Elizabeth Christina, the builder of the palace; Knobelsdorf. Jean Jaques

HIS-STORY of Good Cooking

Russeau, Von Cramer, Herzberg, Von Leuthern, Herzog Leopold von Dessau, talking with the prince Augustus William, Marquis de Mirabeau discussing finances with Jaques Neckar of France. Louise von Schwerin was seen with Von Kleist and Mademoiselle von Pannewitz with Fritz Wendel. Inside the chateau, a chamber music played to the soft penetrating voice of Laura Farinelli, later to be subdued by soprano Anna Prickering with her fioritures and ritournelles.

Note: Anna Prickering received a piteous "back-of-the-hand" applause and silently sneaked out the back door eating anything that night

Great ..... _____

CHERRY CAKE

You will need:
    2 cans dark Bing or Tartariam cherries
    2/3 cup semi-sweet cherry wine
    1/4 cup cherry preserves
    3 Tblsp. cornstarch dissolved in a little water
    2 Tblsp. lemon juice
    Sandtorte or Genoise cake

Drain cherries, reserve juice. Combine cherry wine with cherry preserves and all the cherry juice. Bring to a boil. Reduce heat and simmer for 2 minutes, add all the cherries and bind with cornstarch dissolved in water.

With a wooden spatula, stir the mixture till thickened, add lemon juice. Cool and place in the refrigerator.

Cut a Sandtorte or a Genoise cake into 3 layers. Divide the cherries, put half on the bottom layer, half on the middle layer, then cover with the top layer of cake.

Make the **Whipped Cream (Cream Chantilly)** just before serving.

Francois Boeres, Chef de Cuisine

You will need:
- 1/2 pint of heavy cream
- 1/2 cup powdered sugar, sifted
- trace salt
- few drops of vanilla

Combine the above in a chilled mixing bowl, whip to stiff peaks. Spread cake with whipped cream using a spatula or pastry bag with a big star tip

Optional: Shredded dark chocolate, Kirsch brandy.

STEAK HENRY IV

Prepare Bearnaise (look for Bearnaise)

You will need:
- 7 to 8 ounce filet or Sirloin properly trimmed.
- Bacon and string or toothpick for securing
- Salt
- Coarse pepper from a peppermill.
- Croutons
- Shallots or onions - chopped
- Butter
- Mushrooms
- Artichoke bottoms or hearts
- Salt
- Madeira wine

Wrap steak with a slice of bacon and secure with string or toothpick. Sprinkle with salt and pepper.

In a heavy pan, 'broil' steaks on both sides nice and brown till drops of juice appear...or to your preference. Deglaze the pan with water and save the 'jus'. Remove the string or toothpick and dress on a warm platter on top of a crouton.

In a smaller pan sauté chopped shallots or onions in butter with a few firm selected fresh mushrooms and a can of cut up artichoke bottoms or

hearts. Add a little salt, Madeira wine and the collected pan juice. Reduce and pour over the steaks. Top with the Bearnaise and serve immediately.
Serve with Parisian croquette or stuffed baked potato.

Wine: A good Chateau Neuf du Pape or Pommard.
Music: Chants to the sound of Palestrina or Harp concertos by Petrini.

SALPICON

Salpicon are fricassee or ragout type dishes made from cubed veal, beef, fowl, ham, shrimp, lobster or other boiled meats. Some recipes call for mushrooms and liver, occasionally, boar and deer Salpicon was served. Certain bland meats like veal used in white Salpicon can be improved by adding a trace of mustard, lemon juice or capers. Before the days of potatoes and cornstarch, sauces were 'bound' with seared flour, egg yolks or fine ground breadcrumbs, this was known as "liaison."

WHITE 'RAGOUT' SALPICON
2 - 5 servings

You will need:
1-1/2 pounds blanched or parboiled meat cut into small cubes
2 onions cut 1/2 inch thick
2 crushed garlic cloves
1 bay leaf
Salt; White pepper; Thyme; Chervil; 1 Clove
2 Tblsp. flour
Madeira or dry sherry
Beef or chicken stock

Sauté or boil lightly the meat; add onions, bay leaf and spices. Stir in flour. Add white wine, Madeira or dry sherry and enough beef or chicken stock to cover the meat. Cook till done.

Francois Boeres, Chef de Cuisine

DARK OR RED SALPICON

This is made about the same. Some recipes call for a blonde 'roux'.[2] The stock or the bouillon from the same meat is used, occasionally red wine is added. Burned caramel and Hungarian pepper may be used. Cook meats slowly till done and serve in a terrine. Garnish with parsley, selected firm mushrooms or half moon croutons made of buttered toasts or puff pastry.

Wine: La crima Christi
Music: Dardanus Suite by Rameau

"The best prophet of the future is the past."
Byron

Here are a few of Medici's dishes.

The once popular **SAMAGONDIS** or **SALMAGUNDI** is kin of today's antipasto. This could be reheated meats dipped in a vinaigrette surrounded with hard-boiled eggs, salted meats, white chicken meat, anchovies, capers, herrings, artichokes, marinated little onions, small veal balls and often garnished with cock-combs.

To prepare...COCK-COMBS

Cock-combs, once considered a real delicacy, now have become more of a real gastronomic curiosity. Start preparation by pricking the combs with a needle and soaking them in fresh water. Press all liquids out with the fingers and heat them up, keep warm enough to handle. Rub combs with salt till skin separates then boil for about 25 minutes till soft. Skewers are "spiked" with cock-combs, truffles, quail eggs, crawfish, etc. This so called **"ATTELETS"** do make a statement on any buffet or food display.

---

2. Blond Roux: Fat and flour roasted to a light blond color with stock added.

The **SALAME condire** was done with pickled meats and the **SALAME conditi** made with seasoned meats and prepared with fresh fatback or pork cut into slivers, then turned over in coarse salt and set aside for a day. On the following day, small slices of tender cubed beef are mixed in to the pork with additional salt, crushed peppercorns, chopped garlic and some white wine.

The **SALAMI** as we know it today is a mixture resembling 'dough' made of different meats. This could be made of half pork and half beef mixed with spices, crushed peppercorns, salt and occasionally mixed with saltpeter. This mixture is stuffed in casings to be air-dried or lightly smoked.

SALMIS OF DUCK A LA BIGARADE
(With orange sauce)

Preparing Salmis makes me think of dishes very popular centuries ago. Most Salmis were cut up pieces of fowl, braised or cooked like a stew. Older recipes usually started: **"Take a pair of chickens, pheasants, ducks, partridges. For smaller birds take six ortolans, quails, snipes or six of this or that."**

'Peking' ducks have a lot of fat, so they should be roasted very crisp. After the ducks have been defrosted, take out all innards like hearts, necks and roast them with the ducks. Save and sauté the livers last to be served with the sauce. Sprinkle ducks inside and outside with **salt, pepper, rosemary, sage**.

Roast for almost two hours or until crisp.

While the ducks are roasting, peel the skin of **one orange** with a potato peeler. Cut into thin strips and cook for 5 minutes in boiling water with a little **sugar** added. Add this to the sauce last and save the **orange sections** for decorating.

Take the ducks out of the oven and discard all fat. Cut roasted ducks in half. Chop off all the backbones, take out breastbones and return them with all other trimmings into the pan. Keep the ducks in a warm place.

Pour **4 cups of light chicken stock** into the pan and reduce to half. The boiling will loosen all the black concentrated drippings in the pan that turn into 'jus'. (This is called deglazing.) Strain the 'jus' in a casserole and add:

Francois Boeres, Chef de Cuisine

1/4 cup sugar (lightly caramelized preferred), the juice of 1 lemon, 3 cups of orange juice.

Slowly reduce for 20 minutes and add some **butter**. Thicken with **cornstarch** if needed. The half ducks are to be cut into 6 pieces (which makes 24). Before serving, heat up the duck pieces and cover with the orange sauce. Add orange peels and sections. **Port or orange liqueur** may be added and if you want to "flambee," go ahead...do it!

SALMIS OF PHEASANTS

Season the cavity of **two pheasants** with: **sage; chervil; marjoram; celery salt; pepper and a few juniper berries**.

Top with a piece of **bacon** and place the pheasants in a roasting pan surrounded with **celery and onion cuts**.

Roast them in a 375 degree oven for 50 minutes to an hour, basting frequently.

Take the pheasants out. Cut off all backbones and breastbones and return them to the roasting pan. Add **2 cups of chicken bouillon** and cook for 15 minutes. Strain the sauce and add **one cup of Port or Madeira**. Cut up all the legs (bones removed) into small pieces and add to the sauce with some quartered **mushrooms or chanterelles**. Simmer for 15 more minutes and lightly bind the sauce with a little **cornstarch**.

Before serving, slice the breasts and place them on a platter on top of **croutons**, cover with the sauce and garnish with **fresh basil, kumquats, currant berries or quince marmalade**.

Serve with sweet-sour red cabbage and' mixed' rice pilaf.

Wine: Macon Rouge or a Valpolicella
Music: The Golden Cockerel by Rimsky Korsakov

ROULADES OR VERLORENE VOEGEL
(Lost Birds)
Serves 6

Cut **six 7 ounce steaks** from beef round. Pound and flatten steaks almost as thick as a pencil and 6 inches wide (or let your butcher do this).

Combine **5 ounces of ground beef** with **5 ounces of sausage**. Add **fresh chopped parsley, a little salt, pepper and a dash of white wine**. Mix well.

Arrange the steaks on the table, place on each a slice of **bacon**. Divide the stuffing evenly on the steaks. Roll them up tight, squeeze in the ends to keep the stuffing inside. Bind the roulades with twine. Brown the roulades in a big casserole in **lard or margarine**. Take them out and set aside.

In the same casserole fry: 1/2 sliced **onion;** 1 sliced **carrot;** 1 crushed **garlic clove,** and 2 Tblsp. of **flour**.

Stir for a few minutes then add a **pinch of celery salt, very little salt, pepper and a tsp. light beef bouillon**. Cook for a few minutes then add the roulades. Add enough water to cover the roulades.

Cover the casserole and slowly cook for 2 hours or till done, turning over a few times. Remove the twine before serving.

These can be served with cauliflower, Brussel sprouts, glazed onions, mashed or plain parsley potatoes.

Wine: a Petit Sirah or a Pomerol
Music: by Vivaldi

VEAL PAUPIETTES OR BRAGGIOLES
Serves 6

1 pound and 14 ounces of tender veal. Trim and reserve 5 ounces for the stuffing. Slice the remaining 1 pound - 9 ounces into 12 veal steaks and pound thin using wax paper. On each "veal escallop" place a thin piece of **ham (I prefer Prosciutto type)**. Lay them out and stuff them with a mixture of: **3 ounces ground beef suet, 5 ounces of chopped veal, 1/2 cup chopped fresh breadcrumbs, 1/2 chopped medium onion, 1 ground slice of bacon, chopped parsley, some garlic salt and a pinch of thyme**. Roll and close braggioles firmly and fasten with toothpicks.

Dip them in **flour** and sauté lightly in **lard or margarine** in a casserole. Add **light beef stock** till all are covered. **White wine and green peppercorns** may also be added. Cover and cook for over an hour or till done. Place braggioles in a hot bowl and remove toothpicks. Reduce sauce and garnish

Francois Boeres, Chef de Cuisine

with fresh **broccoli**. Some use **tomato sauce** and others like **white sauce with fresh Parmesan.**

Wine: a Chenin Blanc or a Pinot Blanc
Music: Richard Tucker, the Soul of Italy

CHAPTER 2 ... THE AMERICAN EXPERIENCE

The New Englanders and an old Virginian Story

Long before the Pilgrims, the Indians followed the rite of spring by emerging out of their winter dwellings and woods, to dig clams and collect all kinds of seafood by the beach to make a clam bake. This was a great and happy event for families and people who had not seen each other for some time. While the fire was prepared, cherrystone clams, fresh oysters, sea urchins and other mollusks were eaten raw.

The real clambake started as a distinctly bucolic feast, now often inflated and 'degenerated' into a multitude of different versions, handled and cooked by so called "Bake Masters" to feed heaps of natives and a never ending flow of tourists. No matter what, they all love the clambakes and lobsters. Some of those big clambakes are set up with barrel like contraptions or big boxes, here, everything imaginable is added and served on the side with the "Clambake": fowl, steaks, chops, sausages, salads, beer, wine (Chablis or Rose), champagne, Indian puddings and ice cream. Some conventional New Englanders still are bound to create the old traditional:

NEW ENGLAND CLAM BAKE

To make the pit, dig over a two feet hole in the sand big enough for all the food. Line the hole with big stones like a dry well.

In this "Pit", make a good steady fire from drift wood so to heat the stones as hot as possible. Then most of the embers are removed. The "pit" is lined with a few inches of **rockweed** on which all kinds of **clams: Quahogs, little**

Francois Boeres, Chef de Cuisine

necks, razor and soft shell are placed. Another layer of **rockweed** is laid out with the "catch of the day"; **striped bass, cod, mackerel, lobster, also crabs and corn** are added.

Finally, topped off with the last layer of **rockweed** covered with a tarpaulin and sealed all around with sand and stones. Occasionally, chickens can be added.

Now the real spirit of the clambake begins, sodas, coffee, beer and wine are passed around, some have brought guitars, banjoes and mandolins, others are engaged in conversation, singing or just playing games. Several hours later, it is time to remove the tarpaulin. A puff of steam escapes, mixed with the aromatic scent of seafood and rockweed. The feast begins. Also **salt potatoes** are traditionally served.

The party lasts until late in the evening, with a spectacular sunset. The chill of the late evening has arrived and some are leaving already, thinking about the next clambake that had been going on for centuries.

Note: Some clambakes can be made and cooked a day ahead. It still be hot the day after and all the fish bones will be soft. I always love this parties!

INDIAN PUDDING
Serves 6

Scald a **quart of milk** in a double boiler. Stir in **1/4 cup of yellow corn meal**, cook for 15 minutes, stirring until thickened. Add **1 cup molasses, ½ tsp. ground ginger, ½ tsp. cinnamon and 1 tsp. salt.**

Bake in a preheated oven at 325 degrees for 1-1/2 to 2 hours. Stir pudding only once, after the first hour.

THE AMERICAN EXPERIENCE

The Puritans who came to New England were a devout, hardworking, nervous, "agrarian" people primarily experienced in raising vegetables in "raised beds" and determined to raise farm animals they had brought with them, like: pilgrim geese; goats; chickens; pigs and cheeps. Cows were brought later in 1634 by Governor Winthrop.

HIS-STORY of Good Cooking

By decree, common people could not hunt in Merry Old England, and therefore had no experience doing so, neither were they fishermen. To make things worse, during the first year of winter half the people perished and most of the animals brought for breeding purposes had to be slaughtered. Luckily, the Natives taught them a few tricks to survive and gave them some food, so the legend of Thanksgiving. The less, here we had smart people who learned fast to do the best in a precarious environment, out of this was born Yankee Ingenuity.

Groups like the Shakers were so pious and chaste they barely proliferated and eventually became obscure. Visiting a Shaker village in Massachusetts today, one will find only empty buildings now used as Museums. (What a shame, they could have had a lot of fun dancing, singing and then some more . . .)

The Southern Shore, on Roanoke Island, Virginia, was first colonized by a group of venturesome English settlers, about twelve years before the Jamestown settlement. This first group of settlers headed by Lane, soon were hopelessly lost in the wilderness. Later the island was settled again by a group headed by White. In a short time White took a leave of absence and left his people to their disastrous fate. They probably would have been saved if they attempted to "farm" the land, but all were lost and left no trace.

The Virginian Company of London had encouraged and financed an expedition to establish a Colony to build a Merchant Fleet on the Southeastern Shore. Captain Smith arrived here in 1607 to build the frontier settlement, Johnstown, that progressed for two years.

After most of the resources had been exhausted, Smith also took a leave of absence. By now, shelter, clothing, gun powder and other bare essentials were gone. Governor Lord De La War tried to save the Colony, but it was as if a bad curse had befallen them. Disease, cold, exposure, hunger, high mortality and filthy living quarters finally lead to plague, followed by Indian massacre. It all had been a hopeless venture. It was not until 1630 that a more successful settlement on the York River, Yorktown, was established. To conclude their bungles and mishaps, the Jamestown "Kamikaze" mission was led by pure ignorance and disorder. These people came to a pristine shore of a new continent with an abundance of all kinds of food. Some now have disappeared, like elk, bison, deer, turkey, fox, quail, woodcocks, squirrels and even timber wolves and panthers.

Francois Boeres, Chef de Cuisine

The whole sea, as some early travelers described, was virtually boiling with fish that could be clubbed with an oar or just netted out. Here we had bluefish, croakers, rockfish, shaden, menhaden and so many more. All kinds of seafood washed up on shore....

.... most still alive. These could be flounder, blue crabs, horseshoe crabs, clams, sea urchins, oysters, big turtles and as reported by these early travelers, over three foot long lobsters. The best eating, they said, were one foot long. To the first settlers, the greater part of these strange looking animals did not appeal to them.

Successful hunting and catching of wild animals can often lead to plain survival, like "fishing" with nets, smoking meats, catching small game like birds, trapping rabbits and most of all, getting along with the Natives.

"The world stands aside to let anyone pass who knows what he is doing."

— Dave Jordan

The Oyster Cult and the Preparation of Fish

It is regrettable, that these days such a fine mollusk like the oyster failed to sustain its popularity. This world wide Epicurean delight was served in every place and table in Europe and America alike. Oysters were so prolific they had been depicted in many paintings by great masters like Velazquez, Vermeer, Frans Hals, Heda and others. The ever staggering popularity of oysters started here in the time of Madison. By 1880, the oyster industry employed 53,000 people and three times as much business as the cod or the whaling industry. Eighty percent of the oysters "raked" came from natural beds around the Chesapeake Bay. Regular oyster-cart trains, called the Oyster Express were driving with great speed day and night to bring tons of oysters to towns like Philadelphia, Baltimore and New York because everyone loved oysters. The big cities had rows on rows of oyster bars. On sidewalks, one could see mountains and mountains of oyster-shells in front of oyster bars and restaurants. Some of these shells eventually got ground up for fertilizer, crushed to decorate garden paths or just dumped on nearby shores to gain new land. Fresh shucked oysters in cans were available to prepare stews and chowders served in restaurants. Most oysters came fresh and alive in their shells, the only way known to oyster lovers. Most of these mollusks were eaten fresh, right out of the half shell and served with lemon juice and horseradish or with a vinaigrette. Others were served on "horseback," pickled, mixed with poultry dressings, smoked, steamed and used in chowders.

The common American oyster is known as Ostrea virginia. The European oyster (Ostrea edulis) is circular, flat and easy to open. We also have the smaller Olympic cold water oyster (burido), the thick shell Australian oyster and some from Japan. In the past, many oysters from natural oyster beds came from the Pocomoke Sound of Maryland. Great pressure and demand of the ever growing population has changed this. It would be impossible to supply food to the world in its natural state. Today, only artificial breeding will render it possible to keep up with supply. The Chinese had done this before the Romans. Today, not only oysters, but also mussels and lobsters are raised by artificial breeding. New "Oyster Plantations" are set off with young oysters, called seeds, in beds or so called ponds. Because of preservation and pollution, most of these mollusks and other seafood now are protected and monitored by government agencies.

CLAMS CASINO
12 medium clams per person

Soak and rinse **clams**. Shuck clams by holding clam in the palm of your hand so you can firmly insert the sharp side of the clam knife between the bivalve to open. Remember, the quicker you move, the easier they open. Try to save all the juice, especially if eaten raw.

Dress clams in the half shell on a fireproof plate with **rock salt**. Chop little squares of **onions, green peppers, scallions and pimentos** (canned pimentos can be used). Sauté in **butter** till glazed, adding a little **salt, pepper (some like to add hot tabasco)**. Top mixture over clams and cover with a piece of **bacon**. You can also pour the remaining bacon fat with butter added over the clams. Bake in 425 degree oven for 10 minutes. Serve hot.

Wine: a Californian Claret

Francois Boeres, Chef de Cuisine

"HANGTOWN" OYSTERS

Dip fresh shucked **oysters** in **flour** and fry in **butter**. Sauté **onions** in **butter**, add **eggs with cream** and scramble with oysters. Serve on **buttered toast**.

The Long Island Blue-point oysters from the great South Bay were considered one of the finest. In time the natural beds became depleted. The bay man had to transplant oyster seeds from Chesapeake Bay. It takes four years to grow a marketable size oyster. The Blue-point Company was repudiated to be the biggest exporter of oysters. In the beginning of the '50's the production fell dramatically, but the company was saved by the poor mans oyster....the clam.

BOSTON BROILED DEEP-SEA SCALLOPS

Cut the very big ones in half so they all will be done at the same time. Place in a broiling dish topped with **fresh breadcrumbs** mixed with **thyme, basil, lemon juice, white wine and melted butter**. Broil in the oven for about 10 minutes at 380 degrees or until done. Please don't overcook, scallops should be soft inside. Add a little **salt** and **pepper**. Dress on the plate with **buttered toast** cut into two triangles, serve with **lemon wedges** and a sprig of **parsley**.

Note: Bay scallops cook and are done very fast.

Wine: Riesling-Sylvaner, an Orvieto or a Mersault.
Music: Gaité Parisienne by Offenbach.

MUSSELS A LA MARINIERE

Rinse a small bag of **fresh mussels** in water and scrape off the beards and barnacles, if any. In a pot, sauté in **butter, fine chopped onion, half stalk of celery, 3 scallions and a clove of garlic, minced**. Add mussels with **1-1/2 cups dry white wine** and **some pepper**. Cover and cook until all shells are opened. Don't overcook, discard any unopened shells. Place steamed mussels in a serving bowl. Add **fresh butter** and **chopped parsley** to the boiling juice, bind slightly with **potato starch** and pour over the mussels. The best way, divide mussels in separate soup bowls and pour the sauce over so it can be eaten like a soup or dunked with French bread.

Wine: A rosé or a semi dry wine.

BASS OR POMPANO PAPIOTTE

Cut out a heart from wax or freezer paper the size of a placemat so when folded it makes a pocket. Place **fish** with all ingredients into the pocket, seal properly and tight by crimping the edges (each overlapping). Brush paper pocket with oil and cook in 425 degree oven for about 18 to 20 minutes, or until done. (Don't overcook.) The pocket will look all bloated up. To serve, cut pocket open with a shear, sprinkle with **chopped parsley** and serve immediately.

The main ingredients for a papiotte can be any preferred **fish with butter, lemon slices and some chopped scallion.** With the fish you might use **crabmeat/shrimp/ mussels/oysters/scallops or fresh sliced mushrooms.**

Wine: Pouilly Fume or Fuisse
Music: Carmen by Bizet

NEW ENGLAND CLAM CHOWDER
Serves 4

2 dozen steamed Quahog clams, chopped fine OR 1-14 ounce can of clams
1/4 lb. salt pork cut in small dice
Butter or margarine
1 Tblsp. flour
3 cups water
3 russet potatoes cut in cubes
1 big or 2 small chopped onions
2 finely crushed cloves of garlic
Few coarsely cracked peppercorns
Traces of marjoram and thyme
2 cups of light cream
Chopped chives and parsley

In a casserole fry salt pork till glazed. Add some butter or margarine, all the onions and garlic. Sauté for a minute and stir in flour, water, all the clams and clam juice, the potatoes, crushed pepper and a trace of marjoram and thyme. Cook slowly for 30 minutes. Add 2 cups of "half and half." Cook for 15 minutes more, or until thick enough. Serve with chopped chives and parsley.

FRESH OYSTERS ON THE HALF SHELL

Oysters are best opened with an oyster knife. Hold oyster in a towel in your left hand, secure on the table. Stab knife into the side of the hinge and pry open by rocking motion. Slide the knife under the top shell and separate from the mussel....discard the top shell, cut and loosen oyster from its shell so it can easily be consumed. Clean oysters from all debris left from shucking. If there is a problem, rinse the oysters in the shell under slow running water so not too much juice is lost. Most of it still is retained in the oyster pouch, don't do this to clams, because the juice will be lost forever.....I hear some people shuck oysters by breaking the tip from the thin side of the oyster and opening them from there.....one guy told me, telling them a funny joke will open them laughing....well, whatever. Nevertheless, in no time everyone can open oysters with ease.

To serve, place shucked oysters on a plate laid out with rock salt. The live oyster should be fresh, any already open or unpleasant smelling oysters should be discarded. Serve with lemon wedges, cocktail sauce with horseradish or a vinaigrette.

This is a time for champagne!

OYSTERS ON HORSEBACK

Partially fry **bacon slices** in a pan, drain and cut in half, long enough to wrap around an **oyster**. Fasten with a toothpick and bake in the oven at 450 degrees for 10 minutes. Place oysters on buttered toast triangles.

ANGELS ON HORSEBACK

Marinade **oysters** 4 hours in **white wine** with **crushed garlic and parsley**. Wrap in **raw ham (like Prosciutto)** heat in the oven and place on **buttered toast triangles** and cover with **hollandaise**.

Wine: Frascati or a Sauvignon Blanc
Music: Jesse Norman: With a Song in my Heart.

OYSTERS POULETTE

Melt **4 Tblsp. butter** over medium fire. Add **4 Tblsp. flour, 1/2 cup of white wine, 1 cup heavy cream, a pinch of English mustard, white pepper and a trace of salt**.
Sauté **6 ounces of quartered fresh mushrooms** and add to the sauce, simmer and thicken with **1 tsp. of cornstarch dissolved in water**. Add **2 egg yolks** mixed with a **little cream**. Stir, heat up slowly, but, to prevent separation, don't let it come to a boil. Lightly sauté **oysters in butter with a little lemon juice**. Place them in the shells and top with the sauce. Garnish with **parsley and lemon wedges**.

OYSTERS BIENVILLE

... are done the same way as above except **sliced scallions** are added and the oysters are topped with **breadcrumbs mixed with Parmesan cheese and melted butter**, bake in oven for 12 minutes till golden.

OYSTERS ROCKEFELLER

Dress **fresh shucked oysters** on the half shell on a Pyrex plate with **rock salt**. Sauté **3 medium onions, chopped and 3 chopped garlic cloves with a trace of cayenne, some salt and pepper**. Divide the mixture over the oysters, using a small spoon and top with **fresh cooked spinach** then sprinkle with breadcrumbs mixed with butter and parsley. Broil in the oven for 15 minutes until golden.

Francois Boeres, Chef de Cuisine

OYSTERS MEDIATRICE

.... highly appreciated by our Revolutionary soldiers! Drain and dry **oysters** on a paper towel, dip in **flour, beaten eggs and spiced breadcrumbs**. Fry golden brown on both sides and place oysters on a piece of **toasted French garlic bread**. Pour **Russian dressing** mixed with **Tabasco and horseradish** over the oysters.

Here you need beer!

A buddy of mine boils the **oysters** in **half and half cream** with **salt, pepper,** and **butter**, then thickens with a little **cornstarch dissolved in water**...that's all...simple, but good.

Drink: Cold Sancerre or Liebfraumilch
Music: by Johann Strauss

FILET DE SOLE DORADE OR PIRATE
Serves 4

Select **6....over 6 ounces fresh filets de sole** and marinate them for 1 hour in **white rum**. Cut 9 ounces **small fresh mushrooms** in half. In a **little white wine** steam **1 pound of mussels**, remove them from the shell, save the juice and set aside.

Blanche **2 cups of medium shrimp**, remove just before boiling, cool, peel and set aside.

In a large pan sauté **1 medium chopped onion in butter, add ½ cup of dry white wine, the mussel juice, 1/2 cup of water, thyme, 1 bay leaf, a squirt of lemon juice and white pepper.** Boil for 10 minutes.

Cut sole filets in half (makes 12 pieces, 3 per person) and roll them into little 'turbans.' Secure them with toothpicks. Place soles in the pan with the sauce, cover and slowly cook for about 10 minutes, or until done.

Before serving, take out the sole, remove the toothpicks and carefully place them on a warm platter. Finish the sauce by adding **1/2 cup of cream**. Thicken the sauce with **cornstarch** if needed. Add all the shrimp, mussels, juice and mushrooms. Reheat and pour the sauce over the sole. Garnish with a few **toasted bread triangles, lemon slices and parsley.** Serve with long grain rice.

HIS-STORY of Good Cooking

This recipe is from Uncle Victor.

Wine: California Traminer or a Macon Blanc
Music: Die Moldau by Smetana

Make not your sauce until you've caught your fish.

Anon.

The Cause of our Revolution

The Happening

In the North, the seeds to our Revolution had already been planted on the arrival of the first Pilgrims, the Puritans, who had fled England from religious persecution, followed by Quakers, French Huguenots and German Palastines (Amish, Mennonites, etc.).

In the South, in the year 1649, the same year as Charles I's execution, one hundred Cavaliers fled to the Colony of the old Domain of Virginia to build plantations and became the leading families of Virginia.

I go as far as to say that food is related to our country's destiny. After all, America had been discovered to find a new route for expensive spices (the silk-route had often been blocked by the Turks).

The Rebellion, that eventually turned into a Revolution, started in Boston with a "Tea Party." I regret to say, seldom mentioned, we had one right here in New York, near Murray's Wharf and Sandy Hook, on the 22nd of April, 1774, eighteen cases of tea were dumped overboard by "Mohawks." Another ship was forced to leave with a shipment of tea.

How did this came to be? First, one have to understand this conglomeration of events. Wars between the French and the English Colony had put England under heavy financial burden and the money had to come from some place, and the only place money could be collected by heavy taxes was the colony.

Another was the great rift between England and the Colony that had been molded for the past 150 years to emerge as a self-reliant new civilization. This identity had always been jealously observed by our English "cousins."

Francois Boeres, Chef de Cuisine

The standards of the average American colonist compared to England was beyond comparison when it came to wealth, comfort, culture and abundance of food. The colonists lived a freer and happier life, until a British campaign of taxes and tyranny interfered with existing laws and trade that was unjustly tampered with. One needed a Royal license to trade with Indians. Big marketable trees for building ships became Crown property. (Our first flag had a pine tree). Nails, pots and pans could not be manufactured in quantity and had to be brought over from England because business there left much to be desired. Also, heavy taxes on pewter and silver was implied (pewter was sold by the pound and silver by the ounce). A silversmith, Paul Revere, got very upset and so were the "Natives" who became very restless, because if you push a man against a wall, he will fight back and when a man's spirit is broken, a great physical force is unleashed.

Well, we all know the rest of the story.

Cooking in Fireplaces

In 1850, President Fillmore renovated the White House with hot and cold plumbing and installed a new-fangled "Machine"— a cooking stove. The cooks all quit. They only wanted to work with the old fireplace.

By 1860, everybody that had a decent home had or wanted a cooking stove.

Open Hearth or Fireplace Cooking

Till the mid 19th century, fireplaces had been primarily used for heating and cooking. This was the place families gathered, meals prepared and cooked and the radiant heat from the fireplace made a house a warm, cozy and livable home. The trouble with some fireplaces built was anyone that built them had inherited this experience, or just built them based on tradition. Most worked reasonably well, while others let a lot of smoke inside rooms or used an unreasonable amount of firewood, mainly that the greater part of the heat went right up the chimney. Sitting near a fireplace, this radiant heat could burn or roast your legs, and make your face red hot while your back froze. (This led to the popularity of high-wall benches.) Bigger fireplaces in kitchens weren't any better. The big "throats" in chimneys dispersed heat too fast. A man who really knew fireplaces was Ben Thompson, later known as Count Rumford. Ben Thompson was a real genius and reminds me a lot of Ben Franklin also born near Boston. He investigated everything that moved or stood still.

A devoted Royalist, he had been affiliated with General Gage of the King's troops in Boston, so he did not join the "insurgent crowds and soon left for London. Thompson had so many titles, too numerous to mention here. He was knighted in England, highly decorated in Poland and Strasbourg, elected to the highest position in the Bavarian courts and declared a Count. Most people think of doing things. Thompson made everything happen. The most important, Thompson's knowledge of fireplaces, had no equal. Thompson had a long history of working with the science and the problems of proper combustion and soon was called to fix chimneys in London and everywhere. By correcting the slope of the firebrick and the "throat" often fitted with a damper, and of course, most important, the smoke-shelf that rested on the slope in the chimney.

Ben Franklin was aware of this, so he built a cast iron fireplace (or stove), with built-in dampers and doors, to be placed right into fireplaces. In Europe, Franklin had encountered many variations of fireplaces and their kin. With a studious interest, he was aware of the construction of early stoves.

In northern Europe, built-in Kachel-Ofens still are popular today. Then we had built-in stone constructed cooking stoves with fire holes on top for pots and kettles. This kind of stove was the most advanced pioneer before the cast iron stoves used by our great grand parents. These built-in cooking stoves had fireboxes, ash pits and dampers that resembled stoves known in Roman times. Most early "Patrician" kitchens had no flue or chimney, just a round sky light opening in the center of a vault like ceiling. In the past, referring to the Victorian time, great attention was given to building fireplaces, especially to long lasting "firebricks", bonded with not more than a quarter of an inch of a special formula mortar and lime.

Fireplace cooking was done in kettles or "caldrons" hanging from an iron bar or pivoting crane, to adjust heights, some cranes had two hooks, rings or a chain. More costly and very much sought after today is a cremaillere, an iron bar that can be adjusted by "rack" teeth. Frying eggs or pancakes in the morning was done in a long handled pan called a "spider" that rested on a trivet (three legged stand). A common fireplace inventory consisted of "end-irons," pokers, shovel, broom, bedpan, toasters and many other

Francois Boeres, Chef de Cuisine

variations found in different estates. Some estates of the well-to-do used brass or iron clock jacks that when wound up, turned the roast. A metal cover, called a "curfew" often was used to save and keep the embers for the next morning.

Fireplace roasting on the spit requires a lot of patience and perseverance. A mid size turkey takes about one and a half hours, small birds about 20 minutes on a gridiron (grill on a stand). Roasting on a spit is a tedious job of slow turning and basting. The best thing to do is to pay attention, not get involved in any other chore or extended conversation. Turning and basting is of the essence. If you do this right, the result can be an exquisite, nutty, smoky and crisp flavored roast to remember. A reflector-shield for roasting is recommended, do not forget the drip pan and the pot for basting. Flour mixed with spices was occasionally sifted over the roast to be basted. A 12 pound fresh ham will take about 4-1/2 hours.

A roast piglet should not be over a month old and a roast pig not more than a year. The pig to be roasted is seasoned inside and outside with salt, pepper, marjoram and sage. The skin should be "scored" with a few incisions. Pig roasting on the spit requires a few turns every two to four minutes, and of course can be faster. A roasting piglet averages about 2-1/2 to 3 hours to roast on the spit. As pork is prone to burn easily, special mindfulness is to be given. Once pork and other roasts are scorched, the process is almost irreversible. It can never be cooked properly thereafter and takes longer. Most roasts on the spit should be joined or tied. Allow a quarter hour for every pound roasted. Mutton is best in spring and lamb in July or August.

Boiling meats in kettles or so called "caldrons" should be started with cold water and cooked very slow to assure good flavor and tenderness, occasionally skimming also is important.

I have seen, I regret to say, some people cooking all kinds of food so vigorously to spill and splash all over, messing up everything nearby. This is one of the biggest desecrations of food in a kitchen and should never happen in any household. The right way to cook, not only in fireplaces, but everywhere, is food that "bubbles" slowly on the fire, in plain English . . . simmering!

In his inaugural address, our eighth president, Van Buren, described the new American race as an aggregate of human prosperity, surely not elsewhere to be found. Van Buren came from an affluent society and loved big parties. His table settings were immaculate and of high order. He certainly could have matched that of any European Emperor. There we had solid gold plates, fine crystal and the best of silverware and all the trappings to match the finest in cooking. In the time of Van Buren, we had such an elaborate collection of food, known to us today as an international cuisine and used in many households.

If the great master, August Escoffier . . . called the King of Chefs and the Chef of Kings . . . had lived then, he could easily had written, organized and compiled his culinary masterpieces that became one of the most sought after cookbooks—in other words, the culinary Bible.

Some of the earliest cookbooks in America were written in London by Sarah Harrison in 1755 and by Hanna Glasse in 1760. Some cookbooks around Williamsburg were "The Gentle Woman's Companion," 1772 by Sue Carter. Testimony to more elaborate cooking can be found in the "Virginian Housewife" printed in 1824 by Marie Randolph or "The Direction of Cookery," 1828 by Elya Leslie.

In the North, elaborate food was served on many occasions and no money was spared on weddings. Boston and New York had many (and still have) renowned houses and fine hotels. But somehow the ambiance seemed constantly bequeathed with frugality, while in the Old Dominion, the "Southern Hospitality" in many estates and mansions was more relaxed. Some parties lasted for days, nothing was spared. This often led to financial disaster. Extravagant dinners compared to wealthy houses in Europe often slid toward the abyss of gluttony and disorienting hang-overs.

Here in the poet Marc Antoine's own words:

"I desire to die
in the midst of a great dinner
to be buried under the table cloth
between four large plates
and on my tombstone inscribed;
Under here lies a great poet
killed by indigestion"

from "La Rousse"

Francois Boeres, Chef de Cuisine

Nevertheless, the middle class, the average American, did take their traditional preparation of food seriously, especially on the farm, where people know the value of the food they had planted, grown and harvested with great diligence.

Did I mention the farm...?

CHAPTER 3 ... THE LOST ART OF HOMESTEADING and DRINKING IN THE OLD DAYS

Ooh...The Farm!

... **t**hat nostalgic place, that inner longing for an uncomplicated, robust life, that sublime image that forever seems to be cast in our folklore, stories and songs. In the past, there hardly was anyone not related to the farm, or farm related to any kind of work. It could be of growing, processing or the transportation of food, or connected to a cooper, miller, butcher, baker. . . in other words, America was an agrarian society and there were pioneers pressing for new land to build more farms. If it came from the farm, it was farm-fresh, wholesome, farm raised, country like bread, cheese, sausage, "griddle" cakes and all the blessings from the land. If any chicken, duck or goose was on your next menu, all one had to was to fetch one out of the barnyard and give it the. . . oh no! Please don't give it the ax, I have no idea how this ever got started. It just isn't the right way to do.

As a boy, I still remember late in 1938, Mom had brought home a live goose for the family dinner and Grandpa got the assignment of slaughtering and plucking the animal. Well, all I remember was ,bloody "murder" in the cellar. With much commotion and wrestling, the goose deliberately got the ax on our wood chopping stump and it took almost two long minutes before that bloody, headless flying goose came to rest.

So, if it had been done the proper way, like hanging up the goose with her feet and a quick incision right under the head, the animal would have died quietly without any stress. More relaxed muscles and proper bleeding that can be the difference between a tough and a tender bird.

Now, we all loved Grandpa Boeres. He was pretty smart, had a job as a weightmaster at the steel mill, but killing a goose was not "up his alley" and I think, today, it would not matter that much. People on the farm all know this, besides, all one has to do today, go to the nearby supermarket. They have them . . . all neatly packaged.

As one can see, the food-chain was absolute, from the farm to the table. Vegetables and fruits came right from the producer, delivered to the local stores and farm markets. "Real" live-stock was sold in abundance. Live piglets, chickens, geese and all that. One had to pay a bit more to "dress" the critters. Farmers usually sold the good stuff and kept the "cull" for themselves because, in good or bad seasons, a farmer had to have a strong back, working from morning till dusk, from "kain" to "kain't" till you can or can't see anymore. And most of all, a farmer had to be frugal.

Not every day was a plenty. Young lambs were sold and the old mutton kept. Naturally, most of the milk, cream and butter was reserved for income to keep the farm going. Little milk was kept to make cheese, like white, cottage or farmer's cheese. Clobber (raw milk) was often served with boiled potatoes and topped with bacon bits.

Here is a good

MUTTON OR IRISH STEW

Mutton stew was once very popular and if no mutton is to be had, use **lamb breast, neck or shoulder**, cut into cubes.

In a heavy pot, smother all the lamb meat in **bacon fat** for 6 to 8 minutes. Stir in some **flour** and fill the pot with **water, diced onions, carrots, parsnips or kohlrabi and potatoes.** Add **salt, pepper, bay leaves, rosemary, marjoram, celery seeds and a little dash of white vinegar.** Cook slowly for two hours. Serve this with a good Irish Stout.

Other popular meals were:
    Beans with smoked or fresh ham

Slab bacon, pork or knuckles with sauerkraut
Stuffed cabbage with any kind of meat
A big omelet with onions, bacon or wild mushrooms
"Clobber" with potatoes in a jacket
Boiled beef or corned beef with cabbage or carrots
Dried sliced beef with scalloped potatoes, etc.

Fowl, like chicken, duck or goose, roast ham and domesticated rabbits were reserved for Sundays or family get-togethers.

To make

CREME FRAICHE

This delectable spread is regarded as a special treat on refined breakfast tables.
In a glass jar, combine a small carton of **heavy cream with 3-1/2 Tblsp. buttermilk**. Cover the jar and shake for 1-1/2 minutes.
Keeps for 8 hours at room temperature, stored in the refrigerator this keeps for weeks.

The greatest day of the year was the Fourth of July. On the farm and everywhere in America, people were waiting and preparing for this day. The parade and crowd landed on the village green where the "Um-pah-pah" brass band played the National anthem. Then we had a family picnic. The boys giving the girls the "eye" and all expected and loved that sparkling, profound, patriotic speech given with great eloquence and sometimes peppered with great platitudes by the well known orator, old Veteran Sam. When it was all over, Sam had said it again. It was no surprise that late in the fall, to hear Sam again making his point for the upcoming election. Of course there had to be plenty of food and drinks at hand . . . to bring in the votes.

Francois Boeres, Chef de Cuisine

ELECTION CAKE

(Recipe given to me by a neighbor)

You will need:

2 Tblsp. homemade starter or	one package of yeast mixed with 1/4 cup of warm water
1 cup sifted flour	1 tsp. sugar
1 orange	1 lemon
Orange juice	1/2 cup raisins
1/2 cup brandy	2-1/2 cups flour
nutmeg	salt
1/2 cup hot milk	1/2 cup melted butter
1 cup superfine sugar	1 beaten egg
Syrup and Brandy for topping	

For a **starter**, take **two Tblsp. of homemade** or **one package of yeast mixed with 1/4 cup of warm water**. Stir in **one cup of sifted flour** with **one tsp. sugar**. Let rise.

Peal **one orange and one lemon** in very fine strips with a potato peeler and cook in **orange juice**. Meanwhile, boil **1/2 cup of raisins**. Let cool and add **1/2 cup of brandy**.

In a bowl place **2-1/2 cups of flour** with some **nutmeg and salt**. Make a well in the center of the flour and add: **1/2 cup hot milk, 1/2 cup melted butter, 1 cup superfine sugar**. Add **one beaten egg** to this and mix well. Add all other ingredients. Let it rest for 5 minutes. Mix again, pour into a cake pan and let rise.

Bake at 350 degrees for approximately 45 minutes. Cool and top with **syrup and brandy**.

Here is 'Nipps' O'Connor's emotional outburst of patriotic feelings, looking up at Old Glory!

Oh Thee, O! Mity rag! O beoteous peese of cloth!
Made of red and white and blue stripes,
And stars painted on both sides - - -
All Hail! Again I'm sittin in thy umbrajus
Shadder, and admirin thy granger

HIS-STORY of Good Cooking

and sucking in to my chist the gentle zeffers
That are holding you out well ni onto
Trate. Great flag! When I shet
Mi ize and look at yer, and think
How as when you was lettle, and not much
Bigger than a peese of cloth, and
Almost as tender as a sheet of paper, you
Was karried thru the revolution -
Ary war, and fev sum feu time sense
Held up yer head with difficutty, and
How tremenjus yu are now, I feel
Jest as if I shud bust and fli all round, and want
To git down off the fence, and git shot,
Or stabbed, or hit on the hed with a stick
Uv wood, or hung for my kuntry.

Prodigious banner! Wouldn't I smile to see
A furriainer, or a small unnaterheralized
Aliuns undertake to pull yu down!
If a furreiner, I would fix him, and kut
Of his scalp, and bear it off in tiumf
Before I'd see a split torn in ye, or the sakrilejus
Hands of a fo kuttin you into bullit
Patchin, I'l brace my back agin a waul (or a House
or a fence, or a board, as it mite be!
And fite, and strike, and scratch, and
kick and bite, and tare my klose, an d
loose mi hat, and git hit in the I, an d
On mi leg, and akrost the smaul of
Mi back, and faul down and get up
Agin, and continu the struggle for heff or
three-quarters of an hour, or until
I got Severely woundet.
Teriffic emblem! How prowd you look
And how almity sassy you waiv round,
Snappin and cracken, and skeerin of horses;
I spose yure almost tarrin to get into a

Francois Boeres, Chef de Cuisine

> *Fite with sumbody, and satisfy your kar-*
> *Niverous disposition by eatin up a whole nashun!*
>
> *Great flag! Don't know which maiks me feel the*
> *Most partiotic-yu or the forth of July:*
> *Yu aint made of the same kind of stuff, altho*
> *Yu are about the same age, and are both*
> *Sublimed, and terrible to kontemplate.*
>
> *But I must klose and waive my last adew,*
> *However tryin to my feelins it may be.*
> *And get down off the fence, fo already the*
> *Sharp pints of the pickets begin to stick*
> *Me, and maik me skringe and hitche about, and*
> *Treaten to tare my klose and maik me holler.*

From *The Harp of a 1000 Strings,* 1855
from a compiled konkoktion by Spavery
(Dick & Fitzgerald N.Y.)

The American Chestnut Tragedy

I am not referring to the Chester Gillett tragedy that began here in Cortland, New York, and ended in Raquett Lake, where Chester killed Miss Brown, a story that shocked the whole nation.

Chestnut trees were a way of American life. They shaded our streets, schoolyards, parks, and grew deep in the woods. At Christmastime and long winter months, Grandpa always roasted chestnuts on top of the parlor stove. To prevent the chestnuts from exploding, he notched them with an X. Mainly Italian vendors were selling roasted chestnuts right from a fired up steel drum. One could hear them shouting: "Marroons, canstanias, marroons, canstanias" ...boy, were they hot and delightful, especially on cold days.

At the farm we have an old icebox made out of chestnut, often mistaken for oak. And all our shelves in the food pantry are made out of large chestnut planks, reminding us that they came from large trees. The pantry and the house were built over 167 years ago. Around 1904, a fungus was discovered in the Bronx Zoo in New York. It spread out fast and by the late 1930's, most chestnut trees had died with the beech and elm trees not far behind.

How to make Grandpa's old fashioned

LIVERTERRINE PATÉ

When it came creating real good food in the spur of the moment, Grandpa Boeres was a real wizard. Helping out he often prepared meals we all loved. On long winter evenings, he often roasted chestnuts, or prepared stuffed breast of veal. One of his favored dishes was called a Paté, made out of pork and liver. This is so good and inexpensive to make and it can be served to your guests with pride. If you ever tasted a Paté, this recipe will do it to you. It is uncomplicated and delicious. This wholesome additive free Terrine should not be kept more than three days (like a meat loaf).

You will need:
One small size terrine. A shallow pan with water (a Bain-Marie). A suitable piece of wood to fit the top of the terrine. A stone to weight the Paté down. A grinder with a medium grinder plate.

To prepare:
Take 3/4 pound of pork liver
3/4 pound of pork meat from the shoulder
1/2 pound of fat back bacon
2 small or one big chopped onion
2 eggs
1/2 cup bread crumbs (can be made from stale bread)
1/2 cup dry white wine
salt pepper
fresh chopped parsley
2 tsp. soft green peppercorns or a few dark peppercorns
summer savory
trace of nutmeg.
A few slices of bacon for the layout.

Francois Boeres, Chef de Cuisine

Grind all the meat and add all ingredients. Mix well. Lay slices of bacon on the bottom of the terrine. Fill the terrine with the ground meats, garnish the top with a few bay leaves. Set the terrine in the "Bain-Marie" with water added and cook in a 325 degree oven for one hour or until done. To test, 'puncture' Paté with a needle. If clean juice appears and the needle is hot, it should be done. Take the terrine out of the oven and weigh it down with a board and a stone. After cooling, the Paté should be nice and firm.

Note: To make a finer Paté, use pistachios in the meat, grind fine and use more weight on top.

Serve with rye, French bread, Boston lettuce and pickles.
Wine: Mosel Auxerois, Pinot Gris or Riesling, or a good bottle of beer, but please, no water. (Fish make love in water!)

How to cook a young, plump and delectable

GOOSE

The Goose was usually prepared the day before, after plucking and eviscerating (we don't have to do that any more). The giblets were removed, cooked and chopped up for the sauce. The bile was removed from the liver and the liver set aside for later.

The preparation:
Rub the inside of the goose with **fresh garlic, celery seeds or celery salt, crushed chervil or sage and salt.**

The Goose Stuffing:
Slice cubes from **old bread** and mix with **sauteed chopped onions, chopped garlic, a chopped stalk of celery, cut up apples, peeled and blanched chestnuts cut in half, rendered bacon slices, salt, pepper, sage, thyme and fresh chopped parsley.** Mix all this well and stuff into the goose.
Preheat the oven to 350 degrees and start cooking the goose belly down for 3/4 hour. Turn it onto it's back, baste often with **light chicken stock**. After 2 hours it should be ready. . . nice and crisp. Do not overcook.

Take out the finished goose and dress on a platter. Keep warm. Deglaze the pan with **chicken stock and port wine**. Add chopped giblets and simmer the sauce for about 5 minutes.

Many a smart "Gooser" saves the goose liver for a fine goose liver Paté (Paté de foie) for a special treat.

Sauté the liver in **pork fat** with **salt, pepper and summer savory**. Add some **brandy** and a little **sherry wine**. Be on guard for flames. Cool and grind liver very fine. Mix with **soft butter**. If you have any **truffles**, you are fortunate. This Paté can be served with **round croutons** or a thin **French bread** called a "flute".

You are also invited to stuff the goose neck with your favorite stuffing. This makes an elegant sausage for any occasion. Don't forget to tie both ends when cooking or boiling. Save all the goose fat. It is highly regarded in any kitchen. Use it as a spread, for frying and cooking. It is next to olive oil, the most stable to temperatures and sustainable fat. It has also been used as an ointment to mix with pharmaceutical remedies.

Wine: a Sauvingnon Blanc or a Bolla-Soave

How to use a pig—In my experience.

The popularity of fresh veal in the past was related to the short time production for the market. It took a young veal one to two months and a steer' beefer' over two years to feed. A feeder pig was ready in less than a year and slaughtering was done in late Fall. Pork is pickled, smoked and mostly sold fresh for every desirable taste.

Here, we had raised a few healthy pigs for almost a year. We got them started with a good quality ration, fortified with protein and minerals, some corn and leftover whey from a next door cheese factory, old bread, cakes, fruits and vegetables from a jobber and markets. Of course, not to forget fresh drinking water. Actually, pigs are clean animals. They have a bad reputation for rolling in the mud because that's the way they bathe themselves to get rid of undesirable hosts.

First we had these nice built stalls with cement troughs, none of those "unsanitary" living conditions that later give the meat that terrible barn smell.

Francois Boeres, Chef de Cuisine

After slaughtering, the animal was bled immediately, all the fresh blood was collected in a vessel and mixed with some vinegar to prevent clotting. This was used for sausage. Then the pig was hung up and cleaned out. Care is taken not to cut into the bladder. Hearts, liver and kidneys are set aside and saved. Later, the pig is placed on an outdoor table, hot water is poured over it and any hair or whiskers are shaved off. Then it is hung up again and aerated by spreading out the cavity with a stick. After a day or so, the pig is cut in half, head, tail and heart are saved for head cheese, soups, scrapple or sausages (called charcuterie). Knuckles are smoked or cooked fresh for knuckles with cabbage or sauerkraut. Also the tongue and brains are used for a mixed fare, like hot hors d'oeuvres.

---

*The Cook,
And he could roast and seethe,
and broil and fry
and make a good soup
and bake a pie.*
From the Canterbury Tales

Learning the art:

HOW TO MAKE BLOOD SAUSAGES
(alias Blood puddings or Boudins)

It is amazing what people throw away these days because no one told them how to make blood sausages and other fine concoctions. Start this process by collecting and saving the **blood** from the pig in a big shallow bowl. Mix and stir in some **vinegar** to prevent clotting, strain and set in a cool place.

Slice **2 pounds of soft boiled fat back bacon** into small cubes. Sauté **2 finely chopped onions and 2 fined chopped shallots** in a big pot with pork fat, over medium heat. Add all the fat back and stir for a minute. Take only half the blood and thicken over a slow fire, then add all the fat back with

HIS-STORY of Good Cooking

the onions, then the rest of the blood with **salt, pepper, a trace of nutmeg, thyme, marjoram** and 1/2 a bunch of **chopped parsley**.

Stuff the casings with a sausage funnel by tying one end or slipping the casings over the funnel from the electric sausage maker, tie and close the other end. Boil the sausage in very slowly simmering water for approximately 15 minutes or until they float. Test with a needle to see if they are done and transfer to cold water. After cooling off, take them out of the water and hang them up to dry.

To Cook: Fry both sides in pork fat and cover for a minute. Serve with baked apples and red cabbage. Note; some might burst open, this is normal.

Wine: a Sancerre or Anjou

Note: Besides other foods, blood sausages are traditionally served in Europe on New Year's Eve. Fowl is to be avoided to prevent "scratching" for the rest of the year. So the old tale has it.

HOW TO CURE AND SMOKE HAM

Dad often told me that lousy flour makes lousy pancakes! Fresh ham should come from a clean source or a reputable farm. First, dry the ham and rub in natural salt and sugar for two days. Then place the ham in a nonmetallic tub and cover with the brine, weigh it down with a board and a stone. Turn ham every 4 days. After 3-1/2 to 4-1/2 weeks (according to size) clean with water, rub dry and cover with finely crushed peppercorns and wood-ashes from fruit or maple wood. Place in a fine cheesecloth to prevent skippers. Now is the time to hang the ham in the smokehouse. A slow periodical "smothered"fire should be kept using wood and sawdust. This can take 3-1/2 to 5 months. Preferred "smoke woods" are hickory, maple, apple and "corn cobs."Smoked ham is served like Prosciutto, sliced thin, served with French bread and Boston lettuce at any occasion.

TO MAKE BRINE FOR ONE HAM

To **one quart of water** add **one pound of coarse (Kosher) salt, 4 to 5 ounces of sugar or molasses, 1-1/2 ounces of saltpeter, 3 tsp. pepper,**

Francois Boeres, Chef de Cuisine

3 crushed bay leaves, coriander, rosemary, juniper berries, marjoram and a pinch of cloves.

HOW TO MAKE SCRAPPLE

Boil the **neck, jaw and feet** slowly in water with **salt** added, for two hours. Remove all the meat from the bones and chop fine. Add **3 cups of broth, one cup of cornmeal with pepper and sage**. After cooling, slice and fry in **bacon fat**.

HOW TO MAKE HEAD CHEESE

Boil all "remnants" like the **head, tail and feet of the pig** with **onions, salt and a carrot**, until tender and the bones all fall out. Take out of the broth and cool off. Chop in small pieces and place into a pan or a bread form lined with waxed paper. Add **pepper, sage, savory, marjoram and 1/2 cup of vinegar** to your stock. Reduce and pour over the meat in the pan. Set in a cool place. Cut in slices and serve with pickles and potato salad.

HOW TO MAKE CLABBER

Leave **fresh milk** in a glazed crock in a warm place, all covered up, in the summer on the porch, in the winter near the stove. After it "clabbers", stand it in a cool place. Serve by scooping the thick clabber out carefully and not breaking it up too much. A good combination with clabber is salt-pork, with boiled potatoes or potatoes in the jacket.

HOW TO MAKE GELATIN

Scald, clean and shave off the hair (if any) from approximately **4 calves feet**. Boil slowly in **6 quarts of water** until half is evaporated. Cool and strain in a pan. Clarification for jelly type desserts and flummery is done by adding **beaten egg whites and egg shells** into the gelatin stock. This all should be incorporated and mixed well. Heat up very slowly until the foam surface. Carefully strain through a fine double cheesecloth and keep in a cool place. To make Gelatin for aspic, add and mix **very lean ground beef** to the **egg white**. Combine with the **shells, chopped onions, white wine, celery and salt**. Simmer slowly and strain trough a cloth.

AN OLD RECIPE TO MAKE YEAST

Every woman on the farm had a jar with her home made leaven.
To make a good yeast starter:
1-1/2 cups fresh hops
1 quart potato water
3/4 cups malt flour
1/2 cup sugar

Boil the hops in potato water for 15 minutes. Strain. Stir in malt flour, boil slowly for 10 minutes, cool to lukewarm and add the sugar. Keep in a closed jar and in a cool place. To keep the jar clean, it is a good practice to scald the jar after each use.

Preserving on the Farm and How it Began

Opening the cellar door of my grandparents' was an experience. Under the staircase were dangling slabs of bacon, hard sausages and smoked hams. Downstairs was a bin with two sorts of potatoes. Other large shelves supported bottles of wine, assorted apples, and many jars of fruits and vegetables. Right below stairs stood a big crock with sauerkraut. It had a wooden cover with a stone on top. Once in a while, Grandpa also kept fresh eggs in a crock filled with "waterglass".

Salt, sugar and vinegar are indispensable preservatives on the farm. Honey had been dug out of Pompeii. It was hard and not very good tasting, but it still was honey. As for the salt, some 400 years ago the body of a miner was found in a Salzburg salt mine. Indeed he was very well preserved and "pickled," because he looked very "devilish." The townspeople burned his remains on the village square.

PRESERVING FOOD in its natural state is quite different. It is said that some chef working for Louis XV had an idea of preserving peas and cubed carrots (for a macedoine) to take out to a hunting party. This was done in Champagne bottles and boiled (sterilized) in a water tub. The clever person who brought us real preserving was Francois Appert, a chef-patissier who worked for Christian IX of Denmark in Paris. Appert got the idea from his father, Nicholas Appert. He perfected it and took out a patent in 1852. His idea was the sterilization of food in a conclave (a pressure cooker). Also, the idea of "canning" was first introduced in 1818 by Peter Durant. To produce cans, at that given time was very expensive. The success of Appert and Durant's invention met at the crossroads of mass fabrication during the Civil War. Plenty of real canning was done in households in both World Wars. (The name "can" comes from "ordnance" canister).

TO PRESERVE IN A PRESSURE COOKER

1. Take only the best, freshest, bruise free vegetables or fruits.
2. Inspect jars for nicks and cracks.
3. Clean and sterilize jars in boiling water.
4. Blanch (parboil) fruits or vegetables in water (salt or sugar added).
5. Fill jars to 1-1/2 inches from the top.
6. Close jars firm with a rubber ring on.
7. Cook in the pressure cooker filled 1/2 full with hot water.
8. Cook steady under low fire and watch pressure gauge.
9. Usually, it takes 35 minutes for pints and 40 minutes for quart jars.
10. Please follow instructions from the pressure cooker manufacturer.

TO PRESERVE PICKLES OR GHERKINS

Use **1 pound of 3 inch cucumbers**. Wash and rub clean.

Pack cucumbers in about **6 - 7 pint jars**.

To each jar add: **1/2 clove of garlic, some peppercorns, sprigs of dill, 6 quarter size whole white onions.**

Mix and boil: **1/4 cup salt, 3 cups cider or wine vinegar, 3 cups water.**

Pour boiling solution over cucumbers, filling the jar to 1/2 inch from the top.

Close and cover tightly.

Cook 10 minutes in boiling water.

The Way People Used to Drink

Let it be known from the past, any man dedicated to the toiling of the land was obliged to give fermented beverages not much of a thought unless his cider hardened once in a while. On the contrary, if you happened to be a City Dude, belonging to a "fighting outfit" or a man of the sea, you were in plenty of deep water. For some folk, drinking was a way of life. There were times when a non-drinking fellow was looked upon with great suspicion. A man who did not "imbibe" was not a good man. It got so bad that the "Delirium Tremens" had no boundaries. People drank to everything, the sun that got up and the moon that came out. It was not uncommon to find the parson drunk in the gutter returning from his visit from a temperance campaign.

In the years from 1870 to 1885, PHYLLOXERA and MILDEW-ROT destroyed most of the vineyards in France, some of American origin. Ironically, these vineyards again were saved by American hybrids with a higher strain, affected was the importation of the so-called Sack. It was severely reduced and today almost obscure. Also the taste of whiskey suffered dramatically during the "Prohibition." The speak-easy public used a mediocre hodgepodge, hurly burly version and forgot what good whiskey tasted like. All this, because a men came home drunk, and mistreated his wife, her name was Garry Nation.

Note: Carry Nation's first husband had been a drunk. Her second marriage to David Nation ended in an acrimonious relationship. Her intelligence eclipsed by far both her husbands. Later she became a preacher, writer and a great organizer. Consider that most bad things end up bad, she gained great personal satisfaction in her Temperance Crusade, but prohibition had brought the nation it's share of misery!

The temperance movements had been with us for a long time. The Women's Christian Temperance Union, headed by Francis Willard, gave way to the Anti-Saloon League but the most important to Carry Nation's profile was her straw that broke the camel's back. She died in 1911, in Levenworth, Kansas.

Here are a few of the old timers "bottoms up." Some can give you an uplift, or paralyze you temporarily!

Francois Boeres, Chef de Cuisine

A cabinet member to President Abraham Lincoln: *"I think Grant is drinking too much!"* Lincoln: *"Let all my Generals have some of his brand!"*

OLD TIME DRINKS

RUM LOGGERHEAD (FLIP): Fill a quart pitcher 2/3 full of **strong beer**, add **two tsp. of honey or syrup, 1/2 pint dark rum and a slice of butter**. Stir with a red hot poker.

RUM FUSTIAN (Fustia means imitation): Make a mixture of **1/2 beer, 1/4 sherry, 1/4 gin**. Add a few **egg yolks**, some **sugar** and a **trace of nutmeg**. Stir with a red hot poker.

A quick made **MINT JULEP**: Mix **eggnog** with **1-1/2 ounces green Creme de Menthe** and **1-1/2 ounces Bourbon**. Stir and pour into a goblet filled with ice shavings. Garnish with **fresh sprigs of mint**.

KENTUCY MINT JULEP: Chill goblets and fill with **crushed ice**. Add to each goblet, **2 tsp. prepared sugar syrup** and **2 ounces of Bourbon**. Garnish with **sprigs of mint**.

A SACK POSSET: Mix **ale, Sack, egg yolks and cream**. (Sack is a strong light colored wine from Spain.)

SYLLABUB (one version): Add **sugar** into **7 cups of cream** and beat for half a minute. Grate **4 lemon rinds** fine, squeeze out the **juice of the 4 lemons** and pour into **2 cups of Rhine wine** and **1 cup of Sack or dry sherry**. Pour into the cream and beat for at least 15 minutes. Fill stemmed glasses and refrigerate or keep in a cool place.

PORTER: A strong dark beer, it resembles a light Stout and is made from "browned" malt. This is so good that even the kids used to love it.

PORT WINE: Was very popular and served on any occasion. It is a semi-sweet dark red Portuguese wine fortified with Brandy.

MULLED WINE: This is red wine heated with honey, nutmeg, cinnamon and a slice of lemon.

OTHER PREFERRED CONCOCTIONS WERE: Hot cider with spices, cold cider, Madeira and Sherry wine.

WASSAIL: Usually a traditional non-alcoholic drink served in a big bowl. (An early version of punch.)

NIBBLE AND SIP: A sip of tea and a nibble of a dunked lump of sugar.

—

I'd like to tell a story about WASSAIL (If you don't mind.)

The custom of "wassailing" is quite old and was very popular with the Saxons and Northern people alike, especially on Jule-tide, a celebration known as Jule-fest, that took place on the 22nd of December. On this occasion, huge bonfires were lit on nearby hills and spiced beer, known as wassail, was shared. This tradition still is very much alive.

Charlemagne had a lot of trouble converting nonconforming Saxons to Christianity, besides being very belligerent, he brought about, where Boniface failed, evacuating some Saxons to the land of the Franks and sending some Franks to Saxony where they exchanged traditions. The Saxons taught the Franks different ways of preserving without smoking, like Westphalia ham, building boats and brewing great beer. The Franks taught the Saxons to smoke certain meats, make sausages and different methods of tanning leather they had learned from the Romans, the same people that also taught the Franks to grow vines on the Rhine and the Moselle valleys, here the wassail became more and more like a wine punch.

To make Christianity more appealing to the Saxons and other Northmen, the Jule period was conveniently replaced by Christmas. (Christ was born much later, that is, earlier in the coming year.) The giant woman "Hel" that reigned over the Kingdom of the dead became Hell. Great men and fallen heros were "ushered" directly to Valhalla (Heaven) by the Valkuries (Angels). The Myths of the end of the world became the Last Judgement.

Francois Boeres, Chef de Cuisine

Easter replaced the Pagan Rite of Spring. The holy Oak Tree, used for ceremonies, still is the symbol of strength and the Wassail (wass-heal), which means "be well" still is with us today. Today's wassail resembles more of a concoction made by an Anglo-Saxon who had just returned from India.

Here is a non-alcoholic and good tasting traditional wassail served on academic festivities and other occasions. It was much appreciated by the faculty who had their share of troubles with beer saturated students. Here a cup of kindness is lifted, singing "Auld Lang Syne" and the "Claudiamus."

TRADITIONAL WASSAIL

Brew a **quart of cider** with **a stick of cinnamon, 6 cloves, peels from an orange and a lemon** (peel the fruit with a potato peeler). Cool this in the refrigerator. Fill the punch bowl with the **spiced cider, one liter of ginger ale, two bottles of pink sparkling grape juice, 6 circular slices (wheels) of blood orange, 4 wheels of lemon.**

Optional: one dozen cocktail cherries.

For a hardy company serve a **TRADITIONAL CHAMPAGNE WASSAIL** by replacing the sparkling grape juice with champagne. Your company can drink a lot of this without getting "plastered."

A TEA WASSAIL
for the "reserved" Country Club ladies

Boil **4 cups of strong tea**. Add and dissolve **2-1/2 cups of sugar** in the tea. Pour in a **quart of sweet cider, 3 sticks of cinnamon, 6 cloves** and simmer for about 5 minutes. Add **1-1/2 cups of orange juice** and the **juice from 2 lemons**. Bring to the boiling point. Cool or serve hot.

Music: Brahm's *The Academic Festivals* or Haydn's *The Seven Last Words*.

Served with "cigarettes."

CHEESE CIGARETTES

In a double boiler, melt **mild cheddar** with some **milk, pepper, dash of spicy mustard** and a **few drops of tabasco**, stirring occasionally with a wooden spoon till soft and melted. Take this from the fire and let it rest till warm and spreadable.

Cut thin slices from a firm **white, whole pullman bread.** Lay out the bread slices on the table and spread with the cheese. Roll them up good, like cigarettes and let cool.

Meanwhile, heat up the **fryer fat (very hot)** till it smokes a bit, drop in the cigarettes in the fryer, not more than 8 at a time. Fry till golden. Dry them on a paper towel and serve hot.

Or serve with a BELGIAN FONDUE

Make a firm and thick Bechamel sauce (with butter, flour and hot milk). Add half the volume of grated Gruyere or aged Cheddar, a few egg yolks, a lot of pepper and cook in a double boiler till melted and very hot. (Close to boil.) To test the thickness, place a spoonful in the refrigerator. Pour into a buttered or wax-paper lined sheet pan and cool in the refrigerator. Cut into two inch squares, dip in flour, egg wash and fine bread crumbs. Fry in a deep fryer till golden. Serve with fried parsley.

A POSSET
(A milk punch for the holidays.)

Beat **8 eggs** until foamy. Whisk in **1 cup ale, 1 cup sherry, 1/2 cup superfine sugar, 1 tsp. nutmeg and a dash of salt.** Slowly pour in **4 cups of scalded milk.** Serve in mugs, topped with **cinnamon.**

SANGRIA COOLER

Dissolve **1/4 cup sugar in ½ cup orange juice and the juice of 3 lemons** (strained). Add **one liter good dry red wine and ice.** Serve in a pitcher.

Francois Boeres, Chef de Cuisine

ANOTHER HOT WASSAIL

Dissolve **1/2 cup brown sugar in 2 quarts of cider**, add the **juice from 5 lemons and 6 ounces concentrated orange juice, 6 cinnamon sticks, 1/2 tsp. nutmeg and 6 cloves.** Simmer for 15 minutes and serve hot.

SOUTHERN ARTILLERY PUNCH
(To be prepared at least 2 days ahead.)

In a big stainless steel pot, make **2 cups of strong and hot tea.** Add **2 cups of sweet wine, 1 cup dark rum, 1/3 cup gin, 1/3 cup bourbon, 1/2 cup brandy**. Add the **juice of 2 lemons and 2 oranges.** Cover and keep in the refrigerator for at least 2 days. Serve the punch in a big punch bowl, adding **3 chilled bottles of champagne**. Garnish with **lime wheels**. Maybe you want to shoot "Federal Cannon Balls" with this Artillery Punch. These are cookies made with hot spices, poppy and sesame benne seeds. A word of caution, let a designated "Belle" drive you home. . .

Have You Seen the Elephant?

The folklore expression, almost forgotten in the skirmish of time, was "Have you seen the elephant?" Maybe this meant an encounter with chaos, general disaster, coordinated from hell. Maybe a typhoon at sea, or a tornado, maybe a big battle up front. Then you had seen the elephant.
P. T. Barnum, who coined the phrase "There's a sucker born every minute," owned an ostentatious specimen of an elephant called Jumbo. The whole world wanted to see Jumbo. When Jumbo died, they wanted him mounted, a job never done before for such a huge animal. It was a taxidermist's biggest challenge. They also saw, deliberately speaking, the Elephant. I myself have seen the Elephant a few times, once coming home too late, at 3:30 in the morning.

HIS-STORY of Good Cooking

Here is what happened to Harry Green:

Seeing the Elephant Double

Harry Green was brought in for having been inebriated and asleep on the highway. He had been having an evening's amusement, in the course of which he had been to the circus, and afterward to a bowling alley and shooting gallery with a friend he had picked up. By the kind permission of the Judge, he was allowed to tell his story in his own way, which he did in a very disjointed style, and with a great deal of earnestness and volubility, somewhat after the fashion of the well-known Alfred Jingle.

"My name is Green, Mr. Judge; live in the country, come down here for the first time to see the city; stop at Mr. Astor's Tavern in Broadway Street; fine place, good bartender, big whiskers, does things with a kind of flourishy jerk peculiar to himself; don't know anybody in the city; perfect stranger, got my supper, went out on the steps; man came along, good looking man, shiny hat, big gold chain, stand-up collar, cane with jack-knife in it, introduced himself; said he was a stranger too; wanted me to go with him and pass a pleasant evening; agreed to go; went; took something to drink before we started; got a little ways and he said, hadn't we better take a nip? Took a nip; he said shouldn't we go to the circus? Told him wasn't acquainted with the circus, but trot it out; he said hadn't we better have something first? Had something; got to the door; my friend had left his pocketbook at home; borrowed ten dollars and paid for two; gave me the change, a one dollar bill, three pewter dimes and a smooth cent; didn't understand New York currency, but thought all right; got inside; place near the door with bottles in, also glasses and pumps. Large assortment of pumps with mahogany handles; friend said should we smile? We smiled, stepped along and looked at the performance; men with nothing on but a crown and a pair of tight breeches covered with six pence, and women with petticoats about as long as a turnover collar, all standing up on horseback, except when they were rolling heels over head in the sawdust, trying to catch the tips of their toes in their teeth. Remarkable fact, all the horses had two tails, and all the men were double headers; friend said it was the effect of this last smile, and proposed that we should take something to take the dust out of our eyes—friend said if I'd seen enough we'd go—took a last look. The men in the sixpenny breeches were dancing with the ladies in the short skirts, which seemed all upside down like a bowl-man with whip was cracking it at everybody, especially a fellow with three-cornered patches all over him, who was standing on his head on a pewter platter on top of a pair of stilts-stopped at the place with the bottles in - friend said should we imbibe? We imbibed, went outside, started to go across the street; brought up against oyster cart, tried to kick over the oyster cart, got my leg between the wheels—new hat fell off, couldn't get up, concluded to sit down—did sit down on my hat—friend helped me up, and tied my hat on with a string—friend said shouldn't we take a snifter? Took a snifter—went to a shooting place—tried to kill the cast-iron man with the pipe in his mouth—don't think I did. Fired seven times and all the balls lodged in the ceiling overhead, except one which went through the toe of my boot and struck the floor; friend said, hadn't we better horn? Horned; proceeded for a bowling saloon; got part way; friend proposed that we should stop at milk punch place and take a suck; took a suck; got to a rolling place; thought I'd roll first ball; didn't stay on the alley; the second I let slip behind me, and it smashed a bird cage, and demolished a canary, while the last one hit the pin boy and knocked him through the side of the house, friend said, shouldn't we go to the bar and let 'em up, let em up and kept doing so till the floor looked like a river, and I tried to drink the coal hod, under the impression that it was a glass of brandy and sugar; hot; friend said, shouldn't we julep?—Juleped; he then proposed that we should cocktail—cocktailed; friend borrowed my pocketbook and coat; officer came, and here I am."

Mr. Green was reprimanded and discharged, further punishment being considered unnecessary, in consideration of his loss while seeing the Elephant.

From *The Harp of a Thousand Strings*, 1855

And Give Us Our Daily Bread

In our home, bread was so important and religiously respected, Mom always "crossed" and blessed the loaf before slicing.

Cultivation of grain became the most important and stable food that led to bread making. In ancient Egypt, grain was so precious that slaves handling grain had to wear muzzles. The first grain ground probably was done in a hollowed out stone using a round stone "pestle" just as the Indians and Mexicans had ground corn.

This type of bread was non leavened and looked more like a Jewish style of round bread used for Passover. Although sour-milk bread has been found in 3,000 year old Swiss lake dwellings. . . It looked like a small rye bread.

The burghers of Florence used beer-froth as a leaven to raise dough. Wheat was preferred over barley which was often used for the poor. Rye was linked to the ethnic Germanic group and often used as the "commissioned" bread for the Army. Therefore it was called commission bread. Some loaves were so dark and heavy, one just about needed an iron stomach to digest. As the story goes, Napoleon refused this kind of bread from a soldier, with the remark "Bon pour Nickel". Nickel was the name of his horse - "Only good for my horse, Nickel." And so from then on this bread was called PUMPERNICKEL (I love pumpernickel.)

A few years ago, heading home from hunting, I stumbled on the ruins of a Dutch oven from an abandoned farm house. Of course, a more modern cast iron stove could be had at that time for about forty dollars, but meanwhile, a lot of baking was still done in a Dutch oven. The forerunner of the Dutch oven was referred to as that shallow cast iron kettle that stood in the kitchen fireplace. It had a recessed lid, on which embers or hot coal could be placed. The real conception of the Dutch oven was a beehive compartment, next to the kitchen fireplace.

Francois Boeres, Chef de Cuisine

The main construction of this oven was made of bricks to retain heat. It also had a flue, damper and an iron door.

After the building of the first tiers of bricks that formed the arch about three bushels of ashes and dead coal was laid over with the next tier laid on top so it could retain the heat in the oven for long at baking time.

To brake the oven "in" and cure the bricks, it had to be fired up for at least six hours. This was very important to make it work.

To bake, a steady fire of hardwood had to be done for at least two hours. Then the fire had to be burned down to a low flame and glimmer and spread out over the oven floor. This had to be repeated several times. Before baking, all embers had to be cleaned out and the door closed quickly. Testing for the right temperature is done by spilling some flour on the oven floor. If it got dark too fast, it was too hot. If it got brown, it was ready to "peel" in the bread. The round old fashioned bread was about one foot in diameter.

Right away, if you happened to be my friend, I might call you my companion, from companis, the one I break bread with!

There is a lad here,
which hath five barley loaves
and two small fishes, but
what are they among so many?
St. John

Note:
BUCKWHEAT was first imported by the Dutch in New Amsterdam and extensively cultivated in New York. Buckwheat griddle cakes were common on the breakfast table.

___OATS were introduced by Scottish settlers in America, like oatmeal, porridge, oatmeal-cakes and bread still oats was primarily feed to horses.

___RYE is a popular Northern European grain. It was brought to America by early Scandinavian settlers. Today more and more Americans have discovered the hearty, zesty, country flavor of Rye bread.

____BARLEY is also a very old established grain and has many diversified applications. In old Britain it was the poor man's grain for food. By law, some land was reserved to accommodate growing barley for brewing beer.

How to make your own SOUR-DOUGH STARTER

3 potatoes
1-1/2 cup of hops
4 cups of rye or white flour
½ cup of honey or molasses

Boil 3 potatoes in the jacket. Remove peel and mash into potato water. Cover hops with water and boil for 10 minutes. Strain hops water into potato mush and while still warm, stir in flour, salt and honey or molasses. Put in a covered jar and keep in a warm spot for 4 days until it bubbles.

OLD COUNTRY RECIPE FOR GOOD BREAD

One cup of your own sour-dough starter, (or one package of yeast)
Two cups of warm water
Two teaspoons salt
Two teaspoons of sugar
4 cups of white flour.

Dissolve yeast (or starter) in two cups of warm water, add white flour, salt and sugar. Knead till smooth, cover and let rise in a warm spot for 45 minutes to 1 hour. This is the sponge.

An hour later add:

One quarter shortening (lard)
One cup boiling water
1/2 cup molasses
4 cups of wheat flour

Francois Boeres, Chef de Cuisine

In a bowl, mix boiling water with molasses, soft shortening and wheat flour. Mix well and add the sponge. Knead on the table for 10 minutes. Return to the bowl and let it rise for 1-1/2 hours. Punch down the dough and shape into two round loaves. Cover and let rise for 1 hour. Cut two small incisions in the loaf and "peel" them in. Bake in a 375 degree oven for approximately 45 - 50 minutes. Prior to baking, sprinkle some flour on bread to prevent darkening of the crust.

CHAPTER 4 ... THE AMERICAN CHRONICLES

George Washington

A tree had been planted and cultivated in rich Virginia soil, eventually to branch and reach out to every known place in America. This was no ordinary tree, this was an Oak, a symbol of strength, a man known as George Washington. This man had acquired all the material and ingredients to shape his destiny. His hunger for knowledge, great discipline, polished manners and appreciation for beautiful things not only made him a connoisseur of good food, wine and dancing, George also knew how to use hard and firm confrontation to almost hostile forces. He had learned this in the wilderness from Indians and frontiersmen. At sixteen he was introduced to surveying and at twenty, he ran the whole show on the huge plantation. He was involved in many community affairs, belonged to well known fraternities and, of course, knew a lot of important people. All these things were essential to a man iike George. He was six feet three inches tall and 180 pounds in his prime years; broad-shouldered, with a stout back. His steps were sure and steadfast like a man with both feet on the ground. As Lafayette wrote, he had keen blue-grayish eyes and shaking his hands they were about the biggest I had ever seen on a man.

> A wise man knows everything
> A shrewd one, EVERYONE!

In wartime, he often demonstrated great impudence, no useless words were spoken. His orders were impeccable and admirably understood by his

Francois Boeres, Chef de Cuisine

officers. Often, in trying times, anyone in his position would long ago have given up and thrown, like the old saying, "The musket in the cornfield." This was exactly what many Continental soldiers did as General Howe of the British encircled Manhattan with his army. Washington had been seen galloping through a line of deserters, whipping soldiers and shouting orders to take a stand, right in the line of fire.

It was a challenging period with many of his troops deserting and taking leaves of absence to return to work on their farms. With his army plagued by conspiracy, deprivation, hunger and sickness, his only words, "We are all in God's hands. We must accept and go on doing our duty regardless of consequences."

Don't let anyone be fooled. Washington was a witty man with a heart and soul. As Lincoln later observed, "I seldom met a man with virtues, without vices."

Often he was amused in childlike guilelessness, openly made remarks of nearby pretty women, their attire and hairdos. As curious as he was, it was difficult to guess what was going on in his mind. When informed of Major Andre's discovery of treachery, George walked up and down in his room, sobbing like a child.

He was fond of tea and loved to dance if the occasion permitted and occasionally seen dancing alone with Martha in his Mount Vernon home.

Napoleon said, "an army moves on its belly." This was sadly demonstrated by a paralyzed army at Valley Forge. Men without food and with nothing else but hope to survive.

In normal times a soldier's ration would be:
  1 lb. of salted pork, bacon or beef
  1 day a week salted fish like cod or herring
  1 pint of beans, peas or rice
  1/2 lb. of buckwheat bread, or flour to make bread
  2 quarts of beer, rum or other spirits
  good butter or pork fat, if available
  1 small pouch of salt to last 3 weeks
    soap, vinegar, pots and pans called spiders were divided to each "mess" of about eight men
  Meats were mostly boiled
  Sometimes a soldier's meal depended upon booty from nearby farms.

HIS-STORY of Good Cooking

Consider, Generals, the Prima Donnas of the army, needed more than beans. At the surrender of Yorktown, Washington offered in a gentlemanly manner, a scrumptious dinner to the defeated generals, which they promptly accepted. What had they to loose?

As Rochambeau toasted to the new nation, George Washington toasted to France. "To the King of England," Lord Cornwallis replied, and Washington whispered "May he stay there forever!"

Wherever George went he had with him his traveling "mess-chest." This contained pewter plates, platters, forks and spoons, small kettles, 8 square bottles of assorted liquors, a folding grill, tumblers, a tea pot and seasonings. This chest now belongs to the Smithsonian Museum in Washington.

The day before Christmas in 1783 at Annapolis, Maryland, Washington resigned his commission as Commander in Chief, with tears in his eyes, blessing the new nation for a promising future. He stood there in his uniform, proud and erect with a frilled cravat, powdered hair tied in a neat "queue." The ceremony followed with a great dinner fit for a King, but George never wanted to be a King. When asked about this matter his reply was "I don't want to be another Cromwell."

Jawing with George!

In his years of retreat Washington loved to entertain in a congenial and easygoing manner. His guests were usually received in the Main Hall of his home with great enthusiasm and in the most amiable fashion. In later years George had a lot of discomfort with his badly fitting teeth that gave him a "treat-squeezing" mouth depicted on our one dollar bill. This often hindered his speaking correctly and made him converse in discordant syllables.

Martha, his wife, entertained her guests in the most affectionate manner. She always wore a huge cap made of silk that had the look of a night cap. The reception was followed by a tour in the gardens and stables. Later the group assembled on the big veranda with a breathtaking view of the Potomac River. Here refreshing beverages or Wassails were served. Another bowl of punch with Gin, Rum and Brandy mixed with different juices was more appreciated.

A hunting board in the dining room was "spilled over" with assorted "gourmandies." Close by stood another board, that resembled a buffet loaded

Francois Boeres, Chef de Cuisine

with all kinds of sweets. The centerpiece was a whole Virginia smoked ham that was to be sliced very thin and served Prosciutto style. Near the corner stood a round Queen Anne table with a mahogany box known as a "bar." This contained six square bottles, Port wine from Portugal, Madeira from the Madeira Islands, Sherry wine and Marsala from Sicily, Brandy from France and strong dark rum from the Caribbean Islands.

The dinner preparation for the guests was in progress. Meanwhile, Martha entertained the guests with drinks, baked crab cake balls rolled in spiced bread crumbs, little "barquettes," (pastry boats) filled with spiced meats, canapés topped with ground meats, smoked fish, fried oysters and liver pate made from goose liver, pork fat and brandy.

Dinner was to be served at 4 p.m. but now it was 5 o'clock but no one gave it much thought. At last, the food was brought in on huge silver and china platters carried by "colored" servers all dressed in an array of silk and brocade vests and coats, adorned with lace and ruffled neck ties.

> Today they served:
> Leg of Lamb,
> Turkey stuffed with forcemeat
> Cooked beef tongue in Madeira sauce
> Roast piglets
> One of Martha's favored chicken fricassee
> Roasted chicken and
> Roast beef
> with an assortment of relishes
> vegetables and rolls.
> Red Bordeaux and white Rhenish wine and porter was served.

(One guest thought his chicken was kind of tough.)

Most dishes in Martha's kitchen had all been planned from recipes handed over from her family. They were much treasured and guarded in a small wooden chest containing a few booklets of cookery, stuffed with notes and recipes, yellowed and fringed by use. Most cook books in her time were of English, Dutch or French origin and printed for the well to do. Some cook books contained items like: Pom-kin pie, cram-berries, squash, corn, nutmeg and other indispensable Native American delicacies.

HIS-STORY of Good Cooking

With Martha's great care and supervision, most cooking was done by slaves who were cherished and treated like members of the family. Otis, one of their cooks could perform great culinary delights, especially with fish. Some of these "Afro-Ethiopian" cooks had brought us from their native land a heritage of highly flavored dishes using lively and zesty herbs and spices so essential for cooking in the tropics.

MARTHA'S FAVORED CHICKEN FRICASSEE

Bone out **a good size chicken.** Boil all the bones, adding a little **salt, a half onion cut into cubes, 2 bay leaves, 2 cloves, peppercorns.** Simmer for 1 hour. Cut chicken meat into small pieces. Season them with a **powdered mixture of cloves, salt, pepper, nutmeg and mace.** In a large pan, spread out and fry the chicken pieces in **hot butter,** stirring occasionally until done. Remove from pan. Beat **3-4 egg yolks** with some **Rhenish white wine, add parsley, chervil, fresh rosemary, marjoram and a few tarragon leaves.**

On a low fire, pour this egg mixture in hot butter, stirring vigorously without boiling, so that it will make a nice sauce. Add some more wine, remove from the fire and add the chicken pieces.

With the strained chicken broth, make a **light Béchamel (white sauce).** Then pour in all the meat with the egg mixture and the pieces of onions from the broth, a **dash of vinegar and a minced slice of lemon.**

Let it come to a boil. Serve in a Terrine.

Wine: a Camay.

IN COLONIAL TIMES it was the custom in affluent homes to serve:
    5 main dishes for 6 guests
    9 dishes for 12 guests or
    15 dishes for 18 guests.

Imagine having a party like this in a restaurant today, asking the Maitre d'hotel to serve the entire menu!

SWEETS were of the utmost importance when it came to making a party successful. Sweetmeats included all kinds of candied and syrup prepared fruits, like peaches, pears, apricots, plums in caramel or spiced syrup, confection, whole or ground roasted chestnuts, filberts, walnuts, chocolate truffles, mincemeat, brandy and sherry jelly, etc.

Francois Boeres, Chef de Cuisine

Then came flummeries, made from mushed corn, seminola, oats and jelly, made from calves bones. Much sought after were biscuits, lady fingers, floating islands and plum puddings. Also a great selection of quince, blueberry, elderberry, black currant (cassis) and apple pies were followed by Blanc-mange, cakes, cookies and syllabubs.

TO MAKE A SYLLABUB

Use 1 quart and 1 cup heavy cream
2 cups Rhine wine
1 cup Chablis
Almost 1 lb. of fine bar sugar
Shred the peels of 3 lemons and squeeze out the juice.
Add lemon juice to the wine and heavy cream.
Mix and beat at medium speed for 1/2 hour.
Fill serving glasses and chill in the refrigerator.

TO MAKE A LONDON SYLLABUB

In a bowl, blend **2 cups Port wine** with **1/2 cup sugar, 1/2 tsp. nutmeg and 1 jigger of Brandy**. Whip 2 quarts of **half and half cream** until frothy.
(Pay attention not to whip it into butter.)
Mix all ingredients well and serve in tall wine glasses.
Before serving, add **whipped cream** and sprinkle with **cinnamon**.

Note: The name "syllabub" comes from Sillery, France and "bub" from bubbly drink.

TO MAKE A BLANC-MANGE

Sprinkle **1 envelope of gelatin** over **2 cups heavy cream**, in a skillet. Let rest for a few minutes. Add **1 cup confectioner's sugar, 1/2 tsp. mace and 1 tsp. almond extract**. Cook until mixture comes to a boil. Pour slowly into custard cups.

HOW TO MAKE FLUMMERY

Soak **2 envelopes of gelatin in 1/2 cup cold water**. Add and stir in **2/3 cup scalded milk** and **2/3 cup confectioner's sugar**. Add **2 tsp. rum or almond bitter extract**. Cool in refrigerator until slightly thickened. Make **1 pint of whipped cream** and gently fold into the almost cooled but not too stiff mixture. Serve in a bowl surrounded with **poached pears or apricots**.

We all scream for ICE CREAM!

Sherbet is the earliest known form of ice cream. The Romans made it with ice, fruits and honey. In America, lactive ice cream was known way back in 1700. Dolly Madison loved to serve this ice cream in the White House. In 1851, it was first produced commercially in Baltimore. The same year, Mr. Williams opened the first cheese factory in Oneida County New York. Nevertheless this shows that ice cream had been around for some time in affluent homes. The French born wife of Governor Bladen of Maryland had served ice cream since 1744 and Washington had an ice cream machine in his Mount Vernon kitchen, all made out of wood.

One of the many assignments of my apprenticeship was to make ice cream. As much as I loved to eat it, I hated to make it, because it took a long time to crank. I sure wish I had one of those electric machines of today. First the cylinder was filled with one-third of cream mixture, then the tub alternately filled with chopped ice and thick salt crystals (cheap at that time), then cranked until it turned very hard, sign that it was ready. Note: regular salt can be used.

STRAWBERRY OR RASPBERRY SHERBET

Clean and wash fruits, then puree.
Mix:
2 quarts of fruit
1-1/2 cups fine bar sugar
1/4 cup lemon juice

Francois Boeres, Chef de Cuisine

Beat until sugar is completely dissolved.
Beat 3 egg whites until stiff,
Whip into the mixture and churn.

TO MAKE APRICOT ICE CREAM

Peel and puree 14 apricots
Mix with 7 ounces fine bar sugar
Add 1 pint of scalded heavy cream
Whip together and churn.

THE REAL VANILLA

Ice cream should be made out of vanilla sugar or vanilla pods. The dark looking vanilla pods are the size of a thin pencil and contain hundreds to thousands of little round vanilla seeds. The pods are cut open lengthwise and the seeds scraped out and blended into the ice cream mixture before freezing. The pods can be placed in jars with fine bar sugar and set aside for some time and used as vanilla sugar in puddings and baking.

To make 2 quarts of VANILLA ICE CREAM

Prepare and mix:
6 beaten egg yolks with
1 cup sugar and a little salt.
Add 2 cups of scalded milk
2 tsp. vanilla or 1 tsp. of vanilla seeds.

Beat over a low fire, mixing continually until creamy. Don't let the mixture come to a boil. Remove from the fire and refrigerate, stirring often. After cooling, mix with **4 cups heavy whipped cream**.
With the dasher in place, pour into the cylinder, close and set up the machine with the ice and the salt.

For electric machines, the "humming" of the motor will tell that the ice cream is ready. Shut the motor off immediately. Take out the dasher and freeze the ice cream for a few hours before serving. Make sure that no salt water enters the cylinder.

Note: 1 inch of vanilla pod = 1 tsp. of extract.

Benjamin Franklin

Let me introduce you to Benjamin Franklin. . . because you see, considering that time, any gentleman, should be properly introduced by a friend or a person of good standing, especially to women in social circles. This was the "tune" of good manners and shall we say, precaution. Here he is, that illustrious character. His Quaker-like appearance, high forehead, his head seems a bit too large for his five foot nine inch figure. He has a mole on his left cheek and his long, salt and pepper hair fits well now. (Wigs have become too "ordinaire".) He walks with his ivory knobbed cane, his steel gray eyes have a way of looking right through you as he speaks in his eloquent Yankee accent, asking curious questions: "Where your from, what you do, and your industry in general?" He has an ear for anything and anyone. Ben's stimulating portrayed personality often can be deceiving if confronted by agitated, objectionable persons. Then he would promptly checkmate them with his artful witty way of speech and put them in their place.
Returning home to Philadelphia, his gout gradually worsened. On special occasions, he was seen carried in a chair to attend meetings. (A chair is a two door cabin resting on two shafts carried by two men.) In 1777, there were about 80 pleasure vehicles in Philadelphia. Generally, they belonged to the rich and often were despised and stoned by unruly common folks.
Ben Franklin loved Scottish music and dances, some that started out to become what we know today as Tennessee mountain music. Besides being short sighted, most times Ben wore glasses, but he sure had a keen eye for beautiful ladies and a good look into the future. Way back in Boston he had met Miss Folger, but later married the very first beautiful girl he saw standing in front of a house door entering Philadelphia. She was then the 18 year-old Miss Read. Later, they had two children. Ben died in his house on the 17th of April, 1790.

Francois Boeres, Chef de Cuisine

Benjamin Franklin and Philadelphia

There are more "vignettes" written about Franklin than any other men of his time, not to mention all the streets, schools, libraries and towns named Franklin. One got the notion that it was almost premeditated that young Franklin, a man with great insight and anticipation, arrived here in Philadelphia in 1723 with only a loaf of bread in his haversack. He knew that this town had everything to offer. It was the most important politically, commercially and socially of all the colonies.

William Penn had provided a committee of good manners, arts and education. Penn only hired schoolmasters with sober and useful instructions. What he started, Franklin carried on extensively. Publishing books for the education of youth, organizing banks, mints, hospitals and many organizations most cities only dreamed about.

Ben Franklin's everlasting bursts of energy, "lightning" and revolutionary ideas are symptomatic to his character. He tinkered with fireplaces, fire stations, printing presses and other varied engagements. During the Revolution, Franklin often visited the American Embassy in Paris where he dined with Arthur Lee and John Adams. He found them quite "dull", so to say. Besides they were very suspicious of his behavior and they always got "groggy" if he had a few sips with them. After all, he was commissioned and rather amused to rub elbows with people like Voltaire, Moellet de la Roche, De Condes and mainly Beaumarchais, the author of "Figaro" and the "Barber of Seville", who ended his career that of a keen rascal, making deals with banker Duvernay and Chaumont, dealing in muskets and other ordnance, made a lot of money and had connections to the courts. Indeed, very promising to Ben Franklin, besides it was supporting and the very reason Ben was here in the first place. On his return to America, Ben's popularity in Europe was shown by overwhelming adoration everywhere. Ceramic busts, figurines and portraits were sold all over, commemorating his visits and his friendship.

Ben visited London quite a few times. In 1757, the Lord of trades had sent him as an agent to address the problems of Indian affairs. On a later visit, he was already highly recognized in the academic circles and received his Doctor's degree from the University of St. Andrews. On one occasion, he met Thomas Paine and was very impressed by this young man

HIS-STORY of Good Cooking

with refreshing new ideas. Franklin suggested that he come to America and gave him a recommendation to Mr. Bach in Philadelphia, his brother-in-law. Thomas Paine soon became a great moral support and an enlightenment to the suffering soldiers and the cause of Liberty. As a soldier at Valley Forge, he wrote "The Crisis."

"These are the times that try men's souls."

His "Common Sense" brought him fame. It sold 120,000 copies in a few months.

Ben Franklin, valiant and knowledgeable, of elegant character, with an easygoing unsophisticated truth in his speech and able never to step out of boundaries, rather putting an argument into a story, and when it came to keep a sociable conversation going and lit up with enthusiasm. Ben was the spark to the "firecracker". He was, in one word, a real diplomat and this country couldn't find a better man to send to France to negotiate for its support. On one of his visits to Versailles, his fame had already preceded him and he was better known than most prominent rulers in Europe. His popularity was unprecedented in the courts and in the Royal Academy of Science, where he received the highest honors.

In the courts, he always was surrounded by clusters of high society and the ever- present beautiful ladies. As for the ladies, he was a real charmer, kissing necks and hands, (Cheek and lip kissing was taboo.)

It is said that Ben Franklin had an "affair-du-coeur" with the prominent Madam Helvetia, who was much younger. She lived near Auteuil, where he spent quite some time. Besides, he kept an eternal correspondence with a Madame Brillion and had an alliance with Madame Levoisier.

Not too far from Paris, near Passy, he visited friends like Abbe de la Rochelle, Comtesse do Polignac, D'Estaing and others where he indulged himself in music, parties of chess, promenades in parks, drank tea or Madeira wine. Ben often took baths near by the hot spas and if his gout hindered him to go out, he just opened the big French balcony doors from his chamber and was seen lying on his huge bed, all naked, taking his sun bath.

As a free thinker, Ben was considered more a Presbyterian than a Quaker. He seldom attended religious services, but made sure not to miss any great parties. Ben Franklin had been a vegetarian in his earlier years, but this

Francois Boeres, Chef de Cuisine

was soon eclipsed by all the scrumptious tempting parties he was invited. It was just too much of a good thing to pass by. Here is a small dinner party given by Ben Franklin to friends and family members. Guests invited were the Hopkins and Sherman families, John Rutledge, Bill Johnson, Phillip Livingston, Dr. Shippen and his wife, John and Abigail Adams, Dr. Benjamin Rush, Mr. Burke, Mr. Mackenzie, David Rittenhouse, the great planner and builder Robert Smith, William Bingham with his witty and beautiful wife Anne, not to forget the Philadelphia' belle' Miss Charlotte Biddle.

It started with a fruit bowl with sweet white wine spiked with rum, followed by Oyster stew, then roast turkey stuffed with raisins, apples and chestnuts. A standing "rump roast", known as a balancing haunch of beef. A young roast goat, cooked ham, smoked whitefish and salmon, fried sweetbreads, meat pie made of lamb, pickled beef tongue in Madeira wine sauce and roast pigeons followed by pears cooked in cinnamon, nutmeg and ginger. Floating Islands, trifles and flummeries. Bread puddings, all kinds of jams, quince pies, apple pies with raisins, brown sugar and walnuts. Syllabubs, coffee, tea, all sorts of wine and not to forget the Sally Lunn bread!

In spite of all this great partying, Ben believed in moderation in eating, drinking and avoiding all the extremes and of all, not to waste any time, for that is the very substance life is made of!

Wine served: Rhenish, French "Cahor" or Spanish Rioja.

Chamber music played: Songs of Scotland.

ROAST TURKEY WITH APPLES, RAISIN AND CHESTNUT STUFFING

To make the dressing: mark **chestnuts** across with a knife and steam in a casserole half full of water for 8 minutes. Drain, cool, peel and cut in half. Boil **raisins** for 5 minutes, turn off the heat and let stand another 5 minutes, then drain and cool. Sauté **sliced bacon** with cut up **turkey liver** and pieces of **onion**. Make **croutons** by roasting a few pieces of bread in a pan with **margarine**. Peel and core **two juicy apples**, cut each into 8 sections.

Mix all together with a little **salt, pepper, sage, thyme**. Stuff turkey with the dressing and tie both ends (this was given great attention in open spit roasting.) Roast turkey at 325 degrees for 3 to 4 hours.

Meanwhile, cook **stomach and heart** until tender, reduce the broth in half and later add to the sauce. Chop meat fine and add later to the sauce.

Take out the cooked turkey from the roasting pan, remove all twine, place on the serving platter and keep warm. Deglaze the juice in the roasting pan with some **light bouillon**, reduce, strain (add stomach and chopped heart) and bind lightly with **potato starch**, thick enough to pour over the sliced meats. (I hate thick, pasty, floury sauces.)

Serve first with dressing followed by slicing the meat.

Wine: Chateau La Tour Blanche or Chenin Blanc.
Music: Oboe concerti by Telemann

CUMBERLAND SAUCE

A much preferred sauce for game and fowl.

Prepare: Blanch **one shallot or 2 Tblsp. of finely chopped onion in 3 Tblsp. water, 1 Tblsp. of wine vinegar**, boil until half the liquid is evaporated and add: **1 cup of red currant jelly, 6 ounce can of frozen orange juice, 1/2 cup port or sherry wine, 1/2 tsp. ground ginger, 1 tsp. Dijon mustard, a dash of tabasco, salt and pepper**. Simmer till smooth.

Another BREAD STUFFING for any occasion

Sauté in **butter or bacon fat**: 1 cup of small diced **celery**, 1 cut of small diced **onions,**
2 firm, medium **apples**, sliced. Cook until tender and add: trace of **cayenne pepper and 1/2 tsp. poultry seasoning**. (A poultry seasoning contains: marjoram, thyme, sage, rosemary; basil, chervil and savory)

In a big pan toast **8 cups of breadcrumbs** in a **little margarine** till golden. Combine all 'stuff' together with **1/2 cup of chick bouillon** and **chopped parsley** and mix well.

This can be used for stuffing or baked separately.

Optional: All kinds of nuts and fowl-livers.

Another scrumptious sweet from times past was the famous SALLY LUN (close to a brioche). Other favorites were Apple Brown Betty, or

Francois Boeres, Chef de Cuisine

an Olykoek, (close to a donut), plum pudding (still on the rise), Jumbles, trifles, Floating Islands or Fools (with stewed fruits and whipped cream) or Flummery (a Jell-O-like oatmeal pudding).

SALLY LUNN

Soften one package of dry **yeast in 1/4 cup warm water**. In a bowl: pour 1/2 cup hot **milk** over 6 tsp. of **butter** until melted. Add a little **salt** and stir in 1/2 cup sifted **flour**. Beat smooth, adding the yeast and mix well. Work in 1-1/2 cups sifted **flour** by mixing in two well-beaten **eggs**. Beat vigorously for at least 5 minutes. Scrape the dough into the center of the bowl, cover and let rise in a warm place for about 45 minutes. After it rises to double its bulk, beat again for 5 minutes and fill in a Baba or Kugelhoff (turban) mold, cover and let rise double. Bake at 350 degrees approximately 35 minutes or until done.

Note: Sally Lunn was a real person. She lived near London a few hundred years ago and served her hot Sally Lunn bread near a resort in Bath. It became an instant success.

—

The English poet, Moore, visiting Philly in 1804 remarked that Philadelphia is the only place in America that can boast of literary society. When this hospitable city of Brotherhood had been occupied by Howe, Ben remarked: "I think Philly has taken Howe."

It was also here where Ben Franklin signed the Declaration of Independence. Soon after this, the old had all come to an end and when Jackson had withdrawn almost all the money out of the bank, things never were the same.

And never the same in France.

When our revolution had succeeded, the alliance with France had cost Louis XVI the exorbitant sum of 30 billions (in today's dollars) for the American cause.

HIS-STORY of Good Cooking

In France this had triggered discontent and unrest. Ironically, it started in the higher ranks and filtered down to the already agitated Proletariat. In essence, our cause became their reckoning and the beginning of the French revolution.

> A small Flame can Set
> An Immense Heap of Wood on Fire
> Van Paassen

Are you ready to make a real

SANDWICH FROM THE EARL OF SANDWICH?

Butter up **a slice of bread**, add some **mustard**. On top place a hefty piece of crisp, well done **slice of roast beef or lamb**. Next, cover this with another piece of buttered **bread** and press down firmly. Now, grab it by its ears and take a bite.

Note: Serve not too hot or cold, with **horseradish and gherkins**. Also a finger bowl should be provided.

Benjamin Franklin and The Earl of Sandwich

Drawing up the Constitution was a great challenge with many obstacles. After many debates, Ben was asked about the future of this delicate instrument. "The only thing I can be sure of," he replied, "is death and taxes."

One thing is for sure, Ben knew everything and everybody. This brilliant character of profound knowledge was at home in every affair of state. After the surrender of Bourgogne at Saratoga, he was already in Versailles, charming his way through the court, to appeal for the so much needed support for Washington's army.

Before the Revolution, Franklin lived in London for an extensive time and engaged in many constructive activities, like printing. Besides many friends, he also had encountered the Earl of Sandwich, a man of somber disposition and many vices. Also, his infamous Fire and Hell Club, where he was Master of Ceremonies of many nefarious activities, had brought him a bad reputation.

Especially, card-playing times often lasted around the clock, so time did not permit elaborate or conventional meals. Therefore, quick food was served, wedged between two pieces of bread. Franklin got the idea and on his return to America, brought home the Sandwich.

It became very popular in Philly.

Working all day in the field, a farmer sure appreciated a good sandwich with his jug of ginger ale.

OF LEGUMES AND VEGETABLES . . . that green stuff that we live on.

Thomas Jefferson, the Planter

Oops, I almost forgot one of the most prolific personalities in our young Republic. Every time I work in my garden on our farm. . . excuse me that I am so partial to the past. . . I am always reminded of THOMAS JEFFERSON. . . not only a great politician, but also a man with great knowledge in agronomy, general affairs in cultivation of everything that grows, propagating, introducing, and importing all kinds of fruits and vegetables. Some people in American had never seen such as asparagus. Emperor Augustus liked asparagus. Marie Washington had some in her garden, but here in Monticello, this tender spring vegetable of the Lily family was served in great proportions. The Monticello gardens even had green Rapuncel "wheat salad" most people don't even know today. There were rows of stalk celery, knob-celery, spinach, colander, radishes, pumpkins from the Cote D'Azur, cabbages from Savoy, Mediterranean watermelons, broccoli from Pisa, German Kale, Collard, Turnips and gooseberries, not to mention rows of orchards of selected fruits. In 1787, Thomas Jefferson (now minister to France) traveled from France to Italy through never ending vineyards and mountains of olive trees. This inspired him to plant vines and olive trees in Monticello. His adventure in viniculture and olives ended in disaster. He also was growing potatoes and tomatoes, both night-shade plants that were looked upon with 'shady' suspicion. Mainly, their leaves were known to be toxic. Jefferson served a very diversified menu. . . from hot flambé to freezing cold ice cream first served here to a ever ending flow of guests passing day in and day out in one of the greatest hospitable places in North America.

HIS-STORY of Good Cooking

Jefferson's wine cellars were the best on the continent. His hospitality to accommodate guests from all over the world was beyond reproach. His Presidential salary could not satisfy his never ending expenses and, close to bankruptcy, he was forced to sell some of his best books, including a few books of procedure in cookery. Another low watermark in his life came to him when Cornwallis entered Monticello (Jefferson managed to escape), burned some buildings, stables and ate all the food and livestock, drank most of the wine and carried off his slaves.

The Louisiana Territory purchase was one of the greatest events of his administration. The fifteen million dollar deal (about three cents an acre) was signed by Napoleon as he took a bath in his bathtub.

Personally, Thomas Jefferson is one of my favored presidents who loved Life, Liberty and Happiness.

I had, at the beginning of this chapter, written a fat page about Jefferson's life and legacy. Mysteriously, it got lost, Puff...gone, nowhere to be found, just as mysteriously as the men I had written about. Then it occurred to me, that I really was pleased to have lost the page, realizing that I possibly could not ever have done justice to this man with his exuberant wisdom and greatness and it would be a shame to take away that "mystical" aura by probing the man to death, surrendering all imagination.

Jefferson, of great pleasant and sanguine nature, was also known as a great host, great dancer, inclined to music occasionally playing his violin. His straight posture, sandy hair and sparkling hazel eyes showed that here honest and clear words were spoken and that this was a man with great knowledge, supposedly using his free thinking mind "generously."

To Jefferson, mediocrity was intolerable and his meticulous commitment for excellence often brought conflicts within himself.

John Adams, of quite different political views, recommended that Jefferson draw up a Constitution. By all means! So eventually, that frail piece of parchment, the most important "Instrument" and valuable statement of endeavor anywhere, was born by a pen guided by Jefferson's hand in a Philly tavern in Penn-Sylvania.

In those days, a tavern was an Institution, the place where our Revolution was plotted an schemed. Here great deals and plans were forged, the Marine Corps founded, a bawdy tavern melody adapted to: National Songs and reckoning, that it was not the church, but primarily the tavern that became the center of gathering and socializing. Here people changed

Francois Boeres, Chef de Cuisine

from introverts to extroverts. One could pound his fists on the table using expressive language, saying what was on his mind, eye to eye with great and impressive enthusiasm. It was also the place where judges were judged and fools had their day. The tavern was more than a newspaper, here you got to know what was going on, first hand, where and ,whodunit, and of all, if hungry. . . for it was late and the kitchen closed, the tavern owner still could bring you a piece of cold roast beef with relish and' a piece of bread before retiring.

Note: It was customary to invite an old buddy for a drink if you met him more than twice a day on the street!

Note: Often, popular melodies were adopted for important occasions. This could be old folk or tavern songs, church or Christmas melodies, everyone knew how to sing them.

> *THE PUNISHMENT OF WISE MEN WHO REFUSE TO TAKE PART IN THE AFFAIRS OF GOVERNMENT, IS TO LIVE UNDER THE GOVERNMENT OF UNWISE MEN.*
>
> *Plato*

> *ALL AUTHORITY BELONGS TO THE PEOPLE.*
>
> *Jefferson*

Desserts

FLOATING ISLAND
(for 6 plus)

Separate **whites from 7 eggs** and place in the cooler before whipping, (they do better that way). Mix **egg yolks with 1 Tblsp. of milk, trace of salt, a little powdered sugar and 1 Tblsp. of corn or potato starch dissolved in a little water**. Mix until smooth and set aside.

Beat the **egg whites** until firm and stiff, adding a **trace of salt and powdered sugar**. With a Tblsp., scoop out little "balls" and boil them, a few at a time, for a minute on top of a liter of slow simmering **milk**, then turn them over and boil for another minute. Take them out, drain and set aside.

To make the Vanilla cream: In the slow simmering milk, pour **one cup of sugar**, stir till dissolved. Add some **vanilla extract** and all the egg-yolk mixture, stirring vigorously to thicken. Take care not to boil to prevent the eggs from scrambling and breaking down. Pour immediately into a flat serving bowl and top with the egg white "balls". Cool before serving.

YE GOOD OLD TRIFLE

In a 3 to 4 quart serving glass or crystal bowl, place a small box **(14) lady-fingers**, or pound cake slices along the sides and the bottom of the bowl. Soak in **a cup of Madeira, Port or sweet Sauterne**.

To make the custard pudding (known as Anglaise):

Heat up **two cups of milk with 1 Tblsp. of sugar, some cinnamon, almond extract and blanched grated lemon rinds with 2 tsp. of brandy**.

Mix **4 egg yolks** with **some milk or cream, add 2 tsp. of corn or dissolved potato starch**. . . . add this to the slow simmering milk, stirring vigorously so it does not come to a boil. Take off the fire and cool. Pour all in the bowl on top of the lady-fingers or the cake. Lay out with **peaches, apricots or quinces**. Cool in the refrigerator. Before serving, top with **1 quart of whipped cream, powdered sugar** added. Garnish with **currant,**

raspberry or strawberry jelly. This is almost as good as....feeling like a kid again!

RUM CUSTARD CREAM
for cakes and eclairs

In a stainless steel bowl, mix:

1 beaten egg
1/2 cup of sugar
2/3 cup of half and half
2 Tblsp. sifted flour

Mix well and place in a double boiler with slow boiling water. Whip continuously for 5 minutes, then add 2 Tblsp. dark rum and whip for 5 minutes more, until smooth and glossy. Remove from heat and refrigerate for 1 hour. Fold in 1 cup of whipped cream.

CUSTARD CREAM

In a stainless bowl, mix:

4 eggs
trace of salt
1/4 cup of sugar
1/2 tsp. vanilla

Place in a double boiler with slow boiling water and whip till frothy. Stir continuously over moderate heat until the mixture is thick enough to stick to the spoon. Do not let it come to a boil.

SMOOTH CHOCOLATE FROSTING

To give a nice finish to eclairs, mix:

2-1/2 cups powdered sugar

8 ounces soft butter
1 4 ounce bar of dark chocolate, softened
1 tsp. vanilla
1 Tblsp. milk

Beat till smooth and fluffy, brush over cakes and pastry.

WHITE BUTTER FROSTING

Mix:

3 cups of powdered sugar
5 Tblsp. of soft butter
1 tsp. vanilla
2 Tblsp. milk

Beat till smooth and spreadable.

To Make MERINGUES

In a clean mixing bowl beat on medium speed:
    6 egg whites till foamy,
    beat in 1/4 tsp. cream of tartar
    and a pinch of salt.
Gradually increase speed to moderate fast for about 1 minute.
Add: **2 cups of fine (bar) sugar**...a spoon at a time, then add **2 tsp. of vanilla**.
Increase speed to fast for about 2-1/2 to 3 minutes till it forms very stiff peaks and all sugar is dissolved. (Don't underbeat).
Preheat oven to 250 degrees. With a spoon or a pastry bag with a big star tip*, form 3 to 3-1/2 inch long meringues on a sheet pan lined with wax paper. Turn oven down to 200, after about 5 minutes, place meringues on the middle rack and bake for about 1 hour. They should come out white. The are ready when light and brittle, therefore remove them gently and carefully form the paper and store in a dry place. It is best to use them soon.
Meringues are used in many fine desserts like the famous "Vacherin" (made out of baked egg whites, whipped cream and meringues). The "La

Francois Boeres, Chef de Cuisine

Rousse Gastronomique" mentioned that Marie Antoinette loved them so much that she often made them.

*Note: The pastry bag was not invented till the first quarter of the 19th century. Eventually, it found its place in every Victorian kitchen. Previously they only used spoons.

Here is a nice meringue dessert:

MERINGUE CAFÉ GLACEE

In a dessert cup, place a **scoop of vanilla ice cream**. With a spoon, press a small cavity into the ice cream. Pour over some **espresso or a strong instant coffee**. Place meringue on top and garnish with **whipped cream**.
Optional: ....Kalua, shredded chocolate or sugar glazed violet leaves.

DOUBLE QUICK FRENCH PUFF PASTRY

Use only unbleached low gluten pastry flour to make this pastry, any other will be more difficult.

Sift **2 cups of flour** into a large bowl adding **1/2 tsp. of salt**. With the roller and the heel of your hands, beat and flatten **8 ounces of chilled butter**, cut into small pieces and slowly work into the flour until the mixture looks like coarse meal, then mix in **1/2 cup of ice water**. Roll into a ball, sprinkle with flour, wrap in wax paper and refrigerate for 1 hour.

Roll out the dough into a 6 x 12 inch thick rectangle, keep rolling pin and work space dusted with flour.

Fold the 6 inch side over the center and the other 'third' (of the bottom) on top. This should be 4 x 6 inches and is called the first turn.

Hit and roll out the dough into a 6 x 12 rectangle and fold as before, this is called the second turn.

Make 2 more turns, the same way, ending up with a 4 x 6 rectangle. Now that all the turns are completed, wrap the dough in wax paper and refrigerate. This dough is 'universal' and can be used for a multitude of pastries and dishes.

SIMPLE PIE PASTRY (Pate Brise)

Blend:

3 cups of sifted flour,
1 stick butter
5 Tblsp. Crisco shortening, chilled
a little salt
a dash of vinegar
1 beaten egg

Blend and mix in **4 Tblsp. cold water**. Mix dough just enough so it resembles a rough meal. Form into a ball, wrap in wax paper and refrigerate for 1 hour.

GENOISE

Anyone who can make a good Hollandaise most likely knows how to make 'Genoise', they are all made in a double boiler.

First, butter and dust the cake pan with flour. Preheat the oven to 350.

On top of a double boiler with the water hardly boiling, place a stainless steel bowl with **6 beaten egg yolks** mixed with **1 cup of fine sugar**. Whisk the mixture vigorously until it foams into light fluffy ribbons. Then add **1 tsp. vanilla**. In folding motion, gently sift in one cup of flour a little at a time, add a 'stick' of melted lukewarm butter. Pour batter into the cake pan and bake for 30 to 35 minutes or until done. Test with a small skewer. If it looks 'clean' and hot, it should be ready to be placed on the rack. This cake is used for butter-cream and cream filled cakes, saturated syrup and cordial cakes, filled with glazed fruits, nuts, whipped creams and ice cream cakes, etc.

CREAM PUFF PASTRY (Pate a Choux)

The 'imperative' puff pastry is called for many dishes in fine kitchens, and mostly used to make eclairs, cream puffs, Choux, profiteroles, cheese 'ratons', Dauphine potatoes, etc.

Francois Boeres, Chef de Cuisine

In a heavy pot: Boil on high heat, **2 cups of water** with **2 sticks of butter** and some **salt**. Reduce heat, add **2 cups of sifted flour** and beat vigorously with a wooden spoon until it doesn't stick anymore and forms into a big lump.

Transfer dough into a mixing bowl and mix in: **6 eggs**, one at a time. With every egg, blend mixture till glossy and smooth. This should come out all right, but if it's too thick, add some eggs.

Bake profiteroles, that are little balls used to garnish soups, etc. by making little dots on a baking sheet with the pastry bag.

For eclairs, make 4 inch long stripes, using a bigger pastry bag tip.

With this dough, you can make:

DAUPHINE POTATOES.....
they are delicious!

First, use good '**bakers**' **to make rice potatoes**. Add **salt, pepper** and a trace of **nutmeg**. Add **a few eggs** to give it a 'pasty' texture. Mix with half the volume of the puff pastry dough. In restaurants, we used a pastry bag with a big tip, squeezing and cutting out the dough the size of a cork, right into the fryer until they float. At home I use a small spoon to scoop out the dough to drop it right into the hot fat.

PEACH MELBA

"Prima donna" Melba loved this 'Ambrosia' with strawberries and strawberry syrup...served in a fluted sundae cup. In the sundae cup, place **2 scoops of good vanilla ice cream**, cover with **half a peach**. Pour over with a thick **raspberry syrup** or Melba sauce, then top generously with **whipped cream**. Garnish with a gaufrette roll.

To make MELBA SAUCE

In a saucepan...combine **10 ounces frozen raspberries, 1/2 cup currant jelly with 2 Tblsp. of sugar**. Boil on slow fire for 20 minutes, stirring often. Add **1 tsp. of lemon juice**, place in a jar and refrigerate.

POIRE (PEAR) BELLE HELENE

Same as above, except cover with half a pear instead of a peach and use only chocolate syrup.

COFFEE GLACEE

Place **2 scoops of good vanilla ice cream** in a sundae glass, pour over a **strong mocha type coffee** or some made from instant coffee, top with **whipped cream** and sprinkle with **shredded chocolate**, some gourmands like Kalua. Garnish with a gaufrette roll.

To make GAUFRETTES

To make the dough...mix **1/2 cup of soft melted butter or margarine** with **1-1/2 cups fine sugar with 3 beaten eggs**, beat until frothy, add a small **pinch of salt, vanilla and a section of lemon juice**. Mix with approximately **2 cups of sifted flour**, a little at a time, with **2 cups of water**. Beat until thick but still pourable.

To bake: Preheat gaufrette iron, brush with **melted margarine or pork fat** and pour in some dough, enough not to spill any. The finished golden gaufrettes are then taken out and rolled up quickly before the get brittle. Here, its nice to have a helper. My wife rolled them quickly around a round wooden spoon handle and my uncle Vic let them cool off in tall champagne glasses. Also gaufrettes can be dipped half way in a melted dark or semi sweet chocolate, they look so neat and can be served at tea or coffee hour.

Mother's recipe for GAUFRES

Beat together:

6 eggs,
1-1/2 cup sugar
1/2 cup sifted flour
4 Tblsp. melted butter
1/2 cup of oil
3 tsp. lemon juice
Anise oil or vanilla

Finely grated rind from 1 lemon

Bake in a gaufrette or Pizelle Iron. The iron should be preheated and wiped with a towel dipped in oil before pouring in the dough. This so called gaufres or pizelles can be made into triangles or rolled before cooling off. Serve with coffee, tea or ice cream.

To make CREME CARAMEL
(Custard)

In a pan, caramelize **3/4 cup sugar** to light brown and divide into 8 custard molds.

In a mixing bowl, beat all together:

8 whole eggs
1 cup sugar
3 cups hot milk
1 cup cream
1 tsp. vanilla
trace of salt.

Set custard molds in a pan of boiling water and pour in the custard mixture.

Place in a 350 degree preheated oven for 40 minutes until done and place in the refrigerator for 2 hours. Loosen custard around the edges with a small knife. Remove and serve with the caramel side up.

CHOCOLATE MOUSSE
'mouse' to my Granddaughter Sarah

Prepare **6 ounces of dark chocolate**, melted and runny, but not too hot.

In a chilled bowl, whip **1 quart of heavy cream**. Add **1 cup of fine sugar** at a time.

Beat **12 egg whites** stiff, gradually adding **1 cup of fine sugar** at a time. Beat at high speed until it forms stiff peaks. Gently fold the chocolate into the egg whites and whipped cream. Pour into Hurricane or cocktail glasses.

Chill and sprinkle with dark shredded chocolate. Should make 24 servings that keep for days.

Francois Boeres, Chef de Cuisine

CHAPTER 5....ABOUT VEGETABLES AND SAUCES

BEFORE I MENTION VEGETABLES, I would like to say a few words about potatoes. Of course, potatoes are vegetables. My instant perception of vegetables links me directly to stuff like lettuce, cabbage, peas, beans, or carrots, turnips, rutabagas, knob-celery, and all that. Here potatoes were potatoes, the endless stand-by, the roots of a kitchen. We had fish, meat, vegetables or maybe pasta, but potatoes were potatoes and that was it. A capital to be addressed separately.

So, now I say, a potato is not a potato, now look her. My dad once said to mam, you make so much fuss about a potato. A potato is just a potato, without really giving it too much thought. So, instead getting mad, for good cook she was, she got even. The following day, she served an ordinary of the run potato and guess who got all ruffled up? They are terrible! said Pa. Well, a potato is a potato you told me, said she.

In the past, not every day was a meat day, maybe every other day or so. An average meal in any household could be thick soups or onion soups, creamed potatoes, pastas, croquette potatoes with asparagus or broiled tomatoes, potato pancakes, any kind of dumplings, a salad panache with hard boiled eggs and French bread or a casserole of fava beans in brown sauce, braised Belgian endives, or just a plain Omelet. I remember that day. We only had baked apples, and I loved them. That is why I still remember.

Fall was the time to fill the cellar. First with heaps of two different potatoes. The guy who sold them also sold coal that was needed for cooking the potatoes and other food besides heating the house. And there was cabbage to be cut for sauerkraut, staples of apples and shelves full of white and red wine. Grandpa Phil Hipp had two gardens, one behind his house, square, and as wide as a street, the other, at the end of town, was about the same. In this one, he planted carrots, two different potatoes, onions, red cabbages, peas and tomatoes.

Cooking Potatoes for the trade.

It scares me to see what they do to potatoes being served these days in many food establishments. They have mashed potatoes that look more like plaster, ready to fill a hole in the wall. That is not funny. If instant powdered potatoes are used, please have sufficient boiling water ready in a big pot or mixing bowl with milk, salt, white pepper and hot melted butter or margarine.

Now, pour in the potato powder, stirring and mixing vigorously, a little at a time until it forms little peaks. That is the time to watch for. Stop mixing a few seconds and let the powder absorb all moisture. The mashed potatoes should be light and fluffy. If too thin, fix by adding a little more powder by hand. Finish with a trace of nutmeg, a couple of eggs to correct the blandness of the powder. Pour in a serving tray or pan and top with more butter.

How to make CROQUETTE POTATOES

Just continue from the above procedure, except add enough more potato powder and a few more eggs and fresh chopped parsley, to make the mixture firm enough to handle. Scoop out and make potato balls when warm enough to handle. Spread out some flour on the table, dip your hand in the flour and roll the balls out to a portion big enough so two can compete with one baked potato. Tap both ends flat with the flat side of a knife. Now, they look like corks. With the flour still on, all you do is dip the croquettes in beaten egg and roll them in breadcrumbs. Dip them in the hot deep fryer fat until golden brown before serving. (At home I use real potatoes).

Helping in the Garden

I must've been about eight when I helped Grandpa in his garden. He spaded the first row over and placed the next one into the furrow and made

Francois Boeres, Chef de Cuisine

sure the sod was turned over and mixed with old bedding and composted with some fertilizer. Last, he harrowed and raked all out to prepare the beds. I loved to help him plant beans and peas. As a proud and successful gardener in late fall, Grandpa let me pull his four wheeled wooden hand wagon full of produce through town.

He just paced along, smoking his pipe with a happy face because we got a lot of attention with our potatoes, tomatoes, baskets of green beans and cabbages as big as a head.

I say, vegetables are a finicky affair if they aren't fresh or properly cooked, they're worthless. I had learned this a long time ago working in hotels by cooking green vegetables in a long and shallow chafing pan with not too much water and covered up with a wet kitchen towel that became puffed up by steam, in no time the vegetables are cooked and cooled off in cold running water. The short period of slow boiling retained most of the vitamins, crispness, food value and color. We stayed away as much as possible from deep frying vegetables. It was not too popular and neither very healthy, except for some salsify and onion rings.

___ASPARAGUS is always a royal treat. They should be steamed in a covered pot with a little water and salt added till about tender, served immediately, preferably on a plate on a white napkin. Serve with drawn butter, hollandaise or a vinaigrette.

___BROCCOLI is appropriate to serve with any meal. They look so prominent. If served as "fleurons" on a crudities platter, it is best to pour boiling water with salt added over broccoli and let stand for 7 minutes before cooling. For serving hot, cook for 8 minutes. They should be crisp before serving. I liked to rinse them in garlic butter. If fleurons are made, save the stalks, peal and slice in diagonal pieces and add to the broccoli or mixed vegetables. Cooking vegetables gives away a "mark" of a Chef. In some orders, tomatoes have to be peeled by cutting out the "navel" and score with a cross. Dip quickly into boiling water and peel off the skin. Celery should be peeled and asparagus peeled at the bottom, big mushrooms are peeled by pulling off the skin toward the center.

BELGIAN ENDIVE

Did you ever take a close look at this strange looking yellow cone shaped Belgian Endive in the salad section? They are from the chicory family and are raised in Holland and Belgium in rows of stacked beds with subdued light. Then they are "cut-off" and shipped in crepe paper all over the world. Don't let the price fool you. This is a compact salad that gives a lot of volume, especially if cleaned and chopped into one inch pieces. Wash and drain the broken up leaves.

The salad is prepared with **wine vinegar, a squeeze of lemon juice, pepper, salt** and a trace of **sugar,** thin-sliced **onions, and vegetable oil**. Mix well and let rest 15 minutes before serving. Belgian endive is also used to decorate other salads.

Note: The Belgian Endive is related to the green endive salad and to the wild endive often found by the roadside. It's blue flowers look very much like bachelor-buttons.

BRAISED BELGIAN ENDIVE
(8 endives for 4 persons, 10 for six persons)

Prepare: clean, rinse and trim off the end of the endive. Boil for 8 minutes. Strain and place in a Pyrex or fireproof casserole. Sprinkle and pour over, **salt, pepper, two level tsp. of sugar, a little lemon juice, one stick of melted butter and 1/2 cup chicken bouillon**. Bake in a preheated oven at 350 degrees for approximately 30 minutes or until soft and brown. Don't let this refined vegetable pass you by.

The best FRESH TOMATO SALAD

Tomatoes are best in season. They are plentiful, much cheaper and best of all, they taste like tomatoes! There is nothing like a fresh picked tomato with its distinctive earthy acerbic aroma. In Jefferson's time, tomatoes were known as "Pomme d'amour" or love apple because of its blood red color, soft fleshy skin and if squeezed, able to bounce right back, like the soft skin of a maiden in bloom. I only eat and indulge myself with tomatoes when they are ripe in tomato time, sold by the bushel on the road stand.

Francois Boeres, Chef de Cuisine

Anything out of season, picked green and sent thousands of miles away tastes like biting into a toe of the deceased. The best, all year around, are sold as "tomatoes on the vine."

To prepare:

Core and cut **tomatoes** into large round slices. Lay them out on a large platter not higher than two layers. Sprinkle with fine chopped **onions and parsley or chives, salt, pepper, wine vinegar and your favorite vegetable oil**. Let rest for one half-hour. This is a very good tasting and simple salad to make.

SALADS

A good salad should be made with crisp leafs. If they become too tired in the fridge, loosen leafs and revive them in cold water with some **salt** added. It should come right back, unless it has gone too far. Salads can be served at any occasion and imaginations have no boundaries. The Grecians ate salads with olive oil and wine vinegar. The Roman soldiers ate these tender vegetables dipped in salt, therefore name 'Salada'. Salt at that time was very valuable. It was the custom to compensate Roman Legionnaires partly with salt or a 'salary'.

*Gifted people are the salt of the earth.
Pathetic people aren't worth a grain of salt.*

SALAD PANACHE

Salads used in salad panache are:

CURLY ENDIVE: Use only the 'inside' leaves and discard the tough and bitter outside leaves.

BOSTON LETTUCE: Use most of the tender leaves, discard wilted outside leaves.

ROMAINE: Remove leaves from core, discard spotty and wilted outside leaves, split big leaves in half at the center before cutting.

GREEN OR RED LEAF LETTUCE: Discard all wilted outside leaves.

BELGIAN ENDIVE: Trim off end of the root, cut half into slices, leaving the tender and nice pointed leaves for decoration.

LEAF SPINACH: Enhance and give a colorful tone to any salad, pick through the spinach for wilted leaves.

OPTIONAL: Watercress, radicchio, thin red onion slices, cucumber and tomato slices. Use your favorite dressing.

SALAD MIMOSA

Wash, drain and break up head of **Boston or Bib lettuce**. Prepare a **'Vinaigrette'** (look for Vinaigrette), minced **scallions**, snipped **chives**, mix all with the salad and place into a bowl. Remove the **yolks from 2 hard boiled eggs** and press through a sieve, do the same with the **white**. Sprinkle the chopped white of the eggs around the salad and the yolks in the center.

Optional: **Cherry tomatoes** cut in half, small can of **white asparagus**.

A good piquant DIJON HONEY DRESSING

Mix: 1/2 cup sour cream with
   3 Tblsp. of lemon juice, 1 tsp. of vinegar,
   the grated rind of 1 lemon, 2 tsp. of Dijon style mustard,
   2 Tblsp. of honey, salt, Pepper,
   1 minced garlic clove, chopped parsley,
   dash of Tabasco and basil.
In a stream, stir in 1/2 cup of good **vegetable oil**, 1/3 cup of **olive oil**.

DILLED ASPARAGUS WITH VINAIGRETTE
Vegetables 4 to 6 per person

Cook two bunches of **Asparagus** in boiling salted water for 6 to 7 minutes. Cool off in slow running cold water and drain. Place on a plate laid out with **lettuce leaves**, sprinkle with **snipped dill** and **paper thin red onion rings**. Pour some of the **vinaigrette** over and serve the rest on the side.

Francois Boeres, Chef de Cuisine

To Make VINAIGRETTE

In a bowl, mix and whisk together:
    1/2 cup of lemon juice
    A little salt, pepper and sweet marjoram
    1 minced garlic clove
    1 minced shallot or the white of a scallion
    1/2 cup vegetable oil
    1/3 cup olive oil
    add fresh chopped parsley.

YOGURT DRESSING

Combine 1 cup of yogurt with
    3 Tblsp. orange juice
    2 Tblsp. honey
    1 Tblsp. lemon juice
    dash minced fresh mint
    1/2 tsp. of mild mustard
    salt and pepper, Mix Well.

CELERIAC - - - or Knob Celery

Its difficult to explain this vigorous, ardent and outlandish celery of all celeries, widely known and used in Europe, but its slowly catching on and getting the attention it deserves. There are many ways to prepare this healthy bucolic root. Some people believe Celeriac is an aphrodisiac. To prepare, it can be peeled and cut in one inch cubes and boiled for 10 minutes, drained and sauteed in **oil**, add **salt, pepper** with a squeeze of **lemon juice** and garnished with chopped **parsley**. It can also be served cold, mixed with other salads using a Vinaigrette.

Another CELERIAC SALAD

Serve raw and marinated. Peel and cut Celeriac in two pieces and place flat side on the cutting board (so it is safe to cut with a 'sharp' knife). Cut into flat slices and then lengthwise into 'matchsticks' about half the thickness of wooden kitchen matches. Soak them in some **lemon juice** and **vegetable oil, white pepper and a trace of salt**. After half hour, add enough **mayonnaise** to bind the celery but never enough to be 'runny'. This salad is best served in a glass bowl with hors d'oeuvres or smorgasbord .... so, next time, grab one of these 'knobs' and surprise someone.

TURNIPS AND RUTABAGAS

Surprise someone pleasantly by serving this 'rustic' vegetable. Boil the **turnips** in plenty of water for 15 minutes, drain and discard water, cool off and peel by squeezing the skin off with your fingers. Slice into sections... sauté one inch cut onions and add a **white sauce (bechamel) with pepper, sage and bay leaves and some cream**. Drop turnips in the sauce and cook till tender. Serve with fresh **butter** and sliced **scallions**.

GLAZED PARSNIPS

Cook one pound of peeled **parsnips** for about 8 minutes (parsnips are cut into finger size sticks). Drain and layout in a casserole, sprinkle with **melted butter, pepper, a little salt and brown sugar**. Pour a cup of **chicken bouillon** over and cook in the oven till done and 'glazed.'

Making a RATATOUILLE

This is a nice meat-free casserole and a fine dish for Vegetarians.
Prepare: Cut **3 small Zucchini** in round slices, reserve
Peel **1 big eggplant**, cut in 1" cubes, fry soft, reserve
Optional: **1 big sliced green pepper**, fried, reserve
Sauté 1 big or 2 small **onions** with 2 cloves of crushed **garlic**. Pour in 1 small can of crushed **tomatoes** or 6 fresh pomo 'doro pear tomatoes. Mix with eggplant, zucchini, pepper and bake in a preheated oven at 360 to 400 degrees for 20 minutes (or fry in a pan till some sauce is evaporated).

Note: Some cooks serve this with **grated cheese** or with melted **parmigiana**. Spices are **marjoram, savory and parsley**.

Francois Boeres, Chef de Cuisine

FAVA BEANS

...are available in cans, fresh and dried. The dried have to be soaked in water for 24 hours. The one with tough skin should be avoided but most fava's today are tender and of high protein. They are cooked slowly until tender and best served with **olive oil, garlic and summer savory**. At home, we used to eat them in a brown (espagnole) sauce with smoked pork shoulder or fatback (or a whole slab of bacon.)

FRESH SNAPPY GREEN BEANS

Snap both ends and drop whole in boiling water for 5 - 6 minutes... anyway, they should come out crisp and have a green color. Sauté in **butter, pepper, salt** and a few drops of **lemon juice**. Serve immediately, plain with sliced roast almonds or pieces of red pimentos.

CAULIFLOWER

If we have parties at home, we prefer to serve the entire head of cauliflower. Cook the cauliflower with sufficient water, head down, for about 25 minutes. Drain carefully. To serve place a bowl upside down on top of the pot of cauliflower. Reverse both, and presto, you have a nice head of cauliflower, ready to serve. It can be served with melted **butter and parsley**, or with a **white bechamel sauce** or a bechamel sauce with Gruyere (a la Mornay) or polonaise; with chopped eggs, fresh breadcrumbs, butter and parsley.

Note: For a nice presentation, surround cauliflower with the attractive green color of Brussel Sprouts.

BRUSSEL SPROUTS

Are trimmed of their stems and cooked for about 10 minutes and swirled in butter, pepper and salt (some like almonds and sour cream added.)

CARROTS A LA VICHY

For 1 pound (4-8 people), I use the sweet Nantua type, peel and slice in diagonal slices, cover with **water, salt, pepper, half cup of sugar or honey, 2 Tblsp. of butter**. Cook over moderate heat with lid half open, till most liquid is evaporated.

SAVORY STUFFED CABBAGE
for 4-6 people

From 2 selected heads of **cabbage**, cut out the core and remove the leaves. Use only the big leaves and save the inside for the stuffing.

Blanch the leaves in boiling, salted **water** for about 6 minutes, a few at a time. Cool off in cold water. Cut the left over cabbage in half and simmer for 10 minutes, drain and cut into small pieces.

To make the stuffing:

Sauté a big chopped **onion** with 1 minced **garlic clove** in plenty of **butter** or **margarine**, add the cabbage pieces and 8 ounces of fresh cut up **spinach leaves**, braise all together, stirring often, till most of the water has evaporated. Take from the fire and cool, then add 2 cups of **ricotta cheese** with **1 beaten egg, a trace of nutmeg, basil, chopped parsley, salt, pepper** and mix well.

To dress the stuffed cabbage:

Remove cabbage leaves from cold water, drain and dress them smartly on top of a fresh towel in a circular flower-like fashion, each overlapping with stems outside. Sprinkle center with **grated cheddar cheese** and place the stuffing in the center of the laid out leaves. Lift up the cabbage with the 4 corners from the towel and with the other hand, twist and torque the wrapped up cabbage to remove any liquid and to give it a firm round shape. Remove the cabbage ball from the towel and place all, good side up, into a Dutch oven or a deep saucepan. Brush with **butter or margarine**. Cook for about 50 minutes at 325 degrees or until done, if necessary adding some **bouillon** to prevent sticking.

Can be served with a sauce Allemande, topped with dill. For meat stuffing, sauté ground veal or beef with chopped onions and add to the mixture for the stuffing.

Francois Boeres, Chef de Cuisine

Music: The Village Wedding by Lully
Drink: Scotch on the rocks.

POTATO AND LEEK SOUP
4-6 servings

Prepare: Peel **3 medium baking potatoes** and cut into 1/4 inch cubes. Trim most of the green leaves from **4 leeks**, split the leeks lengthwise into 4 strips, rinse under running water and cut into small slices.

Chop **2 medium onions**. In a casserole sauté onions lightly in **butter** till glazed. Pour in **2-1/2 quarts of light chicken stock** and all the leeks and potatoes. Taste with a little **salt, white pepper and a trace of cayenne**. Cook slowly for 50 minutes, finish with **3 Tblsp. of heavy cream or half and half and 2 tsp of butter**.

Left over soup can be served with pride as a cold Vichissoise by pureeing the soup in a food processor, strain through a coarse strainer and add some milk. Garnish soups with chives.

TURNIPS OR KOHLRABI
4-6 servings

Turnips are all year around, Kohlrabi early in the fall. Use **6 turnips**, trim both ends and boil for 20 minutes, **salt** added. Squeeze peel away under running water and cut into 8 sections.

To make the white sauce (bechamel), sauté **one diced onion** in **butter or margarine**, add some **flour and stir in 2 cups of hot milk** and whisk until smooth. Add **white pepper, salt, a touch of nutmeg, 1/2 cup of cream and a pinch of dill**. Add turnips to the white sauce, simmer slowly for 6-8 minutes (don't overcook). Garnish with chopped **chervil or parsley**.

At home we often served them with pearl onions.

Basic White And Brown Sauces

To make a SHRIMP BISQUE

Place "**green shrimp**" in cold water on the fire, add a **bay leaf and salt**. As soon as they start to come to a boil, strain and save the broth, cool and peel shrimp and use for entree. See what you can do with the broth by not pouring it down the drain.

To make the bisque:

In **butter**, sauté fine chopped **onions** and a small amount of **celery**, add some **flour** and stir in the **shrimp stock**. Add **half and half** so it will be light and creamy. Boil slowly, adding a little **sherry wine, a trace of cayenne, a trace of dry English mustard, a trace of curry powder, a trace of thyme and some tomato paste**.

The bisque should be of peach or light rose color. At the end bind with a little **starch** (potato starch is best and lasts longer). Garnish with a few sliced up **shrimp, a dip of sour cream, fresh parsley and a few buttered croutons**.

An old way to thicken soups, sauces and their like was called "coulis." This used fresh and roasted breadcrumbs from a "pullman" type bread. Another method is to reduce the sauce and bind with a 'liaison' of egg yolks (yolks mixed with some cream.)

To make a LOBSTER-COULIS

Drop live **lobsters** into just enough boiling water so they steam more than boil. Take the boiled lobsters out of the pot and save the broth for the sauce. Take out all the lobster meat and chop fine. The meats are added last. For the final preparation, add **half and half cream and semi-dry sherry wine** to the lobster broth, some **salt, a trace of cayenne, dry mustard, thyme, and some tomato paste** (brandy is optional). Add the lobster meat with some **breadcrumbs**. This is a "thick" sauce and is often used to cover fish, croutons, and little patty shells. The classic kitchens used most of the lobster shells, especially the ones with traces of meat inside, like legs, head, etc. We dried them inside or on the top of the oven for some time until they became very crisp. Then crushed them very fine to the powder in a mortar (now, we would use a food processor.) This powder then was added to the coulis or the lobster bisque.

BROWN STOCK

You know about the stock pot, the one that caught fire on the stove. Well, that was the one we used for all our brown sauces. It contained all the bones from the boned out meat; beef bones, pork bones and veal bones, the most valued and most gelatinous. The **bones** are chopped up into 3 to 4 inch pieces, browned in the oven with cut up **carrots, celery, onions and crushed garlic** till dark brown. Deglaze the pan with the bones, cook for a few minutes on top of the stove, transfer into a pot and fill with **water**. Add a little **salt, a bouquet garnie of thyme, sprigs of parsley, chervil, bay leaves** and boil for two hours before straining.

A quick method for BROWN AND OTHER STOCK

My wife keeps frozen bouillon in ice cube trays saved from her stews and soup stock. Quick stock can also be made out of dissolved bouillon cubes. One cube makes 8 ounces bouillon.** I recommend the natural concentrated bouillon paste sold in one pound jars in selected stores and restaurant supply houses. Don't feel uncomfortable to go there. I often buy them for our church suppers. Get one jar of beef base, chicken base (or fish or lobster base), once open, they keep a long time in the refrigerator, one tsp. of this paste makes 8 ounces of good bouillon.
 ** Note: One of these bouillon cubes contains hydrolyzed soy protein, sugar, garlic powder, beef, corn syrup solids, monosodium-glutamate, caramel color, onion powder, beef fat, autolized yeast extract, natural flavor, partially hydrogenated soybean and cottonseed oils, sodium caseinate, silicon dioxide, disodium inosinate and sodium guanyate.....and B.H.A. and citric-acid......, now I ask you one thing - Do you really want to use this??????

BROWN SAUCE OR SAUCE ESPAGNOLE

Sauté fine chopped **onions in pork drippings or margarine** till glazed. Add **flour** and stir till golden brown, fill in the brown stock and some **tomato puree** and cook for one hour.

MADEIRA SAUCE

Reduce **brown sauce or espagnole sauce** on a slow fire for 15 minutes. Add one part of **Madeira** to 3 parts of sauce and boil for 5 minutes. A 'filet' of dark caramel (burned-sugar) can be added.

Note: Burned sugar can be used for many other brown sauces. To make kitchen caramel, in a small iron pot mix **1 cup of sugar with a little water**. Cook on open flame till brown. Now is the time to watch the next stage, have a half cup of **water** ready when it gets dark-brown. Boil slowly with the water to dissolve. Cool and store in a small bottle. Caution should always be used when burning sugar.

SAUCE PERIGUEUX

Just add chopped **truffles** to the Madeira sauce.

SAUCE BORDELAISE

With the heel of a small pan or a coarse grinder crush **one Tblsp. of dark peppers**, add **3 sprigs of cut up tarragon, 4 chopped shallots or 1 medium onion and 2 cups of red wine**. Reduce by half, strain and mix with **2 cups of brown sauce**. Simmer for 15 minutes and serve with chopped **tarragon, parsley and slices of poached marrows**.

SAUCE DIABLO

Just add **Worcestershire and tabasco sauce** to the Bordelaise.

Francois Boeres, Chef de Cuisine

To CLARIFY STOCK
(called clarification)

In a big pot, cook **lean beef and veal bones** for about 2 hours to a strong broth. Then strain and cool off in the refrigerator. This makes it easy to remove any layers of fat. Any broth used for clarification are processed to clear consomme, madrilene, gelatine aspic and their likes.

To clarify: pour stock into a big pot and add...**beaten egg whites, egg shells** mixed with **lean ground beef, chopped onions, celery, sprigs of chervil and parsley, one cut up leek** if available, some **white wine** and in case of a Madrilene soup...add **crushed tomatoes**. Mix all well into the stock and slowly bring to a boil, then simmer for 15 minutes. This brings all froth and mixture to top. Turn off the fire and slowly strain using a ladle trough a fine rinsed out cloth or cheese-cloth. This takes a little time, so shift the cloth occasionally sideways. The clarified stock should be clear so you can see the bottom without any 'stuff' floating about. For aspic, add gelatine.

Note: Way back, we placed a chair upside down on the table and put a pot into it, then strained the broth through a clean linen or cheesecloth tied to all four chair legs. This always worked out well if using large amounts.

Serving COLD MACEDONIA

My friend, JEAN-PAUL....the one that had that bar in Sao Paulo, served, besides many other refreshments, a cool consomme spiked with **white wine** and mixed with fine **diced tomatoes, (peeled) cucumbers, green peppers, celery and a few red hot peppers** served in a glass bowl with a **slice of lemon**. They all loved it, especially on hot days.

Making White Sauces

Basic white sauces are used in making fricassee's, veloutee's, blanquettes, salpicons, white ragout's and other white sauces. The best of these sauces are not only made with bones, but often with the meat itself, like chicken fricassee, veal blanquettes, veloutee's for meat or vegetable soups.

To make CHICKEN STOCK

Boil **fowl** in a large enough kettle (veal bones are optional). Add cut up **onions**, split **carrots, celery, salt, peppercorns and a bouquet garnie**. Remove the cooked fowl from kettle and save for it's intended use. If fowl is to be deboned or cut in half, add bones to the stock and slowly boil for 2 hours. Strain the stock through a fine sieve, chill and refrigerate till used.

WHITE VEAL STOCK

Is made the same as above, it is best to chop up the veal bones into 2 to 3 inch pieces.

BECHAMEL SAUCE

In a sauce pan, sauté chopped **onions** in **butter or margarine** till glazed, stir in **flour** and cook to a light 'roux' for about 3 minutes. Reduce heat and add **scalded milk**, whisking vigorously until smooth. Add **salt, white pepper, bay leaves** and a squeeze of **lemon juice**. Cook for 15 minutes, strain bechamel through fine sieve and cover with buttered wax paper.

VELOUTEE SAUCE

....is made from chicken, veal or fish stock. Proceed as above with **onions** glazed in **butter or margarine**. Instead of milk, use **stock**. The stock should be thick and smooth enough. Strain through a fine sieve.

Note: The old way of straining certain sauces was done by torsion, using a rinsed out towel in which the sauce is poured so it looks like a pouch. The sauce is then pressed and forced through the towel by torsion. This was done by 2 men holding and turning both ends in opposite directions. Pressing out the sauce in this manner is the hardest, but the best way to strain a sauce.

Life is hectic in a professional working place and time is of the essence, the reason for working efficiently and fast without sacrificing quality. Almost everything related to a white sauce starts with a ready made and previously prepared bechamel sauce.

Making a SAUCE SUPREME, PARISIENNE sometimes called GERMAN 'ALLEMANDE' sauce.

They're almost identical, indispensable and in great demand for entrees like veal, fowl, fish and some vegetables.

The sauces are prepared from sauteed **shallots, or onions** and cut up fresh **mushrooms. White wine** is added. Boil for 5 minutes.......

.....In a sauce pan, heat up the bechamel and add all ingredients above and boil for 10 minutes. Add **heavy cream**, a trace of **mild mustard**, a tsp. of **lemon juice, pepper and salt** to taste.

For fish, add reduced fish stock and for fowl, reduced chicken stock. Before serving, bind sauce with **egg yolks, add cream**. To prevent curdling, keep the sauce hot but don't boil.

To make MORNAY SAUCE

Just add **Gruyere or Parmesan cheese** with **butter**.

To make LYONNAISE SAUCE

Add smothered **onions** and fresh **chives**.

To make DUXELLE SAUCE

Add fine chopped fresh **mushrooms** to a pan with fine chopped smothered **onions**. Reduce and thicken; add trace of **nutmeg, pepper** and very little sauce. Use for stuffing and spreading.

To make SOUBISE SAUCE

Add more **onions**, a trace of **nutmeg** and a pinch of **sugar**.

SAUCE NANTUA

Can be made quickly and is used for all kinds of fish. To the **bechamel sauce** add medium size **shrimp**, reduced **fish stock**, a few **egg yolks** mixed in **heavy cream**, a few drops of **lemon juice** and at last, add a few chips of **fresh butter**. I recommend using fresh or fresh frozen shrimp. They just taste better and when blanched give a good stock for the sauce.

Butter Sauces

...Are served with food like fish, poached eggs, mixed with white sauces and served with vegetables like asparagus, broccoli and artichokes.

Building a HOLLANDAISE SAUCE
for 4 servings

Sociable homemakers should not shy away from complimenting a nice meal with a basic Hollandaise or Bearnaise. It is a step by step process. If you can make a hollandaise, you easily can make a Bearnaise. Make sure the **butter** has the right temperature and beat the **eggs** foamy without making scrambled eggs.

   a. Fill a pot or saucepan 1/4 full of **warm water**, and bring to low simmering.

   b. In another saucepan, melt **2 sticks of butter**, hot enough to put your finger in without feeling 'uncomfortable'. Set aside and keep warm.

   c. In a metal bowl, large enough to place on top of the water pot, mix **5 egg yolks** with a **tsp. of warm water, tsp. lemon juice and a tsp. of white vinegar**. Mix well with a whisk.

   d. Place bowl with the **egg yolks** on top of merely boiling water. With one hand, hold bowl with a dry towel, beat and whisk in steady vigorous motion until eggs are beginning to cream or stick to the whisk. Remove the bowl from the fire and stir in the melted butter slowly in a stream until emulsified. Add **white pepper**, squeeze of **lemon juice** and some **salt**.

Keep warm until served.

Note: Remember, if Hollandaise was separated by being too cold, use some hot water to reconstitute and if separated by being too hot, use warm water.

Francois Boeres, Chef de Cuisine

SAUCE BEARNAISE
about 2 cups

...is served with beef steaks, filet and other fine cuts of meat.

Start with a Hollandaise sauce and set aside....

Crush a heaped tsp. of **peppercorns**, a few cut up sprigs of **tarragon**, 2 chopped up **shallots, thyme** and a trace of **cayenne**. Add all in a sauce pan with 1 cup of **dry white wine** and 1/2 cup of **vinegar**. Reduce to over half. Wait until it is warm and strain slowly into the Hollandaise sauce. (I prefer to strain and wring it out through a towel)

Before serving, add chopped **parsley and tarragon**.

PART TWO

CHAPTER 6... THE LEAN AND LOST YEARS

The Great War and its Consequences

The onslaught of a ravaging battle came like a blizzard over the Ardenne mountains. It became clear to everyone...and so to the German soldiers that this was Hitlers last act before the Götterdammerung.

Here at last, with great joy and anticipation the long years of occupation came to end. The snow from the terrible winter had melted away and many good souls laid to rest .The sun emerged from the dim clouds to embrace the soft dark earth of spring ready to bear new life. At that time, we had made many American friends. Often, Mom cooked good homey meals and cleaned uniforms, the least we could do for them. They were the most jovial and cheerful guys considering being trough hell and back.

Our house was always bursting of peoples . Some brought us chocolate and soap, then that fellow who came with a big can of peanut butter! Ate so much of I was "clogged up" for weeks. I still remember... Charley from Long Island, New York, Jimmy from Ohio, Felix, that dark-haired fellow from Texas, Louis from St. Louis, and Robert our "Dictionary" who spoke French and German and constantly translating our 'pig' English Some came to visit us in later years and many good soldiers we known that time never came back. Occasionally, we "visited" them in the American Military Cemetery in Hamm, Luxembourg. There is now a huge monument. Once a little white chapel stood. Looking down to the right is Patton's final resting place, facing his silent army. I urge every American visiting Luxembourg, to pay a last respect to those gallant soldiers. It's very close to the airport. We also visited a nearby German Cemetery. Here we found these words inscribed in stone:

BECAUSE THE DEAD ARE SILENT
EVERYTHING HAS TO START ALL OVER

As to this, things really did start all over. Wiped out places rebuilt, the economy was put back on track and in no time, we had all kinds of meats and good food on our table. The recent meager ration kitchen made room for new neoclassic cookery. Good restaurants and hotels had desirable items on the menu not seen for years.

Even to this day, people are astonished at the multitude of items served on these menus. The average menu in a fine restaurant had at least 80 main items.

Some of them: Sweetbreads in Champagne, Pike dumplings (Quenelles de brochet l'Armoricaine), Calf's head pieces boiled in a wine and vinegar broth and served with vinaigrette, Frog Legs Provencale, Escargots or Scungili in garlic and wine butter, Ardenne (Virginia type Ham), smoked or pickled beef tongue, real good "marbleized" roast beef with red wine and truffle sauce, fresh live oysters and Foie gras (creamy goose liver pate), and all these heavenly morsels Lucullus had reserved for us. Not to know such trappings and tempting fare is like not knowing the *Odyssey* or *Pilgrim's Progress*.

How it began, why it ever got started? That terrible time of hostility and turmoil, and how could I ever forget that experience of these lean and lost years, fabricated by people with insane ideas that brought us all this misery...the worst to come. I found myself right in the midst of the Battle of the Bulge, known as the Von-Rundstead-Ardenne Offensive, that wiped out many old beautiful places and villages. Some families had lost their loved ones. One of my uncles shot as a Marquisard, another was in the Concentration Camp. I seen many soldiers killed and as for myself, been shot at by drunken soldiers and did not look very healthy either, thin legs sticking out of my shorts and the only pair of shoes I had to fix myself down in the cellar on a shoe anvil. I am not complaining, we all had to pitch in, considering the great parents I had that tried everything to get us through.

HIS-STORY of Good Cooking

During those long war years most meats, fish and dairy products like cheese was kind of scarce and to get them one had to stand in line for hours, not to forget the "coupons" with the money. Mom somehow managed to acquire fresh eggs from a nearby farm where we often worked and helped out. These few eggs reminded me of the fish and bread of Galilee, because it got sooooo stretched out to be made into a multitude of various dishes, like baked goods, noodles, kloesse, spaetzle, cannelloni and gnocchi. The only thing I don't want to see any more Polenta made out of corn meal and semolina couscous, because I have seen so much of it. But I still love to make gnocchi, cannelloni and spaetzle at home.

Cheese, Dumplings, Pasta And Soup

To Make SPAETZLE (LITTLE SPARROWS)

Sift **5 cups of flour** into a bowl. In the center, make a cavity and place **3 big or 4 medium eggs** and some **salt,** stirring and gradually mixing in **2 cups of milk**. Beat smooth with a wooden spoon.

From a board, scrape off the dough with a knife to pencil thick flakes right into the boiling water with some salt added. In about 8 minutes the Spaetzle will "float" and are ready to take out. Swirl them lightly in **butter** and top with **crisp bacon bits**. In restaurants, we forced the dough through a colander with big holes so they all came out the same size.

How to Make NOODLE-DOUGH

Strain over **2 cups of flour** on the working table. In the center, make a cavity and place **1 well-beaten egg, 3 egg yolks, 1/4 cup water, some salt** and gradually mix in with the flour. Knead firm so the dough doesn't stick. Roll in a ball and place in the refrigerator for one hour.

To Make the NOODLES

Break up the dough into lemon size balls. Roll out thin and sprinkle with **flour**. Cut into desired width, heap together and dust with more flour. Boil in water with a little **salt** and **oil** added, cook for about 15 minutes. Strain and prepare to your preference.

Francois Boeres, Chef de Cuisine

To Make CANNELLONI

Cannelloni are generally made with noodle dough as described. Instead of cutting noodles, the dough is rolled out and cut into 2-1/2 by 3-1/2 inch pieces. After boiling, drain, place on wax paper to be filled and rolled.

FILLING FOR CANNELLONI

Sauté sliced **onions** and some **garlic** in good **vegetable or olive oil**, add fine chopped **veal or chicken**, stirring often on a slow fire. Add some peeled, seeded and chopped **tomatoes and tomato paste, salt, pepper and white wine**. Cook slowly and reduce the sauce with the meat. Last add fresh blanched and chopped up **spinach** with **Parmesan cheese**. The filling should be firm enough for stuffing the Cannelloni.

Place finished and rolled cannelloni side by side in a buttered casserole. Pour over a **white sauce** topped with **mozzarella and Parmesan cheese**. Cook in the oven for about 25 minutes at 350 degrees.

Wine: A selected Frascati or Bolla Suave
Music: Vivaldi, a string concerto.

To Make GNOCCHI

Boil one pound **(4 potatoes)**, drain and rice or mash till smooth. Add **3/4 cup sifted flour, white pepper, salt, finely chopped parsley, a trace of nutmeg, two whole beaten eggs and one yolk**. Work in well and blend. Now is the time to test one in boiling water. If too soft, add more flour. The gnocchi should be firm enough so they don't fall apart in the sauce.

On the working table, roll out the dough with sifted **flour,** not less than 1/2 inch thick. Cut into 1 by 1-1/2 inch pieces. Some cooks like to form them with a spoon dipped in hot water. Cook a few at a time in the boiling water, with **salt** added, until they float (approximately 6-7 minutes). Take out, drain well and place in a buttered baking dish. The gnocchi can be gratineed in the oven, topped with cheese sauce and Parmesan or wheeled around in butter and Parmesan cheese or served with tomato sauce.

To Make ITALIAN OR FRENCH STYLE GNOCCHI

These are made with Pate or Choux (look for cream puff pastry). Start with only 1/2 pound of potatoes (**2 potatoes**) and use only **one whole beaten egg**. Mix the mashed potatoes well and blend in twice the volume of **cream puff pastry**. Add: **Parmesan cheese, fine chopped chives, a trace of nutmeg, salt and pepper** to taste. (For green gnocchi, add blanched **spinach**, chopped and well drained.)

Roll out the gnocchi dough and cut into small cylinders and mark them with a fork, then arrange them into a buttered dish and bake in the oven, adding more **butter** and your favored **cheese**. Some cooks also use cheddar sauce. At home, we used Gruyere cheese to make the cheese sauce (a la Mornay). In restaurants, we squeezed the dough out from a pastry bag using a large tip, then cut them off with a knife directly over and into the boiling water. After the gnocchi float, take them out of the water and serve them in a buttered dish with grated cheese or your favored cheese sauce. It is wise to try a few gnocchi in the boiling water. If they are too soft, add more flour.

KLOESSE OR DUMPLINGS

Kloesse can be served with pot roasts, sauerbraten and other "saucy" dishes. They are cheap to make and also can be used in sauces and soups.

Sift **one cup of flour** with **2 tsp. baking powder, add 1/2 tsp. salt and 2 tsp. bread crumbs.**

In another bowl beat **two eggs** with **1/2 cup of milk, 1/3 cup chopped parsley, 1/4 cup fine sliced scallions and a trace of nutmeg**. Mix all smooth and make 1-1/2 inch balls with a spoon or roll them by hand.

Steam dumplings in a covered pot on top of a dish, little water and salt added til done and fluffy.

Note: A Chinese bamboo steamer also can be used.

Francois Boeres, Chef de Cuisine

Another BOILED KLOESSE

Cut **6 to 7 stale rolls** into small cubes, place in a pan with **1/4 cup butter** and add one fine chopped **onion**. Sauté until golden brown. Add chopped **parsley**, take out and mix with **1-1/2 cups milk with 2 beaten eggs and a cup of sifted flour**. Mix very smooth, scoop out the dough with a spoon to make little balls and slowly boil in salt water for about 10 minutes or until soft. Serve with "brown" butter.

Another good tasting and easy on the pocketbook recipe:

LEBERKNOEDEL or LIVERDUMPLINGS

Use one pound of **pork or calves liver**, with **1/4 lb. of fatback** and 1/2 a cut up **onion**. Grind all through a fine grinder (don't use a chopper, it will be something different.) Mix with **3 TBS of bread crumbs, 1 beaten egg, salt, pepper, marjoram and chopped parsley**. The "dough" should be thick enough to form oval shaped dumplings with a spoon. If too soft, add more bread crumbs. Boil slowly in salt water for about 15 to 20 minutes. Scoop out and keep in a warm place until served. Best served with mashed potatoes, sauerkraut or cabbage. Last, pour rendered **bacon bits** over the liver dumplings.

With this I would drink a good glass of beer.
Music: A march by John Philip Susa.

Note: In not so bad times, Mom served this leberknoedel with sauerkraut, mashed potatoes, Kassler-ripchen (smoked pork-chops), Bratwurst, Hacksen (pork-hocks) and boiled pork-belly. You may call it anything you like, but this is known as a Choucroute-garnie or an Alsatian-platter. If you eat this, you never want quiche again, because this is for real men (and real women, of course).

Now, with this, one still can drink beer, but I highly recommend a Riesling or a Riesling-Sylvaner.
Music: The Schweinefurst (Gypsy Baron)

RUSSIAN PASKA CHEESE
A popular Easter cheese dish

Take two pounds of **"Pot" cheese**, (pot cheese is actually a dry ricotta or rigotta), strain through a sieve with a plastic spatula so it is smooth, then hang up in a cloth for 6 hours, to make it firm. Dissolve 1 cup of **sugar** in **1-1/2 cups of milk** and mix with the ricotta, add **4 egg yolks, 8 oz. of sweet grated almonds and fine grated lemon rinds.** Add **1 cup of blanched raisins, vanilla, 10 oz. rendered butter and 1 cup of cream.** Mix well and place in a pot with a hole laid out with cheesecloth, so it can drain (like a plastic flowerpot). Weigh the top down with a big stone for about 12 hours.

This traditional "Ukrainian or Russian" fare is served cold and topped with candied fruits.

Recipe from Uncle Victor

Making Cheese

In spite of a food shortage, an adequate supply of raw milk was to be had. During the war milk was delivered by a horse drawn wagon on rubber wheels. The sound of the bell announced the milkman. The milk was then measured and dispensed right into your milk pot. In 1946, our milkman drove up with his brand new International wagon, no more horsing around, and I didn't have to bring my pot. All the milk now came in bottles, sealed, pasteurized and homogenized. One thing I noticed was the absence of the cream we often used for cooking and in our coffee. Before that, we scalded our milk and often made cheese that called for many of those pastas mentioned. I still remember Mom's large white cheese bag hanging on a hook near the kitchen sink. A good thing she had a few cookbooks stuffed with her own recipes. We made quick, easy to make cheeses at home like cream cheese, farmer's cheese or white cheese and some kind of cottage cheese without using any Rennet (an enzyme).

First the milk was heated to 90 degrees, then put into a crock with a cover in a warm place near the stove for 24 hours. With a long knife, the curd was cut in a criss-cross grid in a bias so to separate the whey. After resting for awhile, it was carefully stirred with a wooden spoon, then warmed up gradually from 86 degrees to 100 degrees in 25 minutes. The best thing is to use your hands to stir slowly from the bottom, break up any big lumps and maintain the temperatures.

The curds are now shrinking and will feel springy and "squeaky." Turn off the heat and allow the curds to settle.

The whey is now slowly removed without disturbing the curds. The curds are then poured into a muslin or cheesecloth that is placed in a strainer or colander, drained for 10 minutes, salt added.

The cheese is tied and hung to drain overnight. At home we called it white cheese by adding cream. Without cream, one might simply call it cottage cheese.

Memories of the NATO Army

Stationed as a NATO soldier in Germany, I can say that our food in the mess hall was not bad. Here we had good onion and potato soups with Kielbasa; Hungarian Goulash, roast pork, and so on. However how good it was, we preferred visiting some of these little restaurants called "Konditorei" that served good wine, beer, pastry, rump steak with fritten (fries), cold platters with assorted meats, garnished with potato salads and little pickles, or KOENIGIN PASTETE: a patty shell filled with chicken and veal in wine sauce. The French call it "Bouchee a la reine." This was not bad at all, besides the waitress sure looked a lot better than that cook in the mess hall.

KOENIGIN PASTETE or BOUCHEE a la REINE

This is so light and delightful, it can be served at any occasion.

You will need:
　　one pound chicken
　　3/4 pound veal shoulder
　　one sweetbread if available
　　6 oz. Fresh mushrooms

First, the sweetbreads should be soaked in vinegar water for about two hours, then cooked separately in salt water with a **bay leaf**. Cook for 45 minutes until soft. Cool, peel and cut into cubes.

Boil chicken with the veal, adding salt, a **stalk of celery** and **half an onion**. Simmer until done. Check and remove the meat that is cooked first. After all the meat is cooked, take it out of the broth, cool, slice into cubes, cover and keep warm.

To make the BECHAMEL SAUCE

In a heavy pot or casserole melt **4 tblsp. Butter**, add a **small chopped onion** and stir until soft. Add **2 tblsp. Flour** and stir with a wooden spoon for 2 minutes. Strain in **2 cups of chicken and veal broth** whisking vigorously until smooth. Add **white pepper, salt to taste**, a **trace of nutmeg** and **1/2 tsp. of mild mustard**. Boil for 15 minutes. Then add **one cup Riesling wine,** boil for 10 more minutes. Sauté and add **cut up mushrooms**. Add and stir in all the meats using a wooden spoon. If thickening is needed, use **cornstarch**. Add **chopped parsley** and fill in to the baked **patty shells**. The Germans love to add capers. Garnish with **watercress** or **parsley** sprigs. Bouchees are traditionally served with French fries. Instead of homemade patty shells, you can substitute the ones found in the freezer compartment at your supermarket. These usually come six to a package.

Serve with a good Mosel-Bernkasteler

—

Soup in the Army

We had our share of soups in the Army and plenty of them during wartime. The German soldiers had their indispensable standby of pea soup called Erbsensuppe that came with ham hocks or chunks of lean bacon. On a very cold day, I stood and stared with longing eyes watching a German soldier tending the field kitchen, known as the Goulash-Kanone. I guess I must have been looking very sorrowful, for he offered me a plate of pea soup topped with a piece of fat back. It was the best I ever had. (Sorry, Mom!)

With the Americans, it was that soul and heartwarming bean soup served with cooked bacon or ham. Here, I also tasted a bean soup made by a Yankee Merlin, performing sorcery with beans, so delightful and mellow without loss of that hearty solid country-like filling quality. I must say it also was better than Mom's but she seldom cooked bean soup, except cut green bean soup, very popular in the old country. I still don't know what makes an Army soup so good tasting. It always has been, since I remember.

REAL YANKEE BEAN SOUP

Soak dry **navy beans** in cold water for 4 hours. Drain and blanche in boiling water for 15 minutes. Drain this again and set beans aside. Cook **slab bacon, ham or knuckles** for 30 minutes. Save only 1/3 of the broth. Or, if fresh pork knuckles or shoulder are used, add a little **salt**, save all the broth and set aside.

In a big pot with **margarine or pork fat**, sauté a "mirepois" of small diced **onions, celery, carrots and garlic cloves**.

Add: all beans and meats with the broth. Fill the pot with water and add **diced potatoes**. Season with **salt** if required, **pepper, summer savory, thyme, bay leaf, some brown sugar and a dash of white vinegar**. Cook slowly for 2 hours or till done, adding more water if needed. For a smoother flavor, reheat soup after a few hours. This soup needs nothing but a good appetite. This soup can be simply glorified by serving it in a nice soup tureen with the meat cut up in small portions.

To make MOZZARELLA CHEESE

Follow the basic procedures for cottage (white) cheese, except use hands to break up the curd in the very hot whey, hot enough to keep hands in, then remove whey and set aside. The cheese is hung up in a muslin or cheese cloth, just like the cottage cheese. After 8 hours, the cheese is put in a press (a wooden cylinder with a "fallower" weighted down with a few bricks). This takes about 20 hours. The cheese is then removed from the press with the muslin removed and put into a preheated 180° whey, then taken from the heat, covered and cooled off. After cooling, take out from the whey and dry for 24 hours.

HIS-STORY of Good Cooking

Here is a QUICK COTTAGE CHEESE

Heat up **1-1/2 gallons of 'turned' milk** that had been sitting in a warm place for 24 hours. Heat up slowly to 115°, hot enough to keep your fingers in it. Let rest for 20 minutes, drain slowly into a muslin laid out in a strainer. Let drain overnight and add **salt**.

RUMPLEDETHUMPS – CABBAGE AND POTATO CASSEROLE

Split **1/2 pound cabbage** in half and remove cores. Chop up the cabbage and boil for 10 minutes in boiling water, **salt** added. Drain cabbage under cold water.

Peel and cut up **1-1/2 pounds potatoes** and boil in water with **salt** added for approximately 20 minutes or until done. Drain, mash, and mix potatoes with the cabbage. In plenty of **butter**, sauté **one chopped onion** and mix in with the cabbage and potatoes, adding **1/2 cup scalded milk**, a **dash of dill weed, 3 sliced scallions, pepper** and **salt** to taste. Place into a gratin dish, top with **grated cheddar** and bake for 25 minutes in a preheated 350° oven or until piping hot.

Drink: A good ale.

To Make QUENELLES A L' ARMORICAINE
(Classic Fish Dumplings)

Use **one pound of cleaned, filleted fish** like Pike, Bass, Halibut, Cod or any other not too fatty fresh fish. If possible, save all the bones for your fish stock (called Court-Bouillon). Boil fish bones in enough water for poaching the quenelles.

To the stock add: **salt, 2 bay leaves, 2 cloves, lemon sections, dry white wine and half an onion** cut up in slices. Boil stock for 15 minutes.

Chill the fresh fish fillets and grind through a chopper.

To this add: **1/2 cup of fresh bread crumbs, 1/2 cup flour, some heavy cream, 3 well beaten egg whites and one yolk, 1/2 an onion** chopped fine and sautéed in **butter, little salt, white pepper, and chopped parsley**. Mix well with a wooden spoon.

Francois Boeres, Chef de Cuisine

With a tablespoon, form the quenelles and drop them into the simmering fish stock. Here it is wise to try one first, if it is too soft, add more flour. Simmer the quenelles for about 8 minutes or till done all through. Take out the quenelles and keep warm.

Wine: Frascati or a Green Hungarian

To Make the SAUCE ARMORICAINE

Start with a **small white roux** (roast flour in butter for 2 minutes). Add as much of the strained fish stock as needed, stirring often.

Add: a pinch of each — **Hungarian paprika; curry powder; dry English mustard. 1 tsp. Tomato paste; jigger of brandy and a jigger of semi-dry Sherry, and 1/4 cup heavy cream.**

Simmer the sauce for about 15 minutes, stirring occasionally. If too thin, add some dissolved cornstarch or the leftover egg yolks. Before serving add a few 'chips' of **butter** to the sauce. In restaurants we add Hollandaise to the sauce so as to give the quenelles, covered with the sauce, a nice color when placed under the grill. Garnish with **buttered crouton triangles** or half-moons of **puff pastry**.

THE VENERABLE PEA SOUP

Soak **dried peas** in cold water for one hour, then drain. Boil in fresh water for 15 minutes. Let stand for 10 minutes. Cool and drain the peas and set aside. Cook **slab bacon, pork knuckles or ham** for 30 minutes, save only 1/3 of the broth and set aside.

In a big pot with **margarine or pork fat**, sauté chopped up **onions**, half the amount of **carrots**, and then add all the meats with the broth and the peas. Add a few small diced **potatoes**. Fill with water and season with **salt or bouillon** if needed, **pepper and thyme**. Cook slowly until done. Soup should be thick enough so that it sticks to the spoon. Serve with fresh **buttered croutons** and crisp **bacon bits**. Queen Victoria ate her pea soup with mint.

MOM'S FRESH GREEN POOL BEAN SOUP

Clean and cut "snappy" fresh **green beans** in 3/4 inch diamond cut pieces, set aside. Render pieces of sliced **bacon** till brown and stir in **sliced onions** till glazed. Add some **flour**, stirring for a minute and pour in hot water. Add **bouillon or beef stock**, small cubed **potatoes** and all the green beans. Season with **summer savory or thyme, salt and pepper**. Cook slowly for one hour. Serve with **sour cream, soy or Maggi sauce** and chopped **cilantro**.

About Soups

Primitive man first seared and roasted meats over the fire. I think that soups brought the first "civilized" people to the table and out of this marmites evolved: boiled meats, beef, lamb and other kinds of stews. Beans and pork soups were commonly cooked in fireplaces hundreds of years ago.

In France, these boiling kettles of meats and vegetables were known as "Pot au Feu." In old Britain, we had thin soups or thick spoon soups. Some of these soups, cooking for hours, gradually became so thick they could be loaded on the spoon. Bean soups became so thick they resembled Boston Baked Beans. All one had to do was to add some brown sugar or molasses and bake them.

Escoffier not only implied an orderly French, but for the greater part a highly organized and comprehensive international kitchen. Not surprisingly, many dishes, thought to be French, originated right here at home, in America, like Veal Cordon Bleu (from the 1939 International Exposition). Vichyssoise was dreamed up by Chef Louis Diat at the New York Ritz Hotel and French Onion soup was served here in the Colonies hundreds of years ago, not with cheese, but with egg yolks.

To Prepare VEAL CORDON BLEU

Ask the butcher or flatten out a few **veal steaks** 1/4 inch thick (from a veal round). On each veal steak, place a thin slice of smoked **Virginia Ham** and a thin slice of **Swiss cheese**. Roll or fold up and secure with a few tooth-picks, **salt and pepper** to taste. Dip each prepared veal steak into **flour, egg wash** and bread lightly with fresh **bread crumbs**. Fry these gently in **vegetable oil** until golden. Turn down the heat, drain the oil if any, and replace with **butter**. Add a filet of **white wine**, cover and simmer for 15 minutes or until done. Uncover and reduce liquids, serve with chopped **parsley**.

Wine: Beaujolais or Rose D'Anjou

Here is a GREAT HUNGARIAN GULYAS SOUP
(Gulyasleves) for 4 to 6 people

This soup is almost as thick as the mud in the bog, but it still can be eaten with a spoon.

In a heavy pot, sauté: 1/2 cup of diced **beef suet till glossy, 2 Tblsp. Butter, 3 medium chopped onions, and 2 minced garlic cloves**.

Stir until soft and then add **1-1/2 pounds beef chuck** cut in 1-1/2 inch cubes, stirring over moderate heat till glazed.

Add: **3 tsp. Sweet Hungarian paprika, 3 tsp. Flour, little salt, pepper, dash of Cayenne pepper**, grated peel from a **lemon** and **5 cups of light beef bouillon**.

Cover and simmer for more than 1-1/2 hours, stirring occasionally. If too thin, remove cover and reduce the soup.

Serve with Italian bread or with fluffy potato dumplings.

Wine: Tokey Szamoridni
Music: Jewish melodies by Perlman

The Evacuation and Uncle Yves

Growing Up

This was the time to remember, being the most important progress of growing up and here I had learned so much in such a short time, to become more and more aware of what the world had to offer—from priceless moments to harsh reality. The most impressive was that the good had prevailed through a bad time, people were clinging to hope, that there would be another day—tomorrow!

Remembering Uncle Yves and Aunt Cecille

Visiting Uncle Yves and Aunt Cecille was always exciting. They lived in a charming place in Nogent, not too far from Paris. Uncle Yves had been a Colonel in the French Army, defending Fort Douaumont in Verdun, but now he was only shooting partridges and rabbits near his hunting lodge where he often took refuge from the hectic life of selling wine as a wine merchant around Paris, and also, sometimes to get away from his wife, he told us, laughing. But, you know how things are; often we try to run away from ourselves.

As long as I can remember, Aunt Cecille was a real "sweetheart," a good cook and a wonderful hostess. Her Coque au vin, Filet Rossini with Gooseliver or even a plain Ratatouille could rival that of the Ritz-Carlton, especially if it was served with a Chateau-Lafitte, a Crucifix, or a La Tache from Yves's wine cellar. Oh, if I had only been older at that time when I had taken it all for granted! Now I'm aware of the ordinary and the extraordinary.

We spent many a sunny day lingering and having dinner in the shade house of his extraordinary garden. The garden itself had several raised beds surrounded by brick walkways. On one side of the garden stood a greenhouse for raising and nurturing seedlings and to keep plants dormant in the winter. Far to the other side, Yves had a small pond with ducks enclosed by an iron fence. The center path was shaded over by a vine trellis facing the greenhouse. Here the sun filtered enough light to play with the shadows of the whispering leaves and the birds rewarded us with songs from all the birdhouses Yves had built.

It was a real enchanted place, a bit in tune with Charles Trenet's song from his "Jardin Extraordinaire." The old estate housed beautiful Regency furniture, an enclosed zinc bathtub, a Credenza with old silver, better still was the "notorious" outhouse, right smack in the garden, all painted green. Coming back to the shade house, we spent hours talking about what had been and what might have been, about family stories, planning vacations, of food, wine and politics. Our opinions were occasionally shared by a bark from "Fiffi" and "Fafflu." Yes, these were the times I always will remember as the carefree, wonderful days enshrouded in an air of tranquillity and contentment known as living like "God in France."

Francois Boeres, Chef de Cuisine
Living in Occupied France

In early May, 1940, the German Army had run over our sovereign country of Luxembourg and the neighboring Belgium, surprising the French Army in surrounding and bypassing the "impenetrable" Maginot Line. This unconventional "Blitzkrieg" over the Ardennes all came to us as a surprise.

Our hometown became under siege of shelling and bombardment, not for too long. We packed a few things and headed for Nogent, in France, to stay with Uncle Yves. Our transportation was a Belgian F.N. motorcycle with a Steif sidecar where I spent the whole trip, while Mom was sitting on the rear seat. From that time on we became refugees, spectators and participants of the greatest war ever fought—followed by chaos and destruction and from then on, things changed a lot! The night sky was lit up by the bombardment of Metz. Soon we became pawns to the tricky play of chess by the oncoming German war machine...finding ourselves all driven into the retreating French Army, blocking and paralyzing all mobility. The French Army, had no other choice but to shove and push all fleeing refugees over the road. Endless caravans of heavy loaded wagons with horses, trucks, busses stuffed with people and all kinds of cars, most out of gas, littered the side roads for miles and miles. Columns of people moving on like herds of cattle...pacing down the road, whole families tied together by ribbons and cords so the children stayed together and none got lost.

By now the route was completely filled and cut off. We waited for hours and hours until Dad decided to take a turn into a rutted, almost overgrown field-way, passing a few farms, finally coming out into a smaller, less congested route. We proceeded slowly, at last we were moving but soon found out this was a dangerous road. Many times we were attacked by low flying planes.

Up front, a French convoy had been under friendly crossfire from French planes and Germans attacking civilians. It was sheer pandemonium. The attacks came fast, just enough time to drive our motorcycle into a ditch to cover it quickly with a blanket and then to jump right over the ravine escaping the spraying bullets. Further on, we passed a bridge with French soldiers discharging hand grenades into the river to secure them from the Germans. The river had scores of dead fish floating around. "That's the end," Paps said, "the end of the French Army." The same day we arrived

HIS-STORY of Good Cooking

late at a refugee station, a huge gymnasium. Here the villagers served us a big bowl of minestrone type soup spiked with beef chunks. "Francois... Francois," a woman in a high voice screeched my way. "Vien manger ta soupe!" (Come eat your soup!) In France, soups are taken very seriously, they mean substance, strength and health, the first and last resort to bring you back on track. Here, a meal without soup is almost heretical. It is the introduction to a good meal, a cook is judged by his soup. If he makes a good soup, he is to be trusted.

—

Here is a POTAGE de CAMPAGNE – (Country Soup)

In a heavy pot, sauté in **butter**: chopped **onions**, diced **carrots**, sliced **pascal celery, a few parsnips** and crushed **garlic cloves**. Fill with half water and half beef stock. In this stock, boil some **beef belly (or brisket) and pork fatback** for one hour. Then add **cubed potatoes**, cut up **leeks** and "diamond cut" **green pool beans, salt, pepper, marjoram, and bay leaves**. Cook for one hour. Before serving, cut up beef and the pork into small cubes.

—

Late, tired and worn out, we finally arrived at Yve's place to be accommodated in the most cordial fashion. After eating dinner, we all "dropped dead" in bed. This kind of hospitable scenario was common throughout the French countryside. In some places, people gave up their beds to sleep on the couch to accommodate refugees during the time of the Occupation. There was always enough to eat and drink!

Uncle Yves, as long as I can remember, always drove a Citroen that looked like a square box on wheels. The car had the soft, plush seats and the two cone-shaped cut flower vases on each side and a loop to hang onto. Later, as gasoline known as Benzene, became as rare as hen's teeth, Uncle Yves converted his car into methane gas. This was produced by a Pepasus-type generator. That ugly looking contraption looked like a gas heater standing out of the rear trunk. It was fired by small sticks of wood that produced the gas, cleaned through centrifugation and channeled into a carburetor like regulator. The damper went "clack, clack, clack" with the car driving down the road at 30 to 35 miles per hour. Tires were equally hard to come by and to repair. A large rubber band was laid over the old tire and on very sharp curves, often this band would dislodge and fall off, followed by profane words. Eventually he took the train.

Outside Nogent, Uncle Yves owned a few nice provincial rental units. We moved into a vacant one to live there for some time. Pops got a job in a Nogent aluminum pot and knife factory that also had made gas masks. Not long after, Grandpa Boeres arrived there out of nowhere, and it looked like the family was back on track. Paps was working, Mom taking care of the house and Grandpa tinkering around, growing vegetables and chopping wood. Behind the house stood a thirty-foot big, fragrant dying Bay-leaf tree. Grandpa cut it into firewood to feed the big kitchen stove with its water tank that stood on the black and white tile kitchen floor.

As for myself, I had already made friends. My best buddy was Guy. Whenever we got together, there was trouble—chasing chickens, stealing strawberries and coming home late. One of our favored plots was to look out for truckloads of peanuts on the way to the peanut oil factory. As soon as one was sighted, an old wooden plank was laid across the road. Then as the truck drove over the plank—kerplunk—down came a pailful of peanuts. I never will forget that place. Here and there we got news from home through the "grapevine." Now the dust had settled and the German occupation was complete. Intolerable and immeasurable was the time for all of us, especially a Frenchman, to endure suppression over four long years in gloomy mediation. A deep-rooted feeling for freedom and patriotism was ever present, like an underground current, wherever people met…at a grocery store, bistro or a church, praying for time to take off this yoke. It just could not go on forever!

It was time to return home. We said "au revoir" to Uncle Yves and Aunt Cecille and left a few cords of wood behind. Grandpa stayed with Yves for awhile. Now we drove and returned through German occupied land, passing through the same villages, if one might call them that, with only chimneys standing, still smoking from people living and cooking their meals in cellars. That's all what was left. We passed a shot-down Army truck with "Putain, Petain" painted over. The former French general Petain was now elected by the new Vichy government as the Governor of France and regarded as the most misunderstood and mistrusted man.

HIS-STORY of Good Cooking

At last we arrived home again where we found all in disarray. A grenade had exploded in Ma's stores and dining room. We decided to go to Grandpa Hipp who had just returned from the evacuation. Grandpa looked very healthy, round face, red cheeks, like he just had returned from vacation. All six of them had found refuge in an old Chateau on the Loire.

There was Grandpa Phil, Grandma Josephine, son Victor, daughter Jeanny and her husband Dyrk (also known as "Jupp"), a Hollander from Rotterdam. "Jupp"had also a nice color, not on his cheeks but on his nose from drinking too much wine in the Loire. Oops! Almost forgot little cousin Clair'chen. So, of all we had been through, here we were all home again—we had made it!

Grandma had given Grandpa eight nice children. One, Kitty, became Miss Luxembourg and went to Atlantic City. Suzette went to London. Vic joined the Foreign Legion where he met "Jupp" who later married his sister, Jeanny. Others became barbers, beauticians, decorators and one a "patissier" (fine baker). One thing they all had in common was, they all knew how to cook! The best of "all" worlds: French, German, Italian, Oriental and what have you.

Grandpa, a busy masonry man, was engaged in building fireplaces, chimneys, train tunnels and relining blast furnaces in the steel mill. He still managed to make sure that his children all had a good profession and so was Grandma Josephine, a seamstress, stitching and sewing on her old pedal operated Singer Sewing machine, helping to get the family through. To no one's surprise, Grandpa did most of the cooking and this he did very well.

"Today" he cooked for all of us, a Pot au Feu, boiled beef with vegetables, a very gratifying and robust meal. This "Sleeping Beauty" should be revived by a kiss from a Culinary Prince.

Francois Boeres, Chef de Cuisine

Here is GRANDPA'S BOILED BEEF (Pot au Feu)
Serves 8 plus

Choose **6 to 7 pound marbleized beef shoulder or 10 to 12 pound beef brisket**, tied. Boil slowly with **salt and peppercorns** for half an hour, skimming often.

Add: **8 whole peeled medium carrots, 6 whole peeled parsnips, 1/2 peeled knob (celeraic) or 6 stalks of pascal celery, 3 big whole onions, 2 bay leaves** "nailed" to the onions with **4 cloves** and **4 large cleaned leeks**, tied. (It is best to add them to the meat when half way cooked so they don't fall apart.)

Boil meats till tender, cook **3 pounds of potatoes** separately. Prepare and serve soup first. Strain most of the beef broth leaving some for the main dish. Cook some **vermicelli** in the broth, serve and sprinkle with chopped parsley or cilantro.

To serve the boiled beef, untie, slice into portions and neatly spruce-up on a big, deep platter surrounded with all the vegetables. Serve with potatoes on the side, spicy Dusseldorf style mustard, horseradish sauce and pickles.

This is the time for a beer!

SAUTÉ CHICKEN LIVERS IN SHERRY WINE

Clean one pound of fresh **chicken livers** by cutting out all blemished spots, fat and little strands. Dry with a paper towel. Slice in quarter size morsels and dip in **flour**.

Sauté **half a chopped onion** in plenty of **butter** till transparent. In the same pan add chicken livers with **salt and pepper**. Stir till half done, squench with semi-dry **Sherry wine**. Cook slowly for a few minutes till almost done, don't overcook. Add pinch of **sage** and fresh chopped **parsley**. If too dry add some water. Sautéed fresh **mushrooms** are optional. This is best served on toast or fluffy long grain rice.

Note: These chicken livers (without the mushrooms) can be made into a delightful chicken liver paté by grinding it fine with butter in a food processor. This paté is best served on Melba toasts or crackers. Do not keep more than two days.

Wine: A Chenin or Sauvignon Blanc

Working years ago was physically very demanding, low pay for long hours worked. Hard work also consumed most of the time known today as recreation. How I ever managed to take time touring on my bike or canoeing...I often ask myself!

We had all kinds of clubs: bicycle; bowling; fishing or swimming clubs, but it was the Canoe Club that stood out from them all. It was the most memorable and the most cheerful.

Our Canoe Club

I loved canoeing, having a good time with friends, eating, drinking, camping, hiking and of all, good companionship. This union of camaraderie was fused by an unwritten code of respect, cooperation and responsibility. It didn't matter if the person was a high profile businessman or just a clerk. Here, we all came to take a vacation from our daily grind. Seldom were somber or intangible affairs mentioned here, like politics, death, hell, taxes or diseases, and if someone happened to do anything stupid, he was never ridiculed or laughed at. We rather laughed all together and thought it to be funny. Most of our topics concerned planning for future outings, episodes from our last trip, sports, new members and other "pleasantries." New jokes were always welcome, neither did we brag or try to prove anything like shooting down into a 12 foot falling cascade of "boiling" water, paddling and fighting yourself out of dangerous white water to save your hide... none of that. We just loved to paddle leisurely along on the "Sure" or the "Mosel."

Canoeing on the "Meuse," the "Somme" or the Marne were for longer outings. Here we rented a small bus where some of our women stayed, following us along the closest route near the river. Come dusk or the end of the voyage, we would load and tie all our boats on top of the bus and usually stopped at a wayside inn on our way home. We used all kinds of boats: kayaks, known to be the swiftest and the best for solo canoeing, also the two seaters to take a friend or your wife along so one could rest

Francois Boeres, Chef de Cuisine

awhile and the other kept paddling. A few had real open canoes manned with two, paddling with short oars. These traditional canoes were made of steam-bent plywood. Navigating these boats needed constant mindfulness. Some even had aluminum canoes. A small factory in Belgium had melted all the shot down Flying Fortresses and Messerschmidts to make pots and pans, window frames and...canoes. These aluminum canoes rumbled and growled a bit, sliding over the stone beds, but they sure were light, especially on "portages" where they reminded me of dinosaurs on four legs. We also had so-called "fold boats" like 'Hammer' and 'Klepper,' disassembled, the whole boat with its rolled up rubber canvas skin and wooden ribs would fit nicely into a bag. Some of us assembled these fold-boats in fifteen minutes to a sturdy kayak that even came with a floating rudder operated by cables.

Of all outings, I enjoyed small parties of up to six boats. A lot of time was spent in our clubhouse known as the Block House, built up on a hill sloping toward the river. Families would take turns spending vacations there; occasionally the whole gang stayed. To get there, one had to walk a mile from the road and cross a small bridge, packed like a mule with all kinds of paraphernalia and provisions.

The smell from creosote and tar with which the block house was painted let you know you were close by. First thing on arrival was to stack all perishable food in a place under the floor, accessible by a trap door. This, our "cellar," wasn't any bigger than the size of an icebox, but it was fresh and cold inside and the food kept quite long in there. Next we fired up the old cooking stove to cook and get rid of all the dampness left from the winter. The wood used first was always replenished by the last people that used the stove. Then there were small tasks to evacuate mice, snakes, porcupines and spider webs, airing all the mattresses and looking forward to a good time. Some time we sat and ate on the front porch till late in the dark, watching the stars above with a "sea" of million lights from glow worms and listen to the chirps of crickets in late summer.

Rain sure can ruin vacations, especially in a natural setting. Thank heaven, it never lasted too long! Well, one day it was raining. I opened the cabin window and looked at the pouring rain, how the big droplets from the roof seemed to explode into a ring of newborn droplets on a stone below. I was grinning at a bird perched on a tree, all resigned and wet, its head tucked in so it looked like a small ball, occasionally ruffling and shaking the rain from his drenched plumage, just like a dog out of the water. Then there was that back and forth swaying buttercup releasing raindrops to return up for another "cup." I looked at a "dreaming" May fly, flying helplessly under the eaves, bouncing back and forth from the wall, then...suddenly, a frigid squall of rain slapped my face.

"Francois, please close that window," a voice commanded. Nothing else to do, I played with that old RCA table gramophone and its fragile record collection with the familiar picture of the dog, listening to his master's voice. With no electricity around, the gramophone had to be cranked and the brad size needle changed often. I still can hear Caruso singing "Carmen," Richard Tauber, "Meine Mutter war'ne Wienerin," Tino Rossi's "O Signore Cosa Che," or "Le Temps n'a rien change." I loved Lotte Lehman's "Draussen in der Wachau," and the "Freischuets"von Weber. I guess I played it too loud. "Francois, turn that thing down," someone shouted. I sure was pleased to see the sun coming out that afternoon. I headed for a place called "Wills Pool." It was a quiet shady spot where the river made a bend and the water was deep. Here the trouts were jumping and baiting and if they didn't, on a hot sultry day, you might as well join them and jump in for a swim.

Nature is an endless cornucopia of good things that can be found all around. Early in spring, when the plow had turned over the earthy, fresh smelling sod clods, bundles of the most tender yellow-white dandelions could be found there. They make wonderful country salad especially if mixed with fresh watercress found alongside brooks.

Then came time to pick bowls full of wild strawberries no bigger than jellybeans with an unsurpassed aroma of sweet strawberries one never forgets. We just added a little sugar with milk. Late summer it was blackberry and blueberry time. Blueberries grew with fern under the tall canopy of trees in the woods no higher than a foot and a half, with berries slightly bigger than peas, so it took some time to pick a pail full but the quality of taste made up for the quantity.

Note: Where do our strawberries come from? It all started in the King's garden of Versailles by crossing the American Scarlet with the Chilean Beauty. Today we have over 1,000 varieties of strawberries all related to a small shrub of the rose family.

A friend of mine (the son of an innkeeper nearby) knew of two big cherry trees, deep in the woods, that only a few people knew of. These trees

Francois Boeres, Chef de Cuisine

had quarter size tartar cherries. We ate so much of them, they came right out of our ears.

Every second day I was sent up through the woods and mountains to a little village called Birden to fetch us some fresh milk or bring home a few potatoes or fresh-made sausage from a farmer. He also had a tavern, made furniture, took care of animals and operated a small still in a shed behind the barn. How he ever had time to take his family out to church on Sunday, I don't know. Now, besides all this, he also took care of little things like felling trees, sawing lumber and stacking up firewood for the long winter. If I ever find a man like this today, I will salute him respectfully. Nevertheless, I returned home the same way, down the mountain, woods and fields, with the singing larks hovering above. I passed paths adorned with colorful foxgloves and bare spots from harvested trees full of red fireweeds. I stopped by a young tree stand covered with grass and moss sprinkled with an abundance of firm yellow Chanterelles (mushrooms). We picked bags full of them and ate them almost every day in late summer.

Passing from the rugged terrain into the richer valley in spring, I brought home lilies of the valley mixed with yellow primroses known as cuckoo flowers. I passed wheat fields in summer and I often picked Marguerites, cornflowers and red poppies.

Everyone loved this rustic bouquet of red, white and blue. Now I will tell you of one of the wonders of the world. To see this, you have to go to the Ardennes, in Luxembourg. In Mid spring, some mountains turn into gold. It is the time nature brags with broome. It resembles Forsythia and is also used to make brooms. Anyone witnessing this spectacle will fall in love with this colorful, incomparable scenery that attracts tourists from all over, just as we go to Vermont to see the foliage.

I loved exciting days filled with action. Then, here and there, my mood longed for inner peace. And here I found it. This serene place with its "mulled" silence, was occasionally elevated by the song of birds, the rustling of tree leaves, the chirping of the grasshoppers, the persistent twitter of the wren, the mocking call of the cuckoo and the hollow owl-like call of the turtledove. "Co-huoo, co-huoo." All this had to come from a divine higher order. I was enchanted by the velvety soft sound of tranquillity and its lasting peace. Resting in the meadows, chewing on a grass stalk, I noticed weird contours of torn up clouds in the sky, of imaginable animals, giants, dwarfs...ouch!! I quickly jumped up as I had been invaded by ants from a nearby anthill. It reminded me that there is no lasting peace.

Our Block House was about the most rustic place one can think of with rough hewn logs on the outside and a cozy veranda facing a big mountain that returned the echo from our yodeling. Here on this veranda, some of the simplest good-tasting natural food was served, like Braised Perch or Pike, Sautéed Trout, small Fish Fry called a Friture, Boiled Pork Knuckles with Virgin Cabbage served the next day as Cold Pork Jelly or Beef Fondu Bourginon from a chafing dish.

An old favored dish was potato pancakes, waffles and onion soup, not to forget the blueberry and strawberry pies. Came dusk, we drank and had little snacks by candlelight and Chinese paper lanterns.

The inside of our Block House was equally primitive. It had big tables, benches, chairs, a few couches and a score of bunk beds leaning against the north wall. We made no fuss having no electricity, water, or even an inside toilet. A hand pump had been installed outside mostly worked just like one of those Parisian elevators in mid season... out of order. Luckily, not too far away was a bubbling cool spring. Believe me, I am not a great water drinker, but this water was the purest. Every morning I brought us two cans full.

Last of all, I will mention a very precarious state of affairs...the outhouse...you know, that place we often have to go to in the midst of the darkest nights. Imagine, running out at three in the morning, all sleepy and drowsy, looking for that place made out of two posts and a rail (called a thunder rail) with a dug out hole behind...have mercy!

Everyday was "something"...taking excursion to nearby castles or maybe a night out bowling in an old village café. Tricky they were, these old bowling alleys, almost built like an hour glass, starting wide, then tapering off in the midst to widen again. To hit all nine, (it only used nine pins) one had to twist the wooden ball so it kind of made a bow in the midst so to hit the left or the right pins and if you happened to hit them all, Great Scott! Then the "Boss" gave you a cigar! Now the pin-boy, the one that set up all the pins and returned the balls in the gutter, always ran fast behind the wall so not to get knocked out by a ball from an eager bowler.

Some nights we had torch-lit processions, each carrying a torch, coming down the mountains to meet other canoe clubs, then we would throw all the torches into a bonfire and sing songs like "Coming Down the Mountains" or

Francois Boeres, Chef de Cuisine

"Give Me a Glass of Beer or I Drop Dead." There were many more I can't remember now. It all ended in a nearby resort near Bourscheid where we ate, drank and danced through the night.

Now and then, I come across the lively picture from the well-known painting of the Canoe Party by Renoir, and somehow, I have the feeling that I know all these people in there!

My First Paying Job

At the end of my three years of apprenticeship, a complete training for professional chefs was required at the State Culinary Institution. This was a full time occupation. I still managed working two days on the weekend for the Consulate. Missing my bus meant three miles of walking to school. Often, this made me so tired, I felt like collapsing, just sitting down. Happy was the day when we received our Diploma. For my first work, I chose a better paying summer season job in an Ardenne tourist hotel called Bel Air. This, a busy resort hotel made all of us five cooks work around the clock. With Chef Charley, Koss, Bill, myself and a salad woman, Kathy, who was also in charge of the coffee kitchen.

Charley had been forced into the Russian front and he told us all kinds of horror stories about the sufficient food they had but it was the cold that got them down. So clothes for the Front had to be collected at home, like leather jackets, long coats and the like, just to keep warm. He always complained about rheumatism and he never had been the same since. Our Koss was a Dutchman and a very pleasant one. Often he got very upset if we made him save leftovers. He told us he had worked on the Holland America Line, there all leftovers were tossed overboard. He came from a beautiful town called Leyden. One day I took him up on his invitation to visit. I never forgot its beautiful botanical gardens and all this birds, flamingos, tulips and all kinds of exotic plants. It was such a beautiful place.

Bill was about my age and full of dynamite. The village was a bit out of the way, but still, all of us...cooks, waiters, and chambermaids, managed to show up in every dancing joint, until closing time. We danced all night...the tango, rumba, fox trot, slow waltz...until we dropped. The latest, I recall, was the Raspa, pushing arms back and forth and jumping all over and never knew who your partner was. Another of our favored places served beer in a glass booth called Stiefel. Often we wagered to drink out all the beer at once, without putting the Stiefel down. Anybody that lost had to pay for the next round. Imagine the hangover the next morning, trying to shuffle and zigzagging into the kitchen. A ten-egg omelet with chives in the morning kept me going. After a bum night and a hard day's work like this, we decided to sober up for awhile and instead of drinking we went night fishing for eels. Some fellows fished from the boat, others from the shore. The river we fished marked the border between Luxembourg and Germany, consequently, a lot of illegal smuggling was going on.

It happened on this dark night, we got surprised and surrounded by a whole garrison of border guards with loud speakers, commanding us to put our hands up. As a sorrowful lot we emerged under the blinding lights, armed only with fishing poles. After awhile, they let us go home with the catch. When we got home, the eels in the basket still were alive, even after cleaning and cutting them into pieces, they still jumped and turned around in the frying pan.

Bill and I often went into the deep woods fishing brown trout with our bare hands, right out of the bubbling creek. If a sweet water fish isn't fresh, you might as well give it to the cat, especially a trout. It still has to retain its slippery coating (so the saying—as slippery as a trout) the gills have to be red and the eyes bright. Therefore, the practice of cooking the trout with the head on is to let you know what a fresh trout should be. Now if you dip the trout to be fried in milk and flour, with salt and pepper, you are going to eat a golden crisp and nutty flavored fish you will never forget. Of course, catching trout like this today is unlawful. So, here, on the hotel premises we had two nice round spring fountain pools. The larger one with salmon trout was a real eye opener, it had a colonnade with columns and an esplanade with marble benches.

The smaller one, nearby the kitchen, was only twelve feet in diameter with a splashing spring fountain that supplied enough oxygen and cold water for our Rainbow trout. They were bigger than the brown trout and it was my job to feed them every day with lean chopped meat. Come feeding time, these trouts really got mad. They jumped up and down and made the pool look like it was going to boil over any time. The trout, once ordered, were caught under the watchful eyes of the customers sitting on the veranda above.

If trout were ordered, Charley would announce: "Francois, two trout!" Then I would run to fetch the trout with my net. Unfortunately, it had rained

Francois Boeres, Chef de Cuisine

the night before and the terrazzo still was wet, so guess what happened. I slipped and sled all over, right into the pool full of trouts. One could hear the screaming and hilarious outburst of laughter from all sides. Well, I had put on a good show on my account. We served fresh trout a la Meuniere (dipped in flour) and as TRUITE au BLEU. Here only fresh killed trout should be used. In preparing the trout, try to keep that slippery membrane on the skin.

In a pot, place enough water so as to cover the **trout**. Add **salt, thin sliced carrot, diced onion, lemon slices, bay leaves and white vinegar**. Boil this stock for ten minutes. Then in this stock, poach the trout for about 10 minutes. Remove, drain and serve trout on a plate on a white napkin. A fresh poached trout should look kind of twisted, have white eyes and have a blue color. Serve with drawn butter, lemons, boiled parsley potatoes.

Wine: a Grave, a Bernkasteler or a Chardonnay
Music: The Trout by Schubert

Our hotel was almost self-sufficient. We cleaned our own hotel laundry. Herbert, a German, had built a stone building to raise pigs, and Jim, our handyman, caretaker and gardener, planted us a real spice garden. The topographic layout of the surrounding landscape is to be known for its harmonious composition of beautiful bizarre shaped cliffs and rocks surrounded by mountains with fertile plateaus dotted with quaint little villages, alluring to tourists from all over. Most of our tourists were Belgians, Wallooners and Hollanders. Some Netherlanders were a bit on the frugal side by just ordering lemonade with their meals. So, here we had these two older fellows, Martin and Jim, our best waiters. They had a good sense of humor and loved to clown around, calling the Netherlanders, "Nur Limonade" (only lemonade). Yep, that's why it said, NL on their license plates. And if some of them ordered Coca Cola or Pepsi Cola, they would holler over to the bar, "Two Ka Ka Cola and two Pi Pi Cola."

One peaceful day, said Chef Charley, "Hey, Francois, take off this afternoon." One can imagine the joy. I took my walking stick and up I go, through the woods and winding mountains until the wood-path turned into a field road that led me into a forlorn little village. There were no tourists in sight, hardly any cars, but just a few draft horses with ladder wagons, carts

HIS-STORY of Good Cooking

with firewood and all that was used years ago. A sheep dog followed me and a small bell was ringing. I thought, it must be late in the evening. A farmer passed with a liquid manure wagon. This whole place reminded me of "Brigadoon," a story of a place lost in time. A white-washed one story building that said "Café" in the window invited me inside. The door with its lock, the old wooden floor and everything inside must have been centuries old, nevertheless, meticulously clean. There was not too much in this room to start with. A fire was crackling in the old oven, a few benches against the wall with a few tables lined up. The small windows were filled with geraniums and the bar (called the counter) had only two shelves carrying not more than 15 bottles of different spirits, like red and white wine, sloe gin, bitters, brandy, white grain spirits, blackberry gin, a few lemonades and a barrel of beer on tap. It was very quiet until the silence was broken by a screechy door. An older woman appeared, cleaning her hands on a large dark apron she wore. After greeting me and inquiring how I got there, she apologized that she had not seen me entering. Today, she said, we have yellow cook cheese, smoked Ardenne ham with sour gherkins and a farmer's platter. I ordered a beer and the platter. It took about 20 minutes before she returned with the plate full of sautéed potatoes with onions plastered with four eggs, sunny side up, and a piece of bacon the size of my hand...and a side order of stewed apples. There was a slight hickory smoked flavor through the place. The woman again apologized, the goat cheese would be ready by tomorrow.

Yes, this is how I remember my little country. I knew at that time that no conditions are permanent and this could not go on forever. Now, stately houses and villas are everywhere. Rustic buildings and medieval castles are now meticulously renovated to their former splendor. Lovely scenic country roads wind through mountains leading to well kept parks and to the most accommodating recreation and camping grounds. Even so, some things have never changed, they still make the best Ardenne ham and sausages, 140 proof of the finest fruit and grain spirits, the best natural Champaigne and Mosel wine, and one of the greatest beers in Europe and...

Gone Fishing!

I never bragged about the "big one" (never caught) like pike and their likes, but sure have hooked many eels, perch, trout, sunfish and quite a few small fries. They are nothing to sneeze at because we know what to do with them. Now and then some fellow from our club showed up with a real winner like a barbel or big pike. If you can get them, you still can fry or oven roast others, properly scaled, cleaned and fins cut off. Some are cooked with heads on and some not because they have very big heads. Candidates to such fine cooked aquatic beasts are any whole fish like striped bass; haddock; cod; whitefish; red drum; weakfish; red snapper and even carp, which is very good if served with a hot or cold sauce like horseradish, mustard, chervil, capers and fresh parsley. Care should be taken in handling fish with sharp teeth and spiny fins.

PIKE OR RED OR WHITE OCEAN PERCH WITH GREEN HERBS

The utmost importance to great 'pan out' in cooking fish, is its freshness and proper cleaning. If not sure, let a fishmonger do this for you. Rinse and dry the **fish** with a paper towel, then rub or sprinkle inside with **lemon juice, salt and pepper**, adding a **few chopped scallions** will do fine. Smaller fish are often baked whole, basted occasionally and sprinkled with **dry white wine**. If a "fish-poacher" is not available, tie larger fish to a wooden board and place in a big roasting pan. Cover and steam with 1/4 of water adding **salt, peppercorns, bay leaf, onion rings, celery, lemon wheels and a splash of white vinegar**. Cover and slowly simmer for 20 to 25 minutes. Lift out of the fish stock and keep warm.

Making the Sauce

In a casserole, sauté ; **1/2 fine chopped Vidalia onion** till glazed, add just a little **flour**, (I love to finish most of my sauces with **potato starch**, it gives a velvety texture). Then add a glass of **dry white wine; a cup of strained fish stock; 3/4 cup of fresh heavy cream; and a dip of Dijon mustard**. Boil slowly for a few minutes adding some fresh **chopped dill and sorrel or chervil**. Dress the whole fish on a big platter and pour over half the sauce, sprinkle with **chopped parsley and roasted almonds**. Garnish with **lemon wheels** dipped halfway with **chopped parsley** and the other half with **paprika**. We often served this with chanterrell mushrooms. I recommend small, fresh mushrooms or artichoke buttons filled with spinach leaves or broiled half tomato provencale (with garlic, parsley and buttered bread crumbs, or asparagus, or smothered pascal celery or braised leeks. Serve the rest of the sauce on the side.

With this we drink a nice Pinot Chardonnay.or a Musigny

Cooking a Small FISH FRY OR FRITURE

This is a real humdinger! It can be made from small fish that I mentioned before. If you happen to travel near the Moselle River in Europe, you should try a "friture," a regional dish much appreciated by the natives.

Clean **fish** and rinse under cold water, heads should be left on. In a bowl, toss fish around with **salt, pepper, some lemon juice** and then let them rest awhile. Sprinkle them with some **flour**, shake well and deep fry them at high temperatures in a mixture of good **oil and Crisco** type fat. They should be floating till crisp and brown. When ready, take them out of the fat, sprinkle with **salt and pepper** and serve immediately. Connoisseurs will eat the whole little fish with heads and tails. Fresh smelts can be used as a good substitute.

Serve a nice Mosel wine like Gray Riesling or a Ruwer.
Fish have to swim, you know!

Note about the Law: Certain fish have to be released if they have not reached minimum length. Yet, plenty of small fish are out there...for keeps!

FRESH PIG KNUCKLES (HACKSEN) WITH SAUERKRAUT

Select a few nice chunky **pig knuckles**, one per person and a few added so you have enough to serve the follow day's Jelly-hacksen. Blanche hacksen for 5 minutes, discard water and start to cook them in fresh water for about 3 hours, adding crushed **peppercorns, salt, bay leaves, some celery and mustard seeds, garlic clove and a dash of white vinegar**. The hacksen should be cooked soft, making the skin gelatious so it easily can be cut with a fork.

Take hacksen out of the broth and place on a big platter with boiled potatoes, sauerkraut or cabbage wedges. Serve with some broth on the side, hardy Dusseldorf style mustard and a good glass of ale.

COLD PORK JELLY-HACKSEN

The leftover hacksen you had saved for the next day's meal are prepared ahead by removing all the bones and the meat cut into 3/4 inch pieces. Boil slowly in the broth for half an hour removing all the onions, bay leaves and adding a **dash of white wine and enough white vinegar** to give it a very piquant and tangy flavor. Preparing cold food always needs a bit more salt or vinegar.

Pour all in a terrine and place in the refrigerator. It will be very gelatinous and firm. Serve this so called pork-jelly with German potato salad and gherkins.

With this we can serve beer or a white madrigal Rhine wine.

COLD BEEF SALAD

On some dog gone hot summer days, you just feel like having something light and refreshing. This salad should do it! Slowly boil a few thick **shoulder steaks**, adding a **bay leaf, peppercorns, salt, celery stalk, a medium onion, chervil and a dash of white vinegar**. Boil until done and soft, cool in the refrigerator.

After cooling, remove the meat from the broth and save the broth for soup. Slice the beef into 1 inch cubes, adding a little **salt, white pepper, mild mustard, thin sliced Vidalia onions, dash of soy or Maggi sauce, wine vinegar and vegetable or olive oil**. Mix all and let soak for about 1/2 hour before serving it in a bowl.

Fondue Cooking in a Chafing Dish

Fondue cooking is really romantic cookery that can be done inside on colder days near a fire place or as we did, outside on the verandah late in the evening by candle light. Fondue, (which means "melt") is to be prepared and served in a special fondue pan or chafing dish, heated up by a candle, propane or "Sterno" type spirituous.

To make a SWISS CHEESE FONDUE

Prepare:
Cut into cubes 1/2 pound of Swiss cheese
1/2 pound of Gruyere cheese

Sprinkle cheese with **3 TBS. flour**, make lightly toasted **French bread slices**. Cut into chunks.
Set up chafing dish and rub inside of the pan with a **garlic clove** and discard. Heat up the pan and pour in:
2 cups of white Chablis wine
And a squirt of lemon juice

Bring almost to a boil and add all the cheese. With a wooden spoon stir continuously until all is melted into a smooth texture, adding a trace of **nutmeg, salt, pepper and a small shot of Gin** (the Swiss prefer Kirsch).
The chafing dish is placed in the center of the table and the guests serve themselves by dipping and twirling a forked piece of bread into the cheese. Needed are....good company and a nice Chablis or Sancerre.

To prepare BEEF FONDUE BOURGUIGNON

It takes about 1/2 pound per person...of lean **sirloin or tenderloin** cut into 1 inch cubes at room temperature.
Fill the chafing dish with **1/2 peanut oil or vegetable oil**, best is to preheat oil on the stove until bubbles appear, place oil in chafing dish with medium high flame. The beef cubes are dipped and dunked into the hot oil using long handled chafing forks. When the piece of meat on your fork is done to your preference, it is then dipped into an assortment of sauces served in side dishes.
Some of the sauces could be Sauce Diablo or Sauce Bordelaise (mentioned in this book). Others are...

Francois Boeres, Chef de Cuisine

QUICK BURGUNDY DIPPING SAUCE

In a casserole boil all the following ingredients together:

1/2 cup of red Burgundy
1/4 cup fine chopped onion
1 cup Chili sauce
small jigger of vinegar
dash of vegetable oil
2 tsp. of brown sugar, some Tabasco,
Worcestershire sauce, garlic powder
and a pinch of English mustard.

Simmer for 15 minutes. This can be served hot or cold.

HORSERADISH DIPPING SAUCE

Mix: 8 oz. sour cream
3 TBS. Dijon Mustard
1-1/2 TBS. finely chopped onion
2 TBS. horseradish
3 TBS. white wine and
some chopped parsley.

CHAPTER 7 . . . FIRE IN THE KITCHEN

What do I want to be?

The retreating Army of the Third Reich had left a swath of destruction behind in the Ardennes of my native Luxembourg. The last days of struggle and desperate fighting had littered the whole countryside with plentiful American and German weapons and ordnance. For some time, I had acquired a nice collection of machine guns, mortars, rifles and to Mother's dismay, in the corner of my high-lacquered Deco-Style bedroom, stood a heavy 42 German machine gun, on a tripod, surrounded by Schmeissers, assault rifles, Garants and pistols of all description that could garnish the walls and match a section of the West Point Military Museum. Soon, this kind of hobby became illegal, so I turned my interests toward hunting weapons and collecting geological artifacts and fossils of all kinds. Now, I had been contemplating the idea of becoming a Forester or Ranger, but soon my enthusiasm was dampened by the fact that you had to undergo four years of military service and a few years attending the "Academy."

By now music had touched a sensitive string in my heart, so Paps sent me to the renowned Music Professor, Mr. Katz. There I performed all kinds of tricks or treats on my "half-size" violin. Mr. Katz, from our town, "Esch," noted that my progress in music left much to be desired and playing the violin sounded more like Katzengejammer (cat mauling)...maybe it came from the cat gut strings, I thought.

Mam suggested piano lessons and sent me to Mrs. Stoyk to learn Solfegio. After all these years I can still hear her playing allegro and singing a coloratura soprano from an aria that put me in awe.

Francois Boeres, Chef de Cuisine

I never did get to have "that" piano, but there was that Black Forest Zither displayed in "Krainzes" store window. I had my eyes on it for quite some time, and every time, passing that store, I had that compassionate longing to have this instrument. It took some time to come up with the 700 francs for that Zither. I fell spellbound by its soft reverberating tunes... like it came from a touch of breath from another time. Many people I knew played some kind of musical instrument, maybe the piano, accordion, concertina, mandolin or violin. There were more bands than stars in the sky. Big bands, orchestras, church and chorale groups. Some restaurants had at least a piano player, playing Debussy, Chopin or Mozart. The one that had a trio or quartet played after the soft melodies of Schubert, often called after his nickname, "Schwammerl-musik." Even in the smallest town one could find a band playing Sunday afternoon in the park. Well, the Germans had their "Schnitzelbank" to sit around, singing arm in arm. In an Italian place one occasionally could hear a customer, singing a well-known aria or someone playing his harmonica on a bus, around a campfire, or any other place. Here we didn't try to save the world and make ourselves miserable. We had enough of our own mishaps to take care of. No matter what, the next day took care of itself. We had, after a hard days work, time to sit around with friends, having a glass of beer, a good time, or swing a leg, with all respect to those "things" I had to find out soon what I was going to do with my life.

As early as 13 years old, I had already learned how to cook a pretty good meal in 25 minutes. Mam had a beauty parlor and often was too busy to cook us a meal when Dad came home for lunch from his office. Lunch was a big meal then and Dad had not to much time. So, here is what I often cooked for us in a short time, and so can you if you're willing: **STEAK, POMME-FRITTE, SALAD** (look up the recipes on how to make a minute steak, French fries and vinaigrette for the salad.)

In the recipes you will notice the absence of the amount and measurement of the ingredients. This I did on purpose, because I know how to make this salad. I want you to decide and learn by trial and experience how much vinegar you are going to use or if you prefer lemon juice, regular or olive oil and maybe add some cream or sour cream. This all will be decided by you and you're given the opportunity to graduate, just like a real chef and when you have mastered this approach, you think like a professional, not like a robot, fooling around with all kinds of crazy gadgets, because the fewer gadgets you will have, the better cook you will be. Professionals in the classic culinary trade always carried with them a so-called "Repertoire of the kitchen" (from repertus, something easy to find in an arranged order,) this, a small sized pocket book produced only the ingredients for the recipe, all you had to do was look it up and instantly you would know how to prepare. I may give a suggestion on the salad, go easy on the salt and vinegar and don't skimp on the oil. Soon you will know exactly how much to use and all of this will be your own creation. All your cooking will be unique and you will receive all the credit and the compliments. As they say in Paris, great success and vive la difference.

Another favorite and quick dish to do for lunch were potato pancakes or so-called "crickets." This we often served with a hardy leek or lentil soup. (look up leek and lentil soup.)

How I Got Myself Into the Soup

My never-ending parochial school years had finally come to an end, most of my summer vacations and other spare time I spent helping out on the farm, haying, hoeing, weeding, digging and harvesting potatoes and rutabagas. The rutabagas we mostly chopped up for cow feed. Mom only liked turnips and so did I. (Look up turnips.)

All this work on the farm had given me many unforgettable moments... jumping into the hay mow from the rafters, going swimming, river fishing with a 14 foot long bamboo pole (I still have) and come dark, sitting all round the campfire, roasting potatoes. Of all importance, I learned and experienced from a never-ending work of a farmer's hand, how the food was planted, grown, taken care of, finely to be harvested. On a late November day, Jeang, the son of Mr. Lucas, invited me to deliver a batch of potatoes and a few slabs of bacon to a big resort hotel. That was the day I got a glimpse into a real big hotel kitchen, with all the chefs and cooks in their white uniforms, engulfed in intoxicating aromatic steam escaping from batteries of shiny copper pots cooking on the stove, people running back and forth, waiters in black, shouting orders, cooks in their whites, hollering. This all seemed like "Pandemonium"...a coordinated mayhem, before an attack. First, I thought it to be funny, on second thought, it seemed to be fun and exciting, besides these guys had a lot of fine things to eat, a nice warm

Francois Boeres, Chef de Cuisine

place in winter and this could be a rewarding artistic profession waiting for me.

Maybe one day I could be a Chef, tasting and creating "scrumdelicious" and exciting menus or testing some of these elevated chocolate soufflés, ooh, gee, gosh!

Soon, plans were discussed and preparations made for enrollment as Apprentice in the renowned and stately Hotel Continental in Luxembourg City. A three-year apprenticeship seemed a long commitment and just enough pocket money to pay for my uniform and basic tools like knives and their like.

Well, the day of reckoning was at hand. Dad drove me to the place with his four cylinder Zundapp (a war relic). Me sitting in the 'Steif' sidecar as Dad leaned over to one side of his "bike" to put his weight against a sharp curve and before we knew, coming around the bend...there it was...in big shiny brass letters, HOTEL CONTINENTAL.

Arriving to the Hotel lobby, Dad inquired about the Head-Chef. Soon we were directed inside the heart of the Hotel...the kitchen itself, with its high ceiling and no windows in sight. Here we met the Chef de Cuisine, topped with his Toque-plissé (high Chefs hat) and his white uniform. He also wore a neat knotted white "foulard" (neckerchief).

I was "mustered" from top to bottom with a half blinking eye, a cigarette in his clinched lips seemed to move up and down as he pressed out these words..."I am Arthur. You might as well start today. Here, Jacqueline," he called to what seemed to be the hostess, "show Francois here up to his quarters." Then I said "Good-bye" to Dad and was glad to have myself a hard working, quasi-non paying job for the next three years.

My live-in quarters were on the seventh floor, paneled with knotty pine. The sleeping quarters reminded me of a berth from an old ship. Naturally, I had to share my room with another apprentice who soon became my best friend. I must say that I saw him more often than I did our sleeping quarters, considering working an average of 10 hours per day. My first assignment was what is called a Cold Pantry, known as a Garde Manger, taking care of all that cold food. I also was called the "Garde Manger." We also had a butcher working inside the enclosed Garde-Manger compartment. Here we prepared all the required cold food for the kitchen. We worked on two butchers blocks and a four inch thick hardwood prep table. The "room" had only one entrance and a pass-through window. Another heavy wooden door

HIS-STORY of Good Cooking

led into a refrigerator called the Icebox and inside the Icebox was another door that led into a much colder Icebox where most of the meat was kept. The first Icebox kept all the prepared food, vegetables and diary. Fresh fish was kept separately on ice in a four-drawer wooden ice chest lined with heavy tin and a drain hole.

The chickens, mostly broilers, came all packed in wooden crates on ice. They only came plucked with the rest still all in there, head, feet, innards, etc. To dress them was no easy job. We served the liver with the bile removed for lunch (look up chicken liver with sherry wine on rice.)

Besides preparing all the salad dressing, mayonnaise, ravigotte sauce, vinaigrettes, etc., I also had to do all the cold "hors d' oeuvres", open oysters, filet the fish, filet and marinate the herring, make all kinds of salads, like potato salad, cooked beef salads, Ocksen-maul salad (Ocks-snout salad,) and many more because the menu changed from day to day.

The midst of the service was the time of high tension and stress because all the food preparation had to be done fast and to order.

The chef usually was the "caller" to call out new orders, like: "Ordering: two steaks, four halibuts, one Bismarck herring, two Russian eggs, flamzam. There they were, in the pass-through window, ready to be picked up by the waiter or for the cooks to prepare.

The kitchen crew consisted of what is called a Brigade, ...an arrangement of 6 to 12 cooks, first the chef, then the Sous-chef, (usually the saucier) the Rotisseur (roaster) the Legumier (vegetables and soups) the Sauteur (fryer) the Patissier, the Butcher and the Garde Manger. Usually a woman was managing the coffee pantry, called the 'office'. She made coffee, tea, coffee-filtres (an espresso type of coffee), folded the napkins, passed out the bread, and made desserts like PEACH-MELBA, CAFFEE-GLACE, POIRE BELLE-HELENE, etc.

My friend Mustique was already in his second year of his apprenticeship. He had mastered making soups, preparing vegetables, roasting meats, cooking fish, making sauces like Béarnaise and playing all kinds of tricks on the "Piano." We nicknamed him "Mustique" (Mosquito) not only because his last name was Musty, but he was also swift in his work. Mustique looked forward to his next and last year of apprenticeship to work next to the Sous Chef, the saucier.

Besides other jobs, every morning I had to fire up the huge 14 by 8 foot cooking stove called the "Piano" in the trade. It sure was a monster. It had

Francois Boeres, Chef de Cuisine

four holes, each covered by three one-inch thick cast iron rings. The fire was started with paper, kindling wood and coal. The inside had water tubes to heat up the water for the dishwasher room and the coffee urns. On one side we had a few gas tops for early breakfast and other emergencies.

Most of the time the heat from the oven was so intense that the oven rings became red hot and temperatures rose to 150 Fahrenheit. Because of hot and moderate spots, cooking pots were rotated for quick cooking to just slow simmering. For protection, the stove was fitted with a beautiful, shiny nickel chromed rail. Another job left to me was taking care of the Marmite, a huge boiling pot with a faucet. This was our Stock pot, that was boiling almost day and night. The stock was used as a base for the most important sauces in the kitchen. It contained split and chopped up bones form beef and calf's hinds, end cuts from onions, carrots, peels from celeriac and a bouquet garnie (a cheese cloth bag that contained garlic, marjoram, bay leaves, cloves, crushed peppercorns and what have you). This boiling pot often had to be skimmed of its grease. On one busy day, I tried to move that huge pot, somehow it got stuck near the rings and a splash of hot grease spilled all over. Oh boy, did you ever see such a flare up. The whole stove seemed to be engulfed in fire. I screamed and got the hell out, fast. All the cooks came running to the rescue to quench the fire with towels, milk, and baking soda. Well, nobody said a word, except I saw Mustique grinning a few times. Besides it was now 11:30, time to stop the works and take a break. The so called Mis-en-place (preparation) for the service was done and now we all walked out through the back door, crossing the street in a goose march toward the Bistro across the street. There we had a hefty Humpen (bumper of beer), repeated a couple of stale jokes, had a few laughs and soon returned to start the 12 o'clock service. Not for too long...all hell broke loose. We had two dining rooms, one on the floor and one upstairs. The food to the upstairs was delivered by a lift, a dumbwaiter, and the order tickets delivered through a pipe post. It then landed downstairs in an old pot where it made a hell of a racket. The chef, the "caller," announced the order and put it on a board so the cooks could read them. You never got to see the second floor waiters, but crazy things always happened there. On one occasion, a filet mignon was sent up, but the customer got lamb chops instead and someone had returned and sent down a halibut. Nobody ever knew what happened to the filet! On another occasion, our temperamental Chef cursed at a waiter upstairs through the lift shaft, calling him all kinds of names; imbecile, putain, schweinhund, etc. The waiter promptly replied, "Chef, your wife is not here."

Downstairs was the worst. The constant contact between hyperactive waiters and revved up, sweating cooks looked like a Civil War. Cooks calling the waiters "Sale espece d' ivrogne", alms receiver (almosenempfanger), in return, the waiter called us "sale cuisteau", (kitchen cats), etc. and when the service was all over, they were the nicest gang of people you ever saw.

Quite often, I had to chop meat on the butchers block with a cleaver, because it said so on the menu: chopped steak. (steak hache), not ground through a machine! For this, top butt steak was preferred and it had to be chopped up fine so to put on the grill, called a Salamander. Also, the meat for the Filet American (sort of tartar steak) had to be chopped on the block to be prepared in front of the customers by a waiter. (Look for....How to prepare a **FILET AMERICAN**).

The owners of the hotel were a kind of "stuck-up" sort, especially Madame Sally, who demanded that her pet, a beautiful, fluffy white, blue-eyed cat named "kitty" also carried a semi-precious rhinestone collar, should be served a filet hache every day at two o'clock. This made Mustique and me very upset. So, come one day when one of the boilers was "laid down", we grabbed "kitty" and threw her into the empty fire box. Oh, la la, what an upheaval we caused. Everyone was looking for the cat. Finally, hearing the 'miau', someone opened the firebox and out jumped a dirty gray cat. Well, all figured out what happened, because we were kind of in the cold for sometime.

French Fries...Simply Done

There are many recipes dealing with "home-spun French fries, some even use clumsy electric fryers while others use deep frying pans filled with vegetable oil that soon will break down.

For "French fry Philo-maniacs, I suggest a 9 inch, heavy-duty, stainless steel bowl with a 7 inch basket with a handle. The bowl should be filled over half full with a 'Crisco' type shortening. If not in use, cover and store in the refrigerator (we have done this for years). The real Belgian fries are fried in beef fat and are the best tasting. It is believed, French fries were first served in a Bruxelle train-station by frying small cut potatoes quick in the fryer because travelers had little time to eat and could not wait too long.

Francois Boeres, Chef de Cuisine

To Prepare FRENCH FRIES

Use the firm **russet type potatoes**, cut close to the size served in fast food restaurants. They will cook faster that way. Soak them 10 minutes in cold water, dry with a paper tower and place in the basket. Turn the previously heated up fat to higher temperatures and carefully drop the basket with fries into the fat, (over 350). Cook until soft but not too mushy. Remove the basket with the fries and set aside. Turn fat on low heat.

Come serving time, reheat fat, (you see some smoke) at high temperatures over 350, hot enough to fry crisp and golden. Shake, **salt** and serve them in a tureen. Soon, you will never forget to do them....just like riding a bike.

Note: Be careful cooking with high temperatures, turn off immediately and let fat cool off where it is at.

To Make the MINUTE STEAK (STEAK MINUTE)

Using sirloin would be great, but the idea of a minute steak is to use less tender cuts like **rump, bottom or chuck steaks**...to be pounded tender. Cut away most fat and beat steaks with a mallet or tenderizing hammer until half the thickness, so it looks like the flag of Fort Moultrie, all ripped apart, shot to 'hell', but still there. All you do is to add **salt, pepper** and place steak into a hot frying pan with a little oil and butter....hot enough so it 'screams', fry quick until nice and brown...when turning steak around, hold it a second with a fork and let the hot fat recuperate so it will not 'boil' instead of frying. Place on the serving platter, it should be pink and juicy inside...or just about. Overcooked steaks are tough! Deglaze the pan with some water and **butter**, pour over the steaks and serve with chopped **parsley**. Now, the whole dinner: Steak, Pomme Frite and salad is served...of course, the salad had been prepared. Now is time to dip the pre-fried fries into the hot fat so all is done on time.

To Make POTATO PANCAKES
for 2 servings plus

Use a high starch **potato**. Peel and wash **3 to 4 medium size** bakers, grate on medium or big hole hand grater (I prefer an electric or hand operated rotating blade). Let rest for 15 minutes, drain and mix with **2 medium fine chopped onions, chopped parsley, salt, pepper, one beaten egg and two TBS. of flour**. Mix well. Use a large frying pan with enough oil so the pancakes will float around. With a TBS., scoop out the dough and flatten it in the pan. In the hot oil, cook both sides golden brown. This can be served with many soups like potato or leek soup.

Here we have an assortment of a few potatoes that can be planted in the Eastern part of the States. I am grateful to the great people from Cornell Extension, who sent this to honor my request.

POTATOES

EARLY:
Andover
Superior (SR)
Norland (SR red)
Carole

MID SEASON:
Chieftain (red, high yielding, large)
Reba
Russet Bake-King (russet, good baker)
Salem (SR)
Yukon Gold (yellow interior)
Yellow Finn (yellow flesh)
Purple #5 (purple flesh)

LATE SEASON:
Elba
Genesee
Katahdin (good yields)

Francois Boeres, Chef de Cuisine

OF SMOKED HAM, HERRING, BISMARK HERRING AND ROLL MOPS

A man I knew had bought a smoked Virginia ham, cooked it for over three hours and turned it into a stringy tough piece of meat. This was very disappointing. First of all, it had been a carefully prepared Virginia ham. To cook certain smoked hams, they have to be soaked in water for some time and boiled very slowly. Aged smoked hams are very desirable and should be sliced very thin and served on rye bread, Boston lettuce, melons and hors d'oeuvres. Another fellow had bought, from a supermarket, a big jar of salted herring. He also was disappointed and told me "They are too salty." This scenario can often be found these days. Nobody ever told these people what it really was and what should be done with it, nor had they any instructions how to prepare. I like to express with great appreciation, a fish of great importance, like the potato, it had saved millions of people from starvation and with respect, rephrasing Bismarck's words "If herrings be scarce, they be greatly in demand and very expensive." Today a good herring is expensive. I think back when they were cheap and came salted in big wooden barrels. Properly prepared herrings can still be found in fine stores and delicatessens. They are prepared from salt herrings just like one hundred years ago.

To Prepare HERRINGS

First, clean and filet the herrings. Some prefer to remove the skin, but this is not required. Soak filets for three days in water, changing it often. Place herrings layer by layer in a serving bowl, adding thin slices of onions, mustard and peppercorns, bay leaves and a few lemon slices. Cover the filets with half dry white wine and half white vinegar, a teaspoon of sugar and place in the refrigerator for four days. They can be served whole or sliced.

Making ROLL MOPS

A roll-mop is a herring filet prepared as above, rolled around a sliced pickle with the skin outside and fastened with a toothpick. Herring can

HIS-STORY of Good Cooking

be served with sour cream, horseradish, potatoes boiled in their jackets or sautéed with butter with dill or caraway seeds. If herrings come with the milky roe, strain and mix with the sauce. Ach du lieber, das schmeckt!

WINE: A dry Riesling, or just a good beer.

Naturally, not all men are created equal, maybe by law. Occasionally, we encounter great people along our way, you know, the ones who leave great impressions.

One of these men was Chef Arthur, of ingenious character, professional excellence and the natural ability to teach in an easygoing manner. Later, he got a Chef's job at the American Embassy. So said he, "Francois, if you want to make extra money on the side, come and help us out, they pay good." And before I knew it, I was helping out to cook parties given by Pearl Mesta and General Eisenhower, some of them in chateaus and lofty residences. Charming she was, that Pearl Mesta, and always smiling. Eisenhower attended a few of those lavish parties and buffets, a very charismatic fellow he was, easy, outgoing and most of all, very diplomatic. Oops, I almost forgot to mention that big guy, Joe, who never left his side. At some parties, I recognized a few people, some of the: Prince "Jang" of Luxembourg, Minister Dupond, Bech, Diderich, the Consul, Bishop Lommell and Marshal Juin. Not all the parties were elaborate, some were given for orphans or other charitable organizations, all donated or paid for by Pearl.

At one of these parties, we cooked BEEF a la MODE, and they all loved it. Around Christmas time, Arthur had cooked, in the kitchen of the Consulate.

TURKEY BALLOTTINE

A Turkey Ballottine is a de-boned and stuffed turkey. It takes time to prepare, but is not that hard to do.

Use a sharp boning knife, cut the wings off at the elbow, cut off the drumstick at the joints and use this meat, with the tendons removed, for the stuffing.

Cut loose and fold over the skin alongside the vertebrae (backbone). Using a pruning or poultry shear, cut out the exposed whole backbone with the neck and lower end attached. Save this with the other bones and the wings for the sauce.

NOTE: In older kitchens, we used a hook on the wall to pull out these tendons.

Now pry the turkey open and remove first the breastbone by cutting it loose and pulling it out with a towel. Remove all ribs, small bones and the wish-bone. As you start boning, scraping and cutting loose all meats alongside the bones, cut them off at the joints and follow to the next bone, cutting and pulling them loose as you go along without piercing the skin. The last bones to be cut out are the ball-joints from the wings.

To STUFF

Arrange the mass of turkey meat on the table and stuff with this stuffing:

1/3 ground meat from chicken thighs purchased extra
1/3 ground veal with some beef suet
1/3 ground pork with some fat back

Use at least 6 cups of stuffing for a 16 pound turkey. A good stuffing should have a reasonable amount of fat.

Sauté 2 medium onions in butter until glazed.
Add 1/3 cup brandy
1/2 cup sweet white wine like Madeira or Sherry

Bring to a boil and reduce to half the volume. Mix into the meats, adding **3 beaten eggs, salt, pepper, sage** (I prefer to add Pistachios). Mix it well so that it looks like dough.

Season the laid out turkey with **salt and pepper** and fill with the stuffing. Roll and close the turkey like a loaf, until both ends meet, with some skin overlapping. (Remember the skin from the backbone.) With strong yarn and a big needle, close and sew the turkey roll so there are no more openings, then tie a twine around to give it a nice round shape.

Roast turkey with all the bones, wings, cut up onion, carrot and celery in a preheated oven at 350 degrees, for 30 minutes. Then lower the heat to 325 degrees and bake for 3 hours, or until done, basting often. Take out of the oven and let it rest a while before removing all the strings.

HIS-STORY of Good Cooking

The sauce is to be made last by deglazing the pan with half water and half chicken bouillon. Strain, reduce and thicken lightly with a little starch and serve in a gravy boat.

Another kind of stuffed turkey is called a **GALANTINE**, and served cold. The Galantine is held together with a towel or cheesecloth, tied down at both ends and kept in shape with twine before cooking it in chicken broth and gelatin made from calf bones.

With the Ballottine, we usually served little Parisienne or soufflé potatoes.

Wine: A California Pinot, a St. George or a Cabernet Sauvignon.
Music: Mendlesohn - Hymn of Praise.

I will never forget the day when Pearl said good-bye, and Arthur, kissing her hand, she handed him a fifty dollar bill. A lot of potatoes for that time. Gee, I wish I had kissed her hand, but that kind of stuff is now out of style like so many other things that got lost in the time machine of progress, like Chips, Shoestrings or Gaufrette potatoes, now available in neatly packaged plastic bags, minus their inherited flavors.

The so-called match or fine shoestring potatoes had to be cut by hand or on the "Mandolin" cutter, then placed in little steel baskets, shaped like nests, to be deep fried into crisp, brown little nests. The nests are kept in a warm place and used to garnish and enhance great dishes. They are filled with all kinds of morsels, like small Parisienne potatoes or soufflé potatoes.

SMALL PARISIENNE POTATOES

...are cut out of big potatoes with a small size melon cutter, then deep fried or blanched and swirled in brown butter.

Other garnishing were made and turned from solid white mushrooms looking like beautiful stars. We blanched them in a little lemon water to keep them white. Here and there, we loved, just for the fun of it, to cut out a foot long, unbroken, solid continuous chain from a big potato to deep fry and used it for decoration. I still know how to do this today, but it never received great attention.

Francois Boeres, Chef de Cuisine

The POMME DE TERRE SOUFFLES

...always got great attention. They looked so "puffed" up. We served them in La Cremaillere Restaurant. Here, two fryers were needed, one with moderate and another with high temperature.

First, peel and slice selected California potatoes into 1/8 inch or about the thickness of 2 quarters. Rinse in cold water and dry with a towel. Place the slices, a few at a time, in the moderate hot fat until they start to float and show fine blisters on the edge. Then transfer them, a few at a time, into a very hot fryer fat until they puff up, crisp and golden. Occasionally they need to be turned over, carefully, with a wire skimmer. Lift them out and dry them on a paper towel, salt and serve immediately.

P.S. - While cooking it is O.K. to have a few sips of old Port wine.

The State of Order

On the high cliffs from the old fortress of Luxembourg...looking down the valley...stands one of the finest hotels in Europe, the CRAVAT. I know... I worked there. The owner, Monsieur Paul Cravat, our patron, was running the place and this he did very well. Naturally, we had managers, Maitre d'Hotel, a Chef and a whole company of dedicated help, but here Paul knew the art of business. He was everywhere and knew at any time what was going on, who made reservations, the next day's menu, the wine in the cellar, the kitchen inventory. He was precise, orderly, concerned and most of all, respected. He would get...for example, very upset if an apprentice or busboy was mistreated. Often he would drive me in his big Buick to the station, so I would not miss the train. It was expected that one kept all in order, wore clean uniforms and kept his station organized. The work tables close to the huge stove had a row of small bins of chopped parsley, garlic, onions, cut up mushrooms, cubed tomatoes and artichokes, lemon slices and all this to use in a jiffy for service. The upper table shelf had bottles of oil, vinegar, wine, sherry, cognac and marsala. The Béarnaise and hollandaise were kept on a warm spot. On the less heated side of the stove stood the "Bain-Marie," a big shallow pan with hot water that contained basic sauces like béchamel, bordelaise, espagnole, tomato sauce and melted butter, all ready for the big rush, often called "coup de feu." A cooks most valued possession in the kitchen were his knives, sharpened with great pride and cleaned after each service to be placed away in a canvas or in a box. Often we stuck corks on the tips of very pointed and sharp knives. Don't ever ask a fellow cook to lend you his knife, you might as well ask for his wife! Each man had his assortment of knives, a big and a medium size Chef's knife, a long ham or roast beef knife, a boning and skinning knife to remove slivers and the silver lining from the meat, fish knives like the "filet de Sole" knife, paring knives, a chopping knife to split lobsters, cut pork chops or portion loin of port or lamb.

Some even had a flattening iron made from a rail-track to flatten veal steaks and other meats. Also needed was a sharpening steel, round melon ball cutters for fruits and Parisian potatoes, braiding and larding needles, flexible steel spatulas and pastry "horns", now made of plastic...to scrape food out of bowls and mortars, this, originally made out of cow-horns, split open and flattened by steam. The real good ones were made of turtle shells.

A kitchen knife was a real piece of art, made by "professionals", for culinary artists. It had to keep a good edge, balance and feel good in your hands. Some still are made this way, but lately I have seen people using knives with plastic handles, resembling a stick from a transmission and guaranteed to trim your fingernails and "cut" the fingers.

Wie der Herr...so das Gescherr!
(like master...so his tools...)
Old German Proverb

Of Mortars, Pestles and Kitchens

Mortars make me think of warfare, no matter what kind of mortars, they sure have been around for a long, long time, used in crushing, grinding, pulverizing, mixing and extracting.

Mongols and Chinese used mortars to mix propellants and explosives for fireworks and rockets...a far cry from real "gunpowder."

Roger Bacon, who lived in Gloucester, invented a good formula for so called gunpowder that could be used to hurl projectiles from a mortar, but it was a monk, Berthold Schwarz, from Freiburg, Germany, who came up with a real "humdinger" of gunpowder, much the same as the black powder we know of. Now, we use Nitro-Cellulose powder.

Francois Boeres, Chef de Cuisine

In the past, mortars had been an indispensable tool in apothecary and kitchens alike. It is to no surprise that a fine kitchen like the Cravat also had a mortar to do all kinds of crushing, extracting, pulping and manipulating ingredients for certain dishes. The marble mortar was built and stuck right out of the wall. It had a yard long pestle, retained by a ring built into the wall. The fine-baker (patissier) used the mortar to crush and make a paste with all kinds of nuts...like filberts, almonds and walnuts. I often used the mortar to extract juices from plants to add to meats, fish and mix in sticks of butter, cut into slices to place on top of fish and steaks, other extracted aromatic juices we used to flavor and color soups and sauces. One of my favored soup was the POTAGE SANTÉ, or good health soup.

The extensive menu from the cravat Hotel kept all the promises a connoisseur of fine foods expects, I remember only a few and here they are.....

Ox Tail Soup/Hollandische veal knoedel suppe
and Pottage Santé (good health soup)
Veal cutlets a la creme with mushroom caps cut like twisted stars and served with artichoke caps filled with hollandaise.
White asparagus with hollandaise served in a "serviette."
Chateau-Briant for two sliced at the table by the waiter.
Beef brochettes flambe (shashlik) served on rice pilaf.
Bouche "Fruit de mer". Sea food patty shell.
Wood cocks with sauce "Cassis".
Marinated "Marcassin" (wild boar) cooked in red wine sauce and juniper berries crushed in a mortar.
Boiled turbot with langustines (shrimplike crustacean)
Poached ray-fish Grenobloise (with brown butter, lemon bits, capers and parsley).

For desserts we carried things like assorted cheese, Napoleons, coup au marron with cognac. Linzer torte, Charlotte-Russe and of all the venerable and much appreciated "Omelet Surprise". (Baked Alaska).

To Make POTAGE SANTE OR GOOD HEALTH SOUP

In a big pot with **butter** sauté one fine chopped **Vidalia onion**. Stir in 1 TBS. **flour**, then pour in **2-1/2 quarts of light chicken broth**. Let it come to a boil and add...all chopped fine... a good handful of fresh **spinach**, a handful of fresh **watercress**, a handful of **sorrel**, a handful of **nettles** that were supplied by our kitchen helper who lived in the country.

Cook for about 35 minutes, then add a **trace of tarragon**, a few leaves of chopped fresh **basil** and a pinch of **sugar**.

Last preparation....in a mortar or food processor, chop and smash a small handful each of......sorrel, watercress and spinach. Place a wet towel on top of a small pot, pour in all the fresh chopped up greens and squeeze or torsion all the juice out of the towel into the soup to retain a nice color and its inherited flavor. Boil up quickly, add some **cream**, a dash of **soy or Maggi sauce**. If too thin, thicken with a little starch. Garnish with **buttered croutons and fresh chives**.

This soup can also be served cold.

The Dover Sole

This funny looking flatfish lives on the bottom of the sea, moving around in an undulatory motion. On top, it has two small cock-eyed eyes, an upper gray skin and a much lighter skin below.

How amazing, many people have never even seen a whole sole besides some "exhausted" pieces of filet of sole displayed in supermarkets. The whole soles were delivered fresh on ice to restaurants and hotels. This was the only way. To filet the fish for filet of sole, it had to be cleaned and filleted. A special, thin and flexible knife called "Filet of Sole" knife was used to loosen the filets with two quick cutting strokes along side the bones, then the bones were cooked out, to make fish stock...a very important kitchen base.

To clean....Place sole on the table and cut off just the tip of the tail. With a small knife, scrape and loosen the tail skin toward the head. Pull the skin off (this is easy) all the way, stopping at the head. Turn sole over and repeat. Now, cut off the head with the skin attached and discard. Clean out the innards (there is not much), and with a strong shear or poultry shear, cut off all the fin bones around the sole.

Francois Boeres, Chef de Cuisine

DOVER SOLE MEUNIERE
One sole per person

Make sure there is a big enough pan, we used a long, oval fish pan.

Dip the whole **sole** in **milk and flour**, season with **salt and pepper** and slowly fry sole on both sides on medium fire in plenty of **butter**, until golden brown and ready. Place sole on the platter. In the pan add some more fresh **butter**, chopped **parsley** and some **lemon juice**. Pour over the sole.

This is about one of the finest fish I can think of!
Wine: Chenin Blanc.

—

The Grand Hotel Cravat had been around for quite some time. Here are some menus given to my grandparents for the farewell party to America. It had been written by a good hand and as you can see, the name was misspelled.

They went to Chicago, on Hoyn Avenue, near a colony of Luxembourg people. Other colonies of Luxembourgers settled in Rollag, Minnesota, near Saint Cloud. There is even a town called Luxembourg.

Grandpa got a job at McCormick Farm Implements. A few years later, Marie, his wife died in child birth, the newborn, Walter, died shortly after. So Grandpa took his two children, Cecile and Philip and returned to Luxembourg to move in with his aunt.

America was not made for everyone. Many returned "home" to Luxembourg. There you can find a place called "Little-America" where most of the returning emigrants had resettled.

Text: (translated) - - Luxembourg le 4. 4. 1913

Grand Hotel Cravat
Monsieur Boever, (Boeres)
By the presence I have the honor to send you the menus requested. If you like to make any change, please call me tomorrow, we can arrange anything to your preference.

HIS-STORY of Good Cooking

MENU A FRS 12

1. Cold consomme Madrilène
2. Poached pike with fine "insigni" butter from Calvados
3. Center cut "Filet" with fresh garden vegetables.
4. A pullet garnished with chicken dumplings, chopped truffles, pieces of sweetbreads, olives, mushrooms, and crawfish.
5. Asparagus with Hollandaise and whipped cream.
6. Young roast duckling.
7. Bib lettuce.
8. Rock lobsters in wine aspic with truffles dressed on a socked of rice "Imperatrice". etc. etc.

MENU A FRS 14

1. Oysters from Colchester.
2. Oxtail Soup.
3. A large chunk of Salmon braised in the oven in white sauce, mushrooms, oysters and crawfish, (truffles preferred).
4. Leg of Venison (Roe Deer) with eggplants and rice pilaf.
5. Fresh asparagus with a sort of light mousseline, lemon added.
6. Roasted pullet from de Mans region.
7. Bib and Endive lettuce with chopped hard boiled eggs and slices of Swiss and Emmentaler cheese.
8. Fresh crawfish braised in spicy butter and wine sauce, etc. etc.

TEXTE: (from the original) LUXEMBOURG, le 4.4.1913

Grand Hotel Cravat

Monsieur Boever

Par la presente, j'ai l'honneur de vous envoyer les menus demandes. Si vous desirez changer quelque chose, vous pouvez me la comm'eniquer demain, on s'arrangera toujours.

MENU A FRS. 12 Vin ordinaire compris

1. Potage Madrilene
2. Brochet au bleu/beurre d'Isigny
3. Coeur de Filet de Boeuf Bouquetiere
4. Poularde a l'Ancienne

Francois Boeres, Chef de Cuisine

    5. Asperges au Branches Sauce Mousseline
    6. Caneton nouveau roti
    7. Salade
    8. Langouste a la Neva
Glaces
Fruits
Dessert
Cafe

            MENU A FRS.14 Vin ordinaire compris
1. Huitres de Colchester.
2. Potage Oxtail.
3. Darne de Saumon Sauce Charon
4. Guige de Chevreuil a la Catalane
5. Asperges nouvelles Sauce Zephir
6. Poularde de Mans rotie
7. Salads de Suisse (?)
8. Ecrevisses a la Luxembourgeoise
Glaces
Fruits
Dessert
Cafe

SAND TORTE

In England, they have Tea Hour and in Germany coffee klatch hour. There are cookies and other sweet cakes are served. Here is the traditional Sand Torte:

In a mixing bowl: combine **3 whole eggs and 3 yolks with 1/2 cup sugar.** Set the bowl in a pot with low boiling water. Beat the mixture occasionally until lukewarm. Place the bowl in the mixer and beat at high speed for 10 minutes, until foamy. Fold in, a little at a time, **3/4 cup of sifted flour, 6 tsp. melted butter, 1/2 cup of fine ground roasted almonds, a few drops of almond extract, grated lemon rinds and a pinch of salt.** After carefully mixing all, pour the batter in a buttered "Turban Kugelhopf" mold and bake in a preheated oven at 350° for approximately 35 to 40 minutes or until done. Cool cake on a rack and sprinkle with confectioners sugar.

Serving Uncooked (Raw) Meats and Fish

Eating uncooked food is so natural we almost take it for granted. We find it in Bacon, Prochiutto, Virginia Ham, Dry Sausages, German Teawurst, Salmon, Shellfish, Japanese "Sushi", Spanish "Seviche" and others too numerous to mention here. This kind of food is prepared and quasi "cooked" in its own marinade, brine, pickled, air dried or smoked.

TARTAR STEAK AND FILET AMERICAIN
for 2 persons

...are made out of fat free selected **Filet of beef or sirloin**, saturated and marinated in a blend of **salt, vinegar and oil** and as good as any salted or marinated meat, its a real Epicurean[3] delight!

First: Prepare the mayonnaise! With a whisk, **mix one egg yolk with a tsp. of sharp mustard**. Add a **squirt of vinegar, white pepper and salt**. Slowly whisk and pour in the **oil** in a thin stream until you have about 3/4 cup full.

Mix mayonnaise into **3/4 pound of sirloin**, add more **salt**, to taste, **2 tsp. chopped onion, 1 TBS. of small capers, 1/2 tsp. of red paprika, a squirt of Worcestershire sauce, a few drops of Tabasco or cayenne powder and a tsp. of chopped parsley**. Mix all well and form into a round chopped steak. Serve it family style, dressed on a round plate on Boston lettuce. Traditionally, this is served with French or Italian bread, Boston lettuce and French Fries. The Tartar steak can be served with tea, coffee or beer, but if you want to make a fuss about this, go ahead and bring that GEWURTZ TRAMINER.

---

3. Throughout the ages, people assumed the name Epicure to be linked with gastronomy. This is unfounded. The Greek philosopher Epicure "only" believed in spiritual culture and virtues.

Francois Boeres, Chef de Cuisine

THE GREATER THE DIFFICULTY THE MORE GLORY IN SURMOUNTING IT.
EPICURUS

ITALIAN CARPACCIO

Clean and trim one pound of beef-filet of all slivers and fat. Cut into paper-thin slices.

Make a cup of homespun mayonnaise using
    1 egg yolk, 1 tsp. of regular mustard,
    1 tsp. of white vinegar. Make 3/4 cup
    mayonnaise using 1/2 olive oil and 1/2 vegetable oil.
    (Some only use lemon juice, olive oil and fresh basil)

Mix filet slices into the mayonnaise and add
    1 tsp. of Dijon mustard
    a few drops of Tabasco
    1/4 cup of strong beef stock.
    salt and pepper to taste.

Mix all well and divide into 6 portions, (serve not too cold) serve on bib-lettuce, garnish with sliced pimentos and olives. Serve with a baked pizza crust brushed with chopped garlic and oil.

Wine: Lambrusco or a Chianti
Music: Berlioz; Harold in Italy or a Scherzo by Brahms.

HOW TO MAKE SEVICHE

Here, all preferred fish is used except some delicate fish like Filet de sole that soon would fall all apart.
The process of preparing the fish to a soft, mellow and spiced acetic "summer" delicacy can be made easy in no time.

HIS-STORY of Good Cooking

Cut **one pound of preferred fish** into strips and cover with a marinade of: **lemon** and **lime juice** and refrigerate for at least 5 hours, turning it around occasionally.

Chop **one peeled tomato** very fine, seeds removed

Two canned and chopped **serrano chili peppers**

1/4 cup olive oil and a **dash of white vinegar**, **pepper**, **salt** and a dash of **oregano** and chopped **cilantro**. Mix all well and pour over the fish. Take out the fish and drain most of the lemon juice and pour over the seviche mixture. Serve with olives and tomato salad.

Have a juicy Marguerita
Music: Tijuana Brass.

MARINATED SALMON WITH GREEN PEPPERCORNS

Cut one pound of Salmon into slices.
    Make a marinade out of 1/2 cup of lemon juice
    1 small, fine chopped onion, 2 tsp. salt,
    3 tsp. of snipped fresh dill or dill weed,
    2 tsp. of crushed soft green peppercorns
    1 pinch of red paprika and 1/2 tsp. sugar.

Mix well and pour over the salmon. Place in refrigerator for at least 6 hours, turning the salmon occasionally.

Don't pay a high price for Lox, make your own!

How to Make LOX

Take about a **3 pound fresh, red salmon filet**. Use a pair of pliers to pull out any pin-bones. Place salmon into a large China-ware platter. Soak salmon filet in the marinade and place in the refrigerator for 5 to 6 days, turning it over every day. After the last day, drain all juices, sprinkle salmon with some **salt** and let it dry some. This salmon can last for over a week... but not too long, because you will like this and by then, it will all be gone.

Francois Boeres, Chef de Cuisine

To Make the MARINADE

Mix:
2 tsp. salt
2-1/2 tsp. sugar
fine ground white pepper
pinch of fresh dill or dill weed
1/3 cup Brandy
1/3 cup Sherry wine

Can be served with Pumpernickel, Rye or French bread, Melba toast or just dressed in a bed of Boston lettuce with sour cream and toast triangles.

Wine: A New York Riesling by Konstantine Frank, or a Great Western Champagne
Music: Fiddler on the Roof or Das muss ein stuck vom himmel sein by Strauss.

SEA BASS OR RED SNAPPER SEVICHE
6-8 servings

Use wax paper to flatten approx. **2 pounds of skinned fresh fish filets**. Cut the filets into small morsels and place in a glass bowl. Add **1 cup fresh lime juice**, from about 10 limes. Place in to the refrigerator. Let the fish marinate overnight, turning it occasionally. Cover with plastic wrap.

Following day, remove fish and dress on a serving dish.

Add:
2 peeled and cubed avocados
2 peeled tomatoes, chopped fine
2 small green hot chili peppers, sliced fine
1/2 cup orange juice
1 tsp. of cumin and salt

Mix all well and serve with thin sliced cucumber salad mixed with pimentos, salt, white vinegar and oil.

Wine: White Pinot or a Pinot Chardonnay.

YUK WHE (KOREAN BEEF TARTAR)
4 portions

In a bowl combine: 2 TBS of beef broth
    2 TBS. of choice sesame oil
    2 minced garlic cloves
    1 TBS. of lightly toasted sesame seed
    1-1/2 tsp. choice soy sauce
    1-1/2 tsp. of salt
    1-1/4 tsp. of sugar

Place **one 1/2 inch thick sirloin steak** in the freezer for one hour, so it is firm but not too hard. With a sharp knife, cut paper thin slices across the grain from the sirloin and mix with the sauce.

Peel and core a **pear** and cut into thin slices. Dress meat into 4 portions and garnish with the pear slices and top with lightly roasted **pine nuts**.

MEDITERRANEAN MARINATED SCALLOPS

In a bowl, mix......1/2 cup fresh lime juice
    one minced garlic clove
    one fine chopped echalotte or scallion
    1/2 TBS Tabasco, little salt and pepper
    1/2 tsp. ground coriander

Mix vigorously, pour **1/2 cup olive oil**...in a small stream until emulsified. Add one minced small **bell pepper**, one minced small **red pepper**. Cut one pound of deep sea **scallops** into slices and marinate overnight or at least for 6 hours.

Dress on **Romaine** leaves surrounded by **scallion** "brushes".

Francois Boeres, Chef de Cuisine

Wine: California Blanc Fume
Music: Rimsky Korsakov...Capriccio Espagnol

ROMESCO SAUCE - (A coulis)

... popular around the Mediterranean and often served with fish.
Cut up into cubes, 2 slices of pullman or white bread.
Roast them in olive oil until golden brown, place in chopper.
Add 1 full cup of olive oil,
1 peeled, squeezed out and chopped tomato,
1/2 cup dry red wine
1/4 cup red wine vinegar,
14 blanched and toasted almonds,
3 crushed garlic cloves,
salt, pepper, ground allspice and a pinch of cayenne.
Blend all till smooth.

TARTAR SAUCE

Chop 1/2 onion, blanch in white vinegar, strain and cool.
Mix one cup of thick mayonnaise with
3 TBS of chopped pickles or relish,
one chopped egg and the blanched onion,
1 tsp. chopped parsley,
1 TBS. cut up capers,
1 tsp. of hardy mustard, salt and pepper.
Optional - chervil, sour cream.

DE RIGUEUR

The first thing we learned was cleaning and putting things where they belong, just being clean and orderly. Naturally, we cleaned everyday, but Wednesday was reserved for the big thorough cleaning day. Waiters cleaned and tumbled silverware, polished candelabras, coffee pots, and creamers. The dishwashers cleaned floors and copper pots. To scrub copper pots sparkling clean, we used a past made of flour, salt and vinegar.

HIS-STORY of Good Cooking

The cooks cleaned the icebox and made soap out of old fryer fat that was slowly heated up and carefully mixed with lye, cooled off in a shallow pan and cut into bars. To make soap water for cleaning, we used a #10 can with holes in the bottom. This can was then filled with cut up chips of soap and hung under the hot running faucet. Chlorine and carbole was used to clean and sanitize. Stainless steel was uncommon that time, our kitchen equipment was made out of an alloy of steel, copper and nickel (Tombac). It became very shiny after scrubbing and cleaning.

Our greatest problem were cockroaches; we did everything thinkable to exterminate this pest. I guess they'll be around long after we're gone. Their kin are found imbedded in fossil Amber known as 'Glass' in the old Celtic language.

So, the most important phases in a kitchen is cleanliness, it is to be addressed with priority for all food preparation. Often I am appalled to see people working with food without washing hands, leaving food out too long in unacceptable temperatures, the greatest sin of all. Besides, I never serve food I don't care to eat—this should be observed even in the most pathetic places!

Drinks: Grape Juice
Music: The Bumble Bee by Ravel

"Order is heaven's first law."
Pope

Francois Boeres, Chef de Cuisine

CHAPTER 8....GOING TO AMERICA

Taking the Big Boat

My mind was set, I was going to America! I had contemplating this for quite some time and was now corresponding with Uncle Lesly from New Jersey who kept my interest alive. I don't know why he always called me Franz, I guess I got kind of used to it. One of his letters read: "Hey Franz, are you going to come over? Chefs like you are much needed here...and the money they make! In no time, you can have your own car, and be all wrapped up nice and snug, like a bug in a rug."

How about that! This all sounded so good to me. I had to wait quite some time to get all my boarding papers from Antwerp. They finally arrived in 1955. Dad and Mom drove me to LeHavre. We all thought my visit to America would be for a year or so, but it turned out to be longer before we all met again. Finally, or was it the beginning, here I stood in line before the Liner. A big ship it was, several stories high and both ends out of sight. I said "good-bye" to my parents and vanished in the hustle and bustle, looking for my cabin on this big new luxury liner, The United States. I had to share a tourist cabin with some religious aficionado, you know, one of those doomsday people. This guy wanted to convert me. I told him that I was already converted some time ago, so he said, "You should come on deck and meet some nice people there," so I capitulated to his wish. He was a bit off the "cuff" but otherwise not a bad fellow...and before I knew it I found myself praying on deck with someone called Billy Graham. I didn't pay too much attention to anything, I was just looking forward with great expectations to embark in New York. As soon as I finished my prayer,

Thank Heaven, I headed for the bar to have a few "stiff" bourbons, a fine drink I had been acquainted with. The bartender liked some of my stories, and gave me one more, but now there was a woman that followed me and put me on guard. The problem was her husband was following wherever I went. I had a tail following me. Well, I cannot tell all the crazy things that happened to me on that big boat. I can only say that real life is stranger than fiction. One bad thing that happened here, I got soooo sick at sea that I thought I was part of the waves. And that nice Porterhouse steak I had last night went away with the waves.

As we were about to enter New York, it started drizzling and it was very hot and muggy. Suddenly I felt a sting on my left wrist, it looked like some doggone female mosquito let me have it and good too, because my arm started swelling and it hurt like hell, looked like blood poisoning. Well, the ship didn't sink and we landed in New York. Here Uncle Less and Aunt Kitty were waiting and so was my little cousin Ralph, who looked up to me with his big, dark eyes like I was a Giraffe or something. I grabbed my two old wooden custom made valises and before I knew it, we were over the bridge toward Fort Lee...my new home. It was not over yet; Uncle Less had to take me right away to his doctor to stop my blood poisoning.

That night I slept like a dog and the following morning we all had a wonderful breakfast starting with good strong coffee and cheeses like camembert, Port-Salue, Pont L'eveque, fresh figs, marmalade, quince jam, hard water rolls and salted butter (new to me). Things started looking better, now the sun was breaking through the morning haze and there was New York, right before our feet. Lesley's place was a bungalow, built right on top of the Palisades. The view was simply breathtaking. Late afternoon, we all took a stroll through Fort Lee, then just a little village where everybody knew each other. We "bumped" into a policewoman Less went to school with, then we stopped by an old "Compa" who owned a nice Italian butcher store. There Less bought about four feet of real Italian sausages, you know the ones that are not too big or too small, just made right, with anise seeds and white wine. To fry them, you just coiled them in a big pan. They never come out too fatty or too dry like some of those "sawdust" sausages of today. Later we visited his office at the motor vehicle bureau, followed by a visit to the Post Office to send away some letters to Europe. I noticed mural paintings depicting early scenes form movies. Less explained that Fort Lee was the cradle of the first moving picture. Here it all started. Not far away from his home was where the first movie pictures were made, right near the Palisades cliffs. This started the phrase of "real cliff hangers". There had been great history made around here, right in his back yard. He showed me a huge, deep well used by Washington's soldiers, covered up by a massive flat stone. I hope it is not forgotten. There are now huge high rise apartments. Not far away, below the cliffs, is the place where Aaron Burr killed Alexander Hamilton in a duel, so, enough of this, we have to make our own history.

What happened meanwhile, Aunt Kitty and Cousin Ralph had left for Europe to visit the family there. From now on, Less and I lived like bums. The only stuff in the refrigerator was Italian bread, Reingold beer, Mortadella and Provolone cheese. All we did was watch TV, drink Reingold, eat Provolone and Mortadella. Well, it was time to look for a job. So we drove uptown, near Warren Street, near the Fulton Fish Market. There they had a row of old buildings with Employment Agencies. Here, we entered into a long hallway with all kinds of jobs posted and tagged on walls. Some read like Boiler men for uptown/good pay/6 days/see Jim in room 105, or Needed immediately/Assistant Chef in Larchmont/inquire at the Clearmont Agency.

Before the day was over, I had an appointment as a broiler cook in the Pick Wick Arms in Greenwich, Connecticut. Having no car, Less drove me down there and praise the Lord, I had a job. I didn't had to go back, I was hired on the spot. Of course, a fee of a week's salary had to be paid to the Agency if the job was accepted. By now, I had acquired the experience to perform all kinds of jobs in a kitchen.

At the Pick Wick Arms, we had five cooks, Chef Hector, Victor the breakfast and lunch cook, Alex the prep cook, another I can't remember and myself, not to count dishwashers, stock clerks, coffee cooks, cleaning women and all that. Funny, at times, Naturalization Officers came to check for illegal workers. Then, like magic, all had disappeared out through the back windows and cellar door, the big kitchen was now empty except of Hector and I still cooking.

The hotel was built after the late "Tudor" style, a fantastic place to behold. I still don't know why they ever tore it down. Everything was executed in the traditional workmanship of the past, a lost art, so to speak. The ceiling had a high relief with the British coat of arms and the motto, "Dieu et mon Droit" (God and my right) and another "On y soit qui mal y pense" (One is as bad as one thinks). Beautiful paneling adorned the dining rooms, the bar and the library. All this was commensurate with the commitment of the people that worked here. The Maitre d'hotel was a real gentleman, the hostess friendly and charming. John the bartender a most entertaining chap. He reminded me of Milton Berle. Here he was known as the "broken arm" because of his peculiar gesture, mixing drinks with his shaker and never to be out of tune with the background music. If you had a bad day, Broken Arm could make it good at his bar.

Here and there, I was asked to help out for breakfast. People used to eat somewhat differently than today. We had a few different cereals, but the most important preparations in the morning were the batter for pancakes, waffles, porridge, soft grits, farina, squeezing oranges for fresh orange juice, serving prune and grape juice. We had fried, shirred, sunny side up and poached eggs, some served with slabs of Canadian bacon, ham, sausages, patties, smoked fish and smoked salmon with cream cheese or sour cream. There we had all kinds of bread, rolls, toast and French toast, muffins, all kinds of jams, coffee, tea, cocoa, melons and other fruits.

Soft-boiled eggs were the order of the day. This was taken care of by the waiters using a contraption that worked like a toaster. The eggs to be boiled were placed into a basket and punched down into a small pot with electric heated boiling water. As the selected time was over, the eggs popped up out of the water with a "ring" to let you know it was ready. I haven't seen a machine like this since.

Every order that came into the kitchen had to be verified and posted. (We had a lot of walk ins and hotel guests). The older lady that took care of this was Helen, a real sweetheart. Often she helped me out with my poor English!

Cooking at the Pickwick Arms

I never really liked to cook breakfast. This was a real hustle. You not only felt like, but often went crazy in the morning, coping with the pressure to meet the demand and get the food out, and when done, you had potatoes and sausages on the floor, grits and porridge smeared all over. You wanted to hit your head with a pan. The waiters got mad at you because you couldn't possibly in any way satisfy the demand of all the customers. This guy's eggs were too soft, the others were too hard. One wanted his meat cut up in small pieces, the other one, oh well, luckily I never was asked to sit on an egg and hatch it for someone. And then, there was a never ending flow of late customers, that came after ten o'clock, just at the critical time to prepare lunch. I can tell you that I would rather like to dig Puffin eggs than cook breakfast. Chef Hector Vasquez was a crackerjack when it came to making buffets or parties, and of all Creole food. He told me that he had worked in New Orleans for some time. Most Creole people around New Orleans and the Bayous are of French and Spanish descent. They have one of the most original cuisines in America and the best restaurants can be found in New Orleans. There was a time, Creole and Indian people that lived here were coerced to reform and to adopt new fangled government regulations. Any kind of doing or even thinking associated with their customs, folklore and language was indiscriminately banned. The only thing left was their cooking and that saved their identity.

Most "Cajun" people came from Arcadia, which is now Nova Scotia. Following an overturn in power in 1755 all French Arcadians were expatriated by English soldiers. Notwithstanding most French being Catholic, they also were despised for their different beliefs and traditions, consequently their families were broken up, Fathers, Mothers and Children were scattered in different directions, some searching for years and years for their family members. The greater part of these descendants are now living in Louisiana's "Arcadia" or Cajun country.
..... have mercy "Evangeline"

I loved to work with Alex, broiling steaks, fish and making sauces. Our menu had prime leg of lamb raised by the Basques from Nevada and Wyoming, ducks from Long Island, filet de sole, soft shell crabs and lobster from New England, frog legs Provencale, prime rib with the bone, squab pigeons, crab cakes, oysters Rockefeller and a very popular MIXED GRILL.

Mixed Grill: One small broiled **lamb chop, pork medallion, small club steak, piece of calves liver, slice of slab bacon, little wine sausages and a broiled tomato.** All topped with au jus and chopped **parsley.** This was served with green beans almondine.

HIS-STORY of Good Cooking

Drink a good Saranac beer from New York or a California Ruby Cabernet.

We had blue fish, pompano and best of all the shad. This fish was so rich, we only broiled it in white wine and butter, topped with fresh seasoned bread crumbs. In the past the shad was treated secondary because there were so many. Our Revolutionary soldiers fed on them and often were saved from hunger and Washington liked them at any occasion. Obviously they have diminished with many other species like the sturgeon and the eel. In spring the shad were "running" by the millions up the Hudson or the Connecticut Rivers. Tons were taken and every restaurant had them on the menu, the shad and its roe.

Here is a Recipe for SHAD
Always start with 2 lbs.

Preheat oven to 350 degrees. **Salt and pepper the filets, add cider or apple juice with butter.** Season in a small amount of **coriander, cumin, ginger and cardamom.** Broil for 20 minutes.

Take out, add some **half and half cream**, reduce the sauce. Sauté a few **apple rings** in **butter** for garnish. Serve with **lemon and parsley**.

Wine" Barbera d'Asti

—

Normally, fresh fish was sold right behind the back door of the kitchen by fishermen who were part of families that had done this for generations. They were all equipped with the necessities to do commercial fishing, big boats, nets and all that. Anyone could go fishing for shad, maybe from a little boat or with a fishing pole, but if someone ever got the idea to interfere with these guys in "commercial kind of fishing", he had it coming to him. First he was harassed, then beaten up, his dog shot, his boat sunk or burned down, and coming to the point he was glad to leave and never to come back!

It all went well with my new job in America. Now I was even the proud owner of a nice light green Studebaker Commander. This car looked like a rocket and seemed to move standing still. Now I could go any place I wanted. Only one thing bothered me, Victor the pantry man kind of "picked" around me, called me a "Marie-con" or something and this had to end. I knew he was a good boxer. This did not bother me any because I happened to be a good French "foot fighter", so come one day, to everyone's surprise, I grabbed him and before you know, we both were entangled on the sawdust floor. The garbage can fell over, spilling potatoes, orange peels, clam shell and other garbage around. It was a tie. Soon they took us apart to break it up. We brushed some of the sawdust off our uniforms, shook hands and from then on became good buddies. That evening we departed off to Port Chester and had a few mean drinks at Tom and Jerry's. I made quite a few friends by now. There we had that old Swiss waiter, Johan. I had the opportunity to use my German. Occasionally he bought me a beer, saying "Hier hast du was..." Another friend was Jean Paul a Frenchman,, also a waiter and close to my age. We got a chance to speak French again. Jean-Paul had a nice joint in Sao Paulo, but went bust. We two got along fine and often painted the town. So, one day we went to this fancy restaurant, the Town House. As soon as you opened the door, you fell into a bar that looked more like a Gazebo, with bar chairs all around. Here Harry, the bartender was presiding. A very pleasant fellow and old enough to retire. Occasionally, we asked for a Campari, Pernod or a Blue Fly. Harry knew them all. Behind the bar was the dining room, all filled up. A guy was playing the piano. I knew that Jean-Paul played the flute and the clarinet and I don't know how he ever got up there to the podium. To my surprise he played the flute with the piano player. He waved to me to come over and embarrassed as I was soon joined them singing a French song........

> "C'est une place, c'est une rue
> C'est meme tout un quartier,
> On y parle, On y passé,...
> Un petie J'aidot, une station de metro,
> Entournee de bistrau, Pigalle...."

I missed a few words, not too many knew French anyway. Our applause was heart warming and in not time we were invited by two fellows having dinner. We figured to have only a couple of drinks here and then split, but no, these fellows insisted we dine with them. What had we to lose? better to have something to eat than running around town getting drunk. Besides, they seemed to be O.K. Our conversation was random and diversified. One of them showed me how they eat in his part of the country. First, you cut your meat with your knife, then place the knife on top of the plate, put your hand in your lap and eat with the fork.

Our evening was a pleasant one. We concluded from their conversation that these two somehow are connected with antiques or decorating and remembered that one mentioned delivering an oil painting. We commented that we too were interested in paintings. By now they insisted that we take a look at the painting they had in their suite at the Pick Wick Arms where they stayed. So with nothing to loose, we also headed that way, it was also our residence.

Jean-Paul and I followed these people we hardly knew for hours and in a short time we all entered into this big suite of rooms at the Pick Wick Arms. Immediately we were confronted with a huge life size oil painting of a lady known as Helen Keller. The picture was simply captivating. The painting was to be delivered to the Helen Keller Institute in New Haven, I believe. I have forgotten the name of the man who did the painting, but we soon found out the name of the other guy in the following evening at the Town House bar where Harry said, "How is Norman Rockwell?" "Who?" said I. .... well, one of the fellows you had dinner with last night."......

*No hand can make the clock
which will strike again for me
the hours that are gone.
Charles Dickens*

My time in Greenwich was memorable. Dancing at the YMCA, going to the beach, visiting the yacht club and of course, working my butt off. I figured that there was no advancement in sight and I probably was going to sling the same hash (we also served that with poached eggs) three years from now. It so happened that I got myself a new job through the grape vine. Not far from here, in a little place in Banksville, a restaurant called La Cremaillere. It was just like coming home, here we became what we really were and wanted to be, proud, conscientious professional people. The comradeship and fraternity was fabulous. Most of us lived upstairs so in the morning we had, like in a big family, coffee together and later, before serving dinner, we all sat in our small dining room , eating quick made food one of us had fabricated, not expensive, but good. This might

Francois Boeres, Chef de Cuisine

be a Cassoulet, Tripes a la mode, Beef Burgundy, Quick Pork steak sauté Provencale, a Ratatouille, a simple ham omelet, a salad Nicoise, cold cut of beef from yesterday, not too much pasta, once in a while spaghetti with meat sauce, risotto or homemade gnocchi with cheese. Every day we ate something different.

Omelettes

Omelets were once popular and in great demand for breakfast and lunch. In hotels we served 2 eggs per person for breakfast and 3 eggs for lunch. First of all our pan for omelets was used only for that purpose. After use, cleaned out with oil and set aside. To break a pan "in", it was heated up to high temperatures and immediately drenched with an oil-soaked towel (Gunsmiths call this process bluing). Today, Teflon coated pans are much in use. I prefer to use my enameled black steel pan. In steel the heat is more "controlled" and gives the omelet a nicer color without making it hard.

To Make an OMELETTE

Beat **eggs** vigorously with a fork, add a little **salt, white pepper** and a squirt of **milk** until bubbles appear. This is the secret of a good omelet. It should also be strained to remove the little white egg-spots.

Heat up the pan and add a good amount of **butter** until it is hot and quiet, then pour the eggs into the pan, stirring it with the fork and shaking the pan with the other hand until the eggs are nearly set, but still soft. (This is the moment to add in the ingredients called for in some omelets.)

Now, tilt the pan and slowly roll the omelet way over the center. Keep it on the heat for a few seconds to give it a nice, firm and golden skin when turning it over onto a hot serving plate. Slip any protruding edges underneath omelet to give it that oval and fluffy professional look.

MEXICAN OMELET

Just before folding add sautéed pencil thick cubed **red onions, red and green bell peppers, chopped scallions** diced **tomatoes**. Option: hot peppers and cubed ham with Tabasco on the side.

CHEF HECTOR'S CREOLE CHICKEN GUMBO

To prepare: cut a **3 pound chicken** into small serving pieces, sauté in a heavy pot until golden brown, then add **3 stalks of sliced celery, two chopped onions, crushed clove of garlic and a big sliced green pepper til glazed, mix with 2 tbsp flour, dash of Tabasco**. Pour in two quarts of light **chicken stock**. Simmer for about 2.1/2.hours .Remove all bones from the chicken, cut in chunks and put back. Shucked oysters can be added last. The gumbo should be thick enough to pour over steamed short grain rice. Serve with parsley and filé on the side.

SHRIMP CREOLE OR CRAB CREOLE GUMBO

Sauté **two medium onions** with **two crushed garlic cloves in 4 TBS. of butter or margarine**. Add TBS. **flour** and stir until light brown, add **two cups water, one sliced green pepper, 5 cups crushed Italian tomatoes, salt, pepper, a trace of nutmeg and 1 pound of sliced okra**. Cook slowly for 3/4 of an hour, then add the **shrimp or crabmeat**, cover and cook for another3 minutes. Serve in a bowl over steamed rice with French bread on the side, filé powder can be added. Should be served very hot..

Note: "Filé" is a powder made from the young leaves of the sassafras tree. This is added last. The Gumbo should not be allowed to boil after the filé is added.

Wine: A Sangria or a Chelois

VEGETABLE AND BEEF GUMBO

In a kettle combine over two quarts of water, two lbs. of boneless **beef neck** or "plate", **two small sliced onions, clove of crushed garlic, 3 stalks of celery, two peeled carrots, salt, crushed pepper**. Boil for 10 minutes, skim off the foam and simmer til done ....then remove the beef and cut into chunks.

In another kettle sauté **one small chopped onion in butter, add 2 stalks sliced celery, one cup of okra**, stir for three minutes. Add one chopped **tomato** and a small can of **tomato paste**. Add the **stock, beef, thyme,**

Francois Boeres, Chef de Cuisine

one bay leaf and a drop of Tabasco. Add 1/4 of a cup of fine tapioca and simmer for 20 minutes. Serve on steamed short grain rice. Sprinkle with sliced **scallions** and serve filé on the side.

PORCO A ALENTEYANE
(Pork loin with clams)

In a bowl mix **2 pounds of cubed loin of pork with 1-1/2 cups of dry white wine, 1 TBS. of sweet paprika, 3 crushed garlic cloves, 2 bay leaves, crushed peppercorns and salt.** Marinade for 8 hours, occasionally turning the meat.

Drain meat and save the marinade, removing the bay leaves.

In a heavy pot, sauté pork in lard on high heat until brown and braised. Take the pork out and set aside. Add the marinade into the heavy pot to de-glaze the sticky "jus". Cook and reduce marinade and add all the pork, bringing it to a boil, set aside and keep warm.

In a pan, sauté **2 medium sliced onions, 1 sliced green pepper, 2 blanched, peeled, seeded and coarse chopped tomatoes, salt, pepper, cayenne** with ½ cup beef broth.

Cook for 3 minutes, stirring often. Add **3 dozen little-neck clams.** Cover and cook for approx. 3 minutes or until all clams are open. (Don't overcook or they will be rubbery.) Take out all the clams, cover and keep warm.

Now, add all the pork to the vegetables and cook for 3 more minutes.

Dress the pork on a nice oval platter or a big bowl. Place the clams around .Remove any froth or excessive fat.

Wine: Rioga, Vina Pomal or Sangria
Music: Malaguena. La Patenera or Serenta Espanola

MOSITA DE PUERCO OMEGA

Slice **4 pounds of pork** into 3/4 inch pieces and soak them in **1/2 cup of lemon juice and 1/2 cup of grapefruit juice add 5 crushed garlic cloves, 2 tsp. salt, 1 tsp. sugar, 1/4 tsp. ground cumin, 1/4 tsp. oregano.**

Mix all pork with "this" marinade and place in the refrigerator overnight. Stir the meat around a few times before cooking.

Melt a **cup of lard** in a saucepan and add **one cup of light chicken-stock**, then put in all the meat and the marinade. Cook on low heat until liquid has evaporated some and the pork is brown and tender. Remove the pork and set aside in a warm place, Remove most fat from the pan and add **1/4 cup grapefruit juice, 1 tsp. of lemon juice and 3 TBS. of chicken stock**. Reduce for a minute and pour over the pork. Can be served with fried plantains and roasted peppers.

Wine: A Valdepenas or a Chilean Semillon.
Music: Pepe et Celini Romero: Spanish Dances or Alhambra.

CHEF HECTOR'S MOSITA DE PUERCO GARCIA

Soak 4 pounds of pork tenders in a mixture of:
3/4 cup lemon juice, 1/2 cup grapefruit juice,
2 crushed and chopped cloves of garlic,
salt, pepper, 1/2 tsp. cumin and some oregano.

Marinate for 14 hours. Roast the tenderloin quick in lard. Add all the juice and let it evaporate. Cook slowly, last, pour in ½ cup grapefruit juice, boil and pour over the pork, it should be pink inside. Can be served with fried plantains or zucchini.

Wine: An Argentinean Rosé or a Sangria.

To STEAM RICE

Bring 3 quarts of water to a boil, add a little **salt** and pour in **1-1/2 cups of rice**. Cook for 17 minutes. Drain in a colander and cool under cold water. Place colander in a big pot with a little water, cover with a lid and steam for about 20 minutes, until dry and fluffy.

WHO CAN ENJOY ALONE.......
Milton

Francois Boeres, Chef de Cuisine

DIRTY CAJUN RICE
for 2 til 4 servings

This rice is usually served as a side dish.

Have ready, at least **3 cups of cooked short grain rice**, 2 cups of previously cooked **giblets**, cooked slowly on a low fire until soft. Take them out of the broth, chop fine and save.

In a large pan or casserole, sauté all vegetables below until half done:
- 1 small chopped onion
- 1/2 cup fine sliced scallions
- 1/2 green pepper chopped fine
- 1/2 celery stalk chopped fine
- 2 minced garlic cloves

Then, add all the chopped giblets to the pan with the vegetables, stir for 1 minute and on hot fire add all the rice to the "stuff". Sauté and swirl the "Cajun" rice around the pan until all the lumps are gone, so it has a nice texture, good enough to shove the rice on your fork without spilling any.

Optional, chopped liver, chili powder, Maggi or soy sauce.

QUICK CRAB CAKES
6 cakes

Clean **1 pound of flaked crab meat**, add **1/3 cup of fresh breadcrumbs, 1/4 cup thick mayonnaise, 1 beaten egg, onion powder, a dash of Worcestershire sauce, a dash of Tabasco, chopped parsley, a pinch of English dry mustard, salt and pepper** to taste. Mix thorough and form in to patties. Pan-fry both sides until golden brown. Can be served with "Hot" sauce.

—

The restaurant La Cremaillere was run by our patron, Mr. Gilly, a crack chef of International credibility and a member of the "Chevaliers des Taste-Vin" (traditional wine-tasters of France.) The gastronomy of this restaurant was the most acclaimed in North America. One can imagine the

HIS-STORY of Good Cooking

regional, diversified and original menu assembled by Chef George Moreas from the Garonne, prepared by Jean-Pierre from the Carcassone, Henry from Strasbourg, Rene and others from the Bretagne and myself from Luxembourg.

It was not unusual to have all kinds of visitors in our kitchen. One day it my be Tom Watson inquiring about a dish Edward G. Robinson addressing you in flawless French or Tom Dorsey inviting us to go swimming in his huge pond. Then we had all these restaurant people who came to visit us, like members of a big family, being exceedingly friendly, patronizing each other and recommending our place to there customers as we would do the same for them. So we got to known many fine Restaurant peoples, from Connecticut, Hudson river right in to Manhattan. After work or on a day off most of us had a rendezvous in Manhattan, maybe to see Pierre Pugol at "The Tunnel" restaurant on 48th Street that was open seven days a week, so we spent Mondays there. Or it could be Fernand at the "Perigord" on 52nd or Marcel at "L'armorique" and there was the "Cote Basque", "Les Pyrennes", etc. Once a while, we visited our culinary Vatel-Club or the Chef's Association all in the same building on 48th Street. Here we played billiards or met other friends. Half of the business around here came from shows near the theater district and if there were none on certain nights, well, there was not too much business and you might as well close some of those days. A little further up, we had "Luchows" that served fine German food. If you liked a good Sauerbraten or Hasenpfeffer, this was the place. Close by was "Mama Leonias", Italian food? Ha, you bet, and the best of it. The inside looked like a Neapolitan garden with beautiful huge marble statues everywhere and here was enough food served to choke a horse. The fish arrived here daily just around the corner from the Fulton Market. Further down was 86th Street, called Germantown, all that loved German food ate at the Café Hindenburg, the Wien-ecke, Kleine Konditorei and that fatal place Café Geiger were I met that lovely girl I got married to.

Thinking, taking your sweetheart out for an evening, they had impressive places nearby La Cremaillere, like Emelie Shaws, Bird and Bottle Inn that served Southern stile dishes, the Ship Lantern and that great place, Leightons' restaurant with a retractable roof over the huge dining room. Here you could dine and dance under the starlight on a hot summer evening. Mr. Leighton was the man that invented the aerosol can you know, the can people now use to spray whip- cream on desserts.

Francois Boeres, Chef de Cuisine

Like I said, I married that German girl I met in Germantown. For awhile we moved and I left all my friends from La Cremaillere to take a job at the Greenwich Country Club. One morning, the whole place burned down to the ground, with my shoes, Sabatier knives and the whole "schmier." Soon I got another job close by, as a Saucier at the Westchester Country Club. Here all the cooks and Chefs came from different places. Our executive Chef, Walter, was German. That time, it was customary having supper before serving dinner. Sitting next to an Englishman, we argued about soups and sauces.

Then, Walter remarked, "You French and you English (they thought I was French) are nothing but pompous A-holes and think you know everything. We Germans just enjoy good food."

Way down the table a Pole mumbled, "You and your snails, truffles and all that garbage. We take simple food like cabbage, potatoes, roots and make miracles out of it."

"Fang-le!" hollered Gino, an Italian sitting next to him, pretending to clean and brush his mustache. "Only Italian food is the best, multo bene!"

I kept quiet, just thought, "All these idiots, don't they know that the best food is served in Luxembourg?" This all was very amusing, thinking there is something here in progress.

A great International Tournament had been planned for the coming week. It was "hel'ter-skel'ter." We had over two thousand people, the press, TV crews, circling helicopters and Ed Sullivan, the host in charge, driving around in his cart. He looked much smaller than I had seen him on TV. We cooked roast beef, even all night through, I mean walls of Prime Rib. It was, besides the Army, the greatest mass feeding I ever participated. For a whole month, even the thought of Roast Beef made me sick. But right now, I wish I had some. Most of my friends know how to cook roast beef, but I thought cooking roast beef should be mentioned here.

NOBODY IN AMERICA WANTS TO STAND STILL
WE ALL WANT TO LIVE BETTER
Humphrey

THE ILLUSTRIOUS ROAST PRIME RIB OF BEEF

    Personally I place the standing rib roast on the throne of King of all meats. There is nothing more enticing and rewarding among friends than a real good juicy piece of roast rib of beef. It reminds me and makes me feel transported to an Acadian party at an old Scottish castle...holding a hefty piece of roast beast stuck on a big fork and dipping a broken chunk of hearty bread into a fat eyed juicy sauce. Ah, John! Throw another log onto the fire and bring us here some more of that dark wine and don't forget the Scotch whiskey.

    A lad plays the pipes after an old Highlander tune, the "crowd" gets rowdier and some start bellowing loud songs.

    That lass, sitting next to me, just reached over for another morsel. I noticed her soft and tender...oh, this beef is almost as good as...oh, almost, but not quite.

    Sorry, I was dreaming about a roast beef again...

Wine: A Siglo or a Sangue Del Toro or a St. Julien
Music: Royal Fireworks by Handel.

    Roasting a whole or a half of a **roast beef** is about the easiest thing to do. Just place the roast in a pan with **salt** for 2 hours and some. Stick a thermometer into it until done. (I still use a skewer needle for testing). The internal temperature should be 120 degrees for very rare or rare, 140 degrees for medium or medium rare. I am sure there is a more refined way of doing this. For a big roast, reduce temperature after one hour; a small one, half the time. For a rare roast all the way through, roast at 225 degrees until done.

    There are two ways of roasting. The first, start the oven at 450 degrees for one hour and then turn it down to 325° until done. The second way is to start the roast at 325° and remain at this temperature till the roast is done. This way you get less shrinkage and the color and texture will be a nice pink all the way through. I personally choose the first method. It gives more flavor, especially when the bones are left on the roast.

    The Roasting: ......I love the beef with the bones in. Tell the butcher you want them this way. It makes it easier to cook in the pan. The bones work like a rack and the meat won't touch the bottom of the pan. I recommend small relief cuts alongside the bones. Place the roast beef, bones down, in the pan and cover with **salt, crushed peppers, rubbed thyme, chervil and rosemary**. Basting can be done a few times, but it is not important. The most important is to watch the time and temperature by sticking in a thermometer in the center of the beef. Remember that a roast beef is still cooking for 15 minutes after it is taken out of the oven.

An eight pound roast beef takes about two hours at 340 degrees.

A five pound roast takes about one hour and fifteen minutes at 325 degrees.

One tied roast beef for two persons takes about one hour.

To make the roast beef juice, take out the beef, remove most of the fat and deglaze the pan with a light beef broth.

POPOVERS
are always nice to serve with roast beef

In a food processor or blender: mix and beat **4 eggs with 2 cups of milk** and slowly combine with **2 cups of sifted flour, salt and 4 TBS. or 1/4 cup of melted butter**.

Divide batter into 12 muffin cups or timbales and bake in a preheated 425 degree oven for 30 minutes or until all puffed up and crisp. Serve hot with butter.

Complimentary to any roast are......

BAKED POTATOES AU GRATIN
for 4 servings

Bake **4 large baking potatoes** until soft. Cut 1/4 from the top, scoop out the inside and mash with **2 TBS. sour cream, 4 TBS. melted butter, 1 tsp. chopped chives, trace of nutmeg, salt and pepper**. Refill the potatoes and bake in the oven till light brown.

Optional: grated parmesan and paprika.

"LUCHOWS" SAUERBRATEN
for 6 servings plus
(German Sour Pot Roast)

Use **4 to 5-1/2 pound rump or top round**. I recommend tying the roast. There will be some shrinkage.

To Make the Marinade

Mix **1-1/2 cups wine vinegar, 1/2 cup dry red wine, 1/2 cup of water, 2 sliced onions, 2 sliced carrots, 2 bay leaves, 1 TBS. salt, 1/2 tsp. sugar, 3 cloves, 3 allspice berries**. Heat up the marinade (do not boil). Place beef in a crock or a big bowl, pour marinade over the meat so it's covered. Place in the refrigerator for 4 days, turning occasionally. After 4 days, take the beef out of the marinade and dry.

In a heavy kettle, brown all sides in **hot fat** and sprinkle with a little **flour**. Pour in the marinade and slowly boil for about 2-1/2 hours or until tender. Some water might be added during cooking.

Remove the braten and keep hot.

To Bind:
In a small pan blend **4 TBS of lard with 4 TBS of flour**. Roast to a blond color and stir this into the simmering sauce until smooth and thick. Place the braten in the sauce and slowly cook for 20 more minutes.

Dress the braten on a big serving platter, pour some sauce over the meat and serve the rest on the side. Traditionally, this is served with potato dumplings, noodles and red cabbage.

The sauerbraten can be sliced or served whole.

Wine: A Piesporter or Niersteiner or a California Pinot Noir... as you like it

Music: German Dances by Mozart

Francois Boeres, Chef de Cuisine

RATATOUILLE NICOISE
(Eggplant melee)

In a big casserole, sauté in plenty of preferred **oil, 2 firm onions** cut into chunks, **6 smashed garlic cloves, 1 big or 2 small peeled and cut up eggplants, 2 small cut up zucchinis**. Sauté and stir for 3 minutes. Add **3 medium size cubed tomatoes**. Cook for 3 minutes. Add **salt, pepper, thyme, oregano** and a small can of plain **tomato sauce**.

Pour into a fireproof casserole and bake for approx. 15 minutes in a 325° preheated oven. This can be served as a vegetarian main dish or on the side.

Recipe from Chef Moreas

STUFFED EGGPLANTS

Puncture and parboil **eggplants** for 5 minutes to take out any tart taste. Snip off both ends, cut lengthwise in half, remove seedy pulp to make a cavity for the stuffing. Sauté chopped **onions** with a few minced **garlic cloves** and some cubed **bread**, using plenty of **oil**. Stir for a few minutes. Add **salt, pepper, thyme, oregano, a pinch of nutmeg** and all the chopped up core from the eggplant. Add fresh parboiled cut **spinach.** Take from the fire and add **1 beaten egg** to the stuffing. Stuff eggplants with the mixture and bake in a 350 degree oven for 15 minutes, then sprinkle with butter, Parmesan and bake for 5 more minutes.

Recipe from Chef Theresa La Cremaillere served this Lobster with great success.

LOBSTER THERMIDOR
for 4 persons

The term "thermidor" is related to the Robespierre Republic...from the 20th of July to the 18th of August, 1794, the last phase of terror in the French Revolution. Actually this dish was created to celebrate Victorien Sardou's play "Thermidor". The play fell flat, but the lobster kept on going.

Tie **four 1-1/2 pound lobsters** to flat pieces of wood to keep them straight after boiling and cooling. In a big pot with not too much water, boil or more likely, steam lobsters for approximately 10 minutes, add **salt, a bay leaf, 2 lemon wheels**. Keep pot covered tightly. Remove ,cool, untie lobster from the wood and split in half. Clean out the sack near the head and discard. Save, if any, the green, delicious "brainy" stuff called "tamale" or coral. Mix this smooth with **butter and two egg yolks** and set aside to bind the sauce. If there is no "tamale" replace it with a mixture of **flour, butter and two egg yolks**. Remove tail and claw meat, cut up into slices and set aside.

To Make the Sauce:

In plenty of **butter**, sauté fine chopped **shallots or 1/2 chopped onion**, until glazed. Add **1 cup of dry white wine, 1 tsp. of Dijon mustard, a trace of tarragon, pepper, a little salt, a trace of cayenne**, a few fresh cut up **mushrooms and 1/2 pint of heavy cream**. Reduce the sauce so it is thick enough to be able to stick to the lobster. Bind the sauce with the "tamale"and trace of flour mixture without letting it come to a boil. Fill the shells with the lobster mixture. Sprinkle the lobsters with fresh **breadcrumbs, half Gruyere and half Parmesan cheese and melted butter**. Bake in a 425 degree oven for approximately 15 minutes or until done. Garnish with parsley.

Serve with asparagus, French bread or Boston lettuce. Some people use cheddar cheese instead of Gruyere.

Wine: A Mersault or Monterey
Music: "Midsummer Night's Dream" by Mendelssohn.

Francois Boeres, Chef de Cuisine

LOBSTER AMERICAINE
for 3 to 4 persons

....or is it really L'Armoricaine....once part of French Brittany, this is still a debate. Personally I believe the tomatoes in it make it more American.

Get **four 1-1/2 pound lobsters**, tear off and crack all the claws, split lobsters in half. Remove the sack and the intestine tube that runs down the tail. Separate the head from the tails. If there is a 'tamale 'or green coral, save, mix with butter and little flour to add last to bind the sauce.

Prepare and cut very fine (a brunoise) **1/4 stalk of celery, 1/4 of a carrot, half an onion,**[4] the **white of two scallions and two garlic cloves**. Sauté this all in **butter** until soft. Add a glass of **white wine, trace of cayenne, tarragon, pepper and a little salt**, if needed. Then add ½ **cup of clam or fish stock**. ½ cup semi dry sherry. Reduce the sauce, add **1 chopped fresh tomato** and some **tomato paste**.

Place the lobsters into the sauce, cover and cook for 8 minutes or til done, last bind sauce with the "tamale" mixture.

Place the lobsters in a terrine and flambe with a full "on the rock glass"of hot **brandy**.

Wine: Puligny Montrachet or a Blanc de Blanc
Music: Chamber music by Handel

Note: A sauce that is too thin can be corrected with a little dissolved potato starch.

---

4. Note: "Brunoise" are finely cut cubes of vegetables the size of the head of a match.

"CAFE GEIGERS" WIENERSCHNITZEL
for 4 portions
(OR ESCALOPES VIENNOISE)

Flatten **four 8 oz. tender veal steaks** pencil thin between wax paper. Sprinkle with **salt, pepper**, dip in **flour**, shake well then dip in beaten **eggs**, bread them in fresh **breadcrumbs**. Shake and tap loose all crumbs. In a large pan with plenty of **margarine and oil**, sauté schnitzels in moderate heat until golden. Take out the schnitzels. Discard all the oil in the pan and replace with fresh butter. Turn the schnitzels a few minutes in the butter, remove and place on a warm serving platter. Pour some more butter with fresh chopped **parsley** in the pan. Deglaze with the **juice of half a lemon** and pour over the schnitzels. Slice lemon wheels dipped in **paprika**, with a rolled **anchovy** and **caper** on top .Place on each schnitzel and garnish with **parsley**.

JEAGER SCHNITZEL or VEAL STEAK "HUNTER" STYLE"
4 portions

Get **four nice 8 oz. veal steaks**, don't flatten to much, sprinkle with **salt, pepper** and dip in **flour**. Shake well and sauté both sides lightly in **butter or margarine**. Take out the steaks and keep warm.

In a pan render a few thick and lean cut up pieces of **bacon** til transparent. Add one medium **onion** cut into 1/2 inch pieces. Stir and add a few pieces of cut **chicken livers**. Fry them for a few minutes adding **a few fresh mushrooms**, sliced in half. Sauté all this for a few minutes. Add a little more **pepper, a pinch of paprika**, a glass of **dry white wine**. Cook for 6 minutes. Add all the steaks and a **half pint of heavy cream**. Reduce and slowly thicken the sauce for 3 minutes. Dress and pour the sauce over the steaks.

Note: Make sure the sauce don't granulate. If so, bring it back with some cold milk stirring vigorously. Decorate with a few nice mushroom caps.

The schnitzel goes fine with a Rhine or Moselle wine.
Music: Rosamunde by Schubert

Francois Boeres, Chef de Cuisine

OSSO BUCCO - - VEAL SHANKS - - OSSI BUCCHI
One shank for two or 2 shanks for 4 to 6 people.

The Osso Bucco is a braised veal shank with the bone in. It is very popular in Italy, also all over Europe and the States.

Before "tackling" this bucolic, piquant chunk of roast, I like to describe how it was served with great success in our restaurant. It was served "Chateaubriand" style by the waiter for the few connoisseurs that also appreciated the marrow. We had already made relief cuts into the thin side of the bone. First, score little crosscuts with a boning knife around the veal-shank to cut some fibers to relieve contraction of the meat. The shanks are braised in a heavy "Creuset" type pot and finished in the oven for better results.....like a beautiful puffed up roast, compared to a dry, lifeless piece of "deflated tire" on the plate.

In a pot, roast all sides of the **shank** light brown in **olive oil**. Add **salt and pepper**, take out the shanks and keep warm.

In the pot, add **4 TBS. butter, 2 fine chopped onions, 1 carrot** cut in round slices, **2 crushed garlic cloves, 1 bay leaf**. With a wooden spoon stir on moderate heat for 4 minutes. Add **1/2 cup flour, 2 cups dry white wine, 1 ripe, cut up tomato, 4 oz. tomato paste, 1 TBS. fresh basil or a pinch of dried basil, grated rind from 1 lemon, 3 cups of light beef bouillon.**

Boil and place shanks in the sauce. Cover and simmer for 15 minutes. Then, place the pot in a 325 preheated oven for about 1-1/4 hour or until done according to size.

Do not overcook, the meat should stay on the bone. **Salt and pepper** to taste. Can be served with risotto or gnocchi's. Instead of veal shanks, use Veal breast .....Called **PETTO DI VITELLO**, it can be made the same way.

Wine: Pouilly-Fume or a Sauvignon Blanc
Music: Minuet by Bocherini or F. Concerto by Corelli

VEAL SCALLOPINI PIQUANTE
for 6 persons

Let the butcher cut 24....3 to 4 inches of **veal scaloppini.** Beat thin under a piece of wax paper. Dip scaloppini in **flour and in 2 beaten eggs.** Sauté them, a few at a time. in a lot of **butter** on high heat. In the last batch, add all and pour over plenty of **Marsala or Sherry Wine.** It might ignite, but this is natural and part of the fun.

Place all previously cooked scaloppini in the pan, shake and add some **lemon juice and fresh ground pepper.** Before serving add **prosciutto,** sliced in julienne (or Virginia ham), chopped **parsley**, fresh basil, chip of butter and more wine.

Arrange scaloppini on a hot platter, overlapping each other and top with the sauce. I recommend, previously prepared Duchesse potatoes that can be dressed neatly around the scaloppini using a pastry bag with a star tip or served with rice or Rosa marina that looks like rice.

Wine: A white Suave or a light Bardolino
Music: Paganini

LINGUINI GORGONZOLA
for 4 persons

Cook over **1/2 pound of Linguini** in boiling water with **salt** and a squirt of **oil**. Cook for about 15 minutes or until done. They should be a little al'dente inside. Drain and top with the prepared sauce.

The Sauce:
In a casserole pour **3/4 cup of virgin olive oil**. In the oil render 6 oz. cubed **bacon** cut from slab bacon. Add **1 minced garlic clove**, reduce heat and add **6 oz. of crumbled gorgonzola** until melted. Stir in **3/4 cup of heavy cream**. Smooth out and add **pepper, Tabasco sauce and a trace of basil**.

Dress linguini on a hot serving platter or shallow bowl. Top with the sauce, **parmesan cheese and chopped parsley**.

Can be served with garlic bread or a green salad.

Francois Boeres, Chef de Cuisine

Wine: A good Chianti or a Pinot Grigio
Music: Concerto Andaluz by Rodrigo

A quick and good CHEESE FILLING
for cappalletti, shells, raviolis and other pastas.

Combine **1 cup ricotta cheese with 1 cup grated Gruyere, 1/2 cup fresh parmesan, 1/2 cup heavy cream, 1 beaten egg, chopped parsley, salt, pepper and a trace of nutmeg.**

Optional: fresh chopped spinach.

ITALIAN EGGPLANT ROLLS

Slice **two fresh eggplants** in long, half inch slices, dip in **flour** and sauté both sides in **olive oil** until soft. Reserve.

To Make the Filling:
Mix **2 cups of ricotta cheese with 1/2 cup Romano cheese, 1 minced garlic clove**, sauté lightly. Add fresh **basil** and fresh chopped **parsley, a trace of nutmeg, oregano, a little salt and pepper.**
Lay out the eggplants and spread the cheese mixture over the slices. Roll the eggplants and line them in a long Pyrex or chafing dish. Top with the homemade tomato sauce and grated Romano, sprinkle with a little olive oil. Bake in a 350 degree preheated oven for approximately 20 minutes.

Wine: Rose D'Anjou

To Make a Real Good Italian Tomato Sauce:
Open one **14 to 15 oz. can of Italian tomatoes** and crush with your hands. Add **one 10 oz. of canned tomato sauce and 3 oz. (half can) tomato paste**, mix well.
In a heavy pot, sauté in **1/2 olive oil and 1/2 vegetable oil**: 1 fine chopped up **carrot**, 1 small and firm chopped up **onion, 2 minced garlic cloves** (sprout removed).
Add the "tomato sauce" with little **salt and pepper**, a pinch of fresh **basil, 2 sprigs of parsley and oregano.** Simmer for 45 minutes on slow

fire, stirring often, adding water if needed. Please, never add any sugar to this sauce with an Italian nearby, he might "kill" you. The carrot will give "dulci" to it.

This was my first dinner in America...served by Aunt Katherine in Fort Lee, New Jersey. We also had fine Italian sausages, but they are not needed with this wholesome meal.

Main Street USA

Did I ever told you about an honest to goodness American town back East? Well, here it is and it's all true because I will tell it that way! I will start from the East side where the first settlers came from, like the Taylors, the Hicks, the Merrills, and Sam McGraw, who came from Plymouth, Vermont. Of course there are churches, a Town Hall, undertaker, schools, an academy and all that makes a decent village, but here there was something different. One still had the feeling of the spirit lingering, of remarkable and industrious people, like a phantom of the past.

The village was known as the "Box" the "Corset" or Academy town. Here this is just the beginning. In the past, it had three blacksmiths, a few doctors, a band, a Butter-Firkin plant, a corn popper factory, grist and cider mills and a box factory (still here), making jewelry and silverware boxes. Gillette had a shirt factory (Chester Gillette...the American Tragedy). The secretary to President Cleveland, Daniel Lamont resided here in his beautiful Grecian revival home (now the Library). Then there was that fellow "Garey" who invented the CO-RAY-VAC heating system and Howard White, a main figure in the development of nitrocellulose, rayon and cellophane.

McGraw was a busy, palpating Main Street with restaurants, garages, hardware stores, a drug store and so on. It was a real hustle bustle village. How could one forget people like our jovial barber (he died in a strawberry patch), the most helpful librarians from the Lamont library, and our beloved doctor. She still made emergency calls. Tompson, who died in a fire, he always had a joke to tell...not to forget that garage on the end of town where "Homer" could fill her up for five dollars worth, wash your windshield, check the oil and tires and on top of this give you a glass. Then there was the Village Coffee Shop next to the bank where older folks hang around all day on a fifteen cent cup of coffee and quite a few ones for free....still can hear em..."Hey Frenchy, could you heat this one up again?" It was the same building where Mr. Smith had made the first corsets for Dr. Warner. Yes! Right here in the cellar, a new industry had started.

Next to the creek was "Raul's" Antique Store, originally a tobacco store. Inside this store still stood that heavy marble counter that Raul's brother Frank had used in his butcher store. At that time, a butcher had to know slaughtering, how to cut up a whole carcass into sections, know how to make sausages, cure briskets, tie roasts, flatten veal into scallops and occasionally cook Dutch meat loaves. It was also the custom to treat the kids who came in with their mothers with a thick slice of Bologna. They loved it.

From the butcher block over the marble counter, Frank sold all kinds of cuts.

Tender meat cuts like:
Porterhouse, T Bone, Rib or Shell steaks, Delmonico, Tenderloins and Sirloin steaks

Second Cuts:
Chuck or rolled chuck roast, Top Butt, Top round and Tip steaks or boneless rolled belly plates

Then came:
Boneless Rump "Arm roast", Chuck, Short ribs and fresh Briskets, preferred for stewing, braising, marinating. Eye and heel rounds are often used for Sauerbraten and Beef a la Mode. Innards like kidneys, sweetbreads and liver were much in demand. Marbleized beef was highly preferred.

For Pork:
The carcass was cut into whole hams, loins, chops, boneless rolled shoulder butt, then shoulder "Picnic" roast, spare ribs, bacon slab and pork hocks, other good trimmings were made for stuffing and sausages.

For Lamb:
The most tender are Rib loin, leg, chops and boneless roast shoulder. Neck, Breast, etc. are used for stews like Irish stew or soups like Scotch Barley soup.

HIS-STORY of Good Cooking

Veal:
Was also known in every household. The best pieces were the chops and cuts from the hind, cut into tender roasts, steaks and medallions. Here and there, Frank had to prepare a whole breast of veal. For this, all the bones had to be pulled out, and the inside cut open to a pocket so to make "stuffed" breast of veal. This was usually served on Sunday for a family party.

Ask your butcher if he can do all this?

Fowls like chicken were seldom sold in real butcher stores, they were sold in special grocery or "comestible" stores. It was not fitting or "kosher" to mix fowl with other meats!

Behind the counter, Frank had a few kinds of different meats hanging on hooks on a steel bar. The store was kind of on the cool side, it was the ice that kept it so. Today, we all have refrigeration. Up till the first half of the last century, many stores still had ice boxes, a small room with ice where meats and other food was kept. Ice was delivered in blocks, called "cakes". These were about 22 by 32 inches and cut from nearby ponds, then kept in insulated underground chambers built with double walls filled with sawdust to keep the ice through summer. The delivery in the past was, of course, by horses. The "ice-man" wore a leather apron or heavy chaps. He used an iron tong to lift the ice blocks. To cut the "cake" in half, he used an awl sized pick. Right away, teamsters also delivered "cakes" of beer, that is, they also wore leather aprons or chaps. The ice-men were about the size of you or me, beer-men were rather heavy and broad shouldered "chaps" able to swing a big barrel of beer to Kingdom Come. The beer barrel was yanked from the wagon and dropped on a leather pillow below, then grabbed by two hooks to be lowered into the cellar trap door or rolled inside. One thing they had in common, the ice and the beer-men all delivered "cakes" and like the butcher, we all needed them. In the days of Frank's butcher store, the ice came from ice making plants, delivered by trucks, naturally. Today, ice cakes are still needed for ice sculptures and summer picnics.

Oops, almost forgot the old mill that Cliff used for storage. Here, up in the attic, he had plenty of pigeon coups. He loved to eat pigeons. Across the street was his son's haberdasher store. The mill (now a grocery) got its power by the notorious Mosquito creek that ran right under Main Street and came out near the bank. Come spring, that innocent little bubbling creek often would turn into a mean, disastrous turbulent cascade of white water, flooding many buildings, tearing and spoiling everything in its path. Further on, this mad creek would run into the already flooded trout creek to drown a greater section of the village and this is where Knips place comes in. The two story building of Knips bar stood near the bridge. It had sometime before fallen into the creek, but pulled out again. You see, these old buildings were all "pegged" with heavy timber, so they would seldom fall apart. "Knips" ran the place, it was a cozy old joint with a long bar to the bridge side, had a few tables with popcorn and a lively fireplace. The most interesting of all was "Knips" himself, a witty fellow he was. I still see him walking around the place like he was going to climb a mountain. One had to wait some time before he brought you a drink. One day, sitting alone at his bar, I asked a second time, "Hey Knips, did you forget my bourbon?" He gave me a disturbing look and said "Hey, hold your horses, everybody's turn."

Not too long after, we had another nasty flood. This time "Knips" old bar, now owned by Bucky, went down the creek again—for good, lock, stock and barrel.

With all festivities, barbecues, celebrations and fairs, we also had our troubles with fires, floods....and Halloween. Then kids went crazy having fun with eggs, toilet paper, shaving cream and if this was not enough, at night driving a manure spreader through Main Street to let it "loose" and oh my, even some of the old guys wanted to be kids again.

The Main Street bank had been held up twice, one time by a "desperado" who was apprehended in no time, and the other one, no one else but our dear good old Roul. Just for the fun of it, he had pulled a woman's stocking over his head and went right into the bank, shouting "Trick or Treat. No one moves. This is a Hold Up!" Of course no one recognized old Roul behind the mask and in no time the bank was surrounded by six police cars and Roul put at bay by heavily armed "cops." After some haggling and hulla bulloo, Roul was finally released on his own recognizance and later seen sitting with some of his friends on a bench nearby, all laughing their heads off. Wonder what they would do to this guy today?

We had just bought a farm in Taylor, New York. To get there, I had to drive through a quaint little village, McGraw. I was getting very tired after four hours of driving and a good cool beer was on my mind.

Entering Main Street McGraw I noticed a sign: "Pete's Place since 1914"....Very inviting. In no time, I found myself inside a crowded noisy

HIS-STORY of Good Cooking

bar with smoke as thick as molasses. Immediately, I was confronted by an annoying chap with deep set, starry eyes, thick beard and dressed in a dark sports jacket. Apparently, he didn't like the way I wore my beret. "You're a funny looking guy," says he. "Somehow, you just don't fit right in here." Biting my teeth, I tried not to have an argument. Besides there were too many of them.

Pete, who tended bar, coasted a mug of beer my way. "Here Frenchy," he said. "This one is from Jim over there." I managed to pour this one down just the same, so hence, I was known as "Frenchy" like it or not. Now I was chatting with a raggedy looking fellow chewing "Pouch Tobacco". He inquired what I was doing up here anyway, so I told him that I was on my way to a farm up in Taylor to hunt and trap muskrats and beavers. "Oh, trapping," said he, with his eyes popping out. "I'm a trapper and belong to a local Sportsman's club." So, I told him about a nice beaver pond up Potter Hill near the State land and he mentioned a place in Freetown. "Did you ever save the beaver tails?" I asked. "You know, they're delicious. Some day you should try one. They're the best eating part of any critter you ever tasted and you know , they used to serve them in the Chateau Frontenac in Quebec for big bucks."

"You don't say," he replied.

"Oh, yes," said I. "Certain times of the year, many trappers, raconteurs and voyageurs went there to meet for a rendezvous to do all kinds of odd things - singing, "Oh Susanna" and "Allouette," "Au Pres de Ma Blonde," "Home on the Range" and then they would sit on the floor rowing and pretending to be in a boat, singing "Row, row, row your boat," and the place would serve all kinds of food, mostly game, not to forget the most acclaimed of all, the beaver tail."

"You don't say," he replied again, looking kind of stupefied, "all those crazy French "Canucks" eating tails!"

Ah-hem, as I cleared my throat, thinking "I hope he chokes on his last meal today, that bum."

At that time I was not aware that I would spend a good part of my life in Mc Graw.

I sure do miss the old Main Street with all the "Ma and Pa" stores and what have you. Now one has to drive for miles to a superstore and spend hours looking for a "gizmo" that could easily be had in Main Street. We had old fashioned family restaurants, not too fancy, just homey, affordable and with good and plentiful food served. Family places charged 95 cents to $1.25 for a regular meal. Little girls loved their "Shirley Temples" and the boys would ask for a Birch or a Root beer. Most beverages like coffee or juices were included. Here and there a beer or a glass of Gallo wine was served. The plates were cleaned bare and the tips were meager.

   A typical menu featured meals like:
      Beans, barley, or chicken soup,
      Pot roast or Fresh Pork roast,
      Goulash made with macaroni and ground beef,
      Irish stew, referred to as "Mulligan" stew,
      Scalloped (creamed) potatoes with ham pieces,
      Corned beef & cabbage with mustard or horseradish sauce
      Pork chops with apple sauce,
      Beef liver smothered with onions and bacon.

   On Friday it was fish, like broiled haddock or scallops
   Fried Chicken or Chicken a la King on rice or toast,
   not to forget the good old Meatloaf served with
   plenty of gravy and mashed potatoes.
   No menu was without the good old fashioned homemade
   apple or blueberry pie a la mode (with ice cream.)

   A typical Sunday menu would be:
   Broiled chickens with stuffing,
   Sweet potatoes and squash,
   Oven roasted Pork Loin, Pot roast or Pork roast
   A whole cooked ham with cider sauce or pineapple gravy,
   Roast Leg of Lamb, cooked almost done,
   served with green beans, roast potatoes and mint sauce,
   and not to forget, the good "home-style" prepared
   Chicken croquettes with a white sauce.

   It sure was a pleasant sight to see all these nice dressed up people coming from church on the way to their favorite family restaurant.

It's been many years now since I first came to McGraw. At this time there is no more barber, drug or hardware store. The "haberdasher" building is gone, the bank also closed its doors. Worst, I miss most of the people I shared my daily life with, now many are no more. Thinking about them gives me many unforgettable memories, but also, somehow it makes me sad. Then I get that "Hollow" harsh and silent feeling about these people who now are gone and remain only motion pictures in my mind, like "gone with the wind."

The Empire Inn, Library, Post Office and a small grocery, and oh, yes also good old "Pete's Place" is still here. Now, I have traded my beret for a lot of gray hair.

Somehow, I feel like starting all over, entering "Pete's" bar, to be confronted by a "nondescript" who challenges me: "Say, old guy, you're new around here. Somehow you don't seem to fit in here."

Note: To protect the individuals, names have been changed.

Personally, I'm not partial to snobs that have marred and ignored so many of our "good, old-fashioned" dishes like meatloaf and chicken croquettes. Another killer to these dishes was greed. I mean, trying to cash in on big profits by adding left overs and other "garbage" that doesn't belong in there!

—

TO MAKE CHICKEN CROQUETTES
3 or 4 persons

According the portions served, a good size one half chicken makes about six or eight croquettes. Boil **chicken** with **1 bay leaf, 2 cloves**, a few **peppercorns** and half an **onion**. Add little **salt** because the stock will later be reduced. Remove chicken from stock and cool off enough to handle and pull all the meat from the bones. Discard most of the skin and cut meat into small pieces.

Reduce the chicken stock to half the volume and strain. Use half of the stock for the croquettes and the other half for the white sauce.

Make a thick white sauce from a "roux" (roasting flour with butter in a pan). Add half of the **chicken stock** and some **cream**. To test the sauce,

Francois Boeres, Chef de Cuisine

place some in a small plate and put in the refrigerator. When cold, it should be thick enough to handle and form the croquettes.

In this thick sauce, add all the cut up chicken, some fresh **parsley**, a squeeze of **lemon juice, white pepper, a trace of nutmeg** and maybe some **salt**. Slowly bring all to a boil and pour the mixture in a shallow square dish and place for a few hours in the refrigerator.

Take out and form the mixture into golf ball size using a lot of flour on hands and on the table. Now, roll them into cork like cylinders, patting each side with the flat side of a knife so they all look tidy. Dip them into **egg wash** and fine **bread crumbs**. You can place them in the refrigerator till needed. Use the other half of the chicken stock to make the white sauce that is served separately.

Fry croquettes in very hot fryer fat until golden. Serve piping hot....with rice, broccoli or asparagus.

> Wine: a light regional Rose or a Sauterne
> Music: Potpourri by Boston Pops.

TO MAKE A GOOD MEATLOAF
for 6 servings plus

Use at least **3 pounds of ground beef** or it will be a "Nitty-meathy-laughfy." The meat should be at least 85% and of acceptable quality or it will be too dry after cooking.

First, soak a good size **Kaiser roll** in just enough **milk** to soften. Squash roll to pulp. Add **2 beaten eggs, 1/2 fine chopped onion, chopped parsley, sage and one bouillon cube** dissolved in 1/2 cup warm water. Add all to meat, mix well to prevent holes and cracks after cooking. It should come out O.K. If too soft, add some bread crumbs. Shape into a loaf, place into a pan, cover with a few **bacon slices** and bake at 350° oven till done (about 40 minutes).

To make a fancy Meatloaf: Stuff and line the inside with hard boiled **eggs**. Best, cut off both ends of the eggs, so each slice will have a yellow sliver of the egg.

The Meatloaf can be served with brown, tomato or white horseradish sauce with capers. Serve with mashed potatoes, glazed onions with peas or fresh carrots.

An Encounter

There we had cooked for a party in a swanky residence, not far away from Greenwich, Connecticut. This guy "Joe" was affiliated with a big newspaper and he knew how to live. His place had three bars, four tennis courts and a swimming pool big enough to navigate a boat in, not to mention all the "mermaids" hanging around.

It had been a hectic day and I was glad to see myself driving home, hardly keeping my eyes open. I was forced to stop off the roadside and promptly "knocked out," soon to be awakened by the flashlight from a State Trooper. "Can I see your license?" Fumbling around, I presented my New York license with Connecticut plates on my car and a New Jersey registration. "I don't know about these things," I said, in an accent.

There was no reply.

I noticed the trooper was driving a Harley Davidson and wore a riding outfit that gave him the distinguished appearance known as "Mussolini's Paratroopers."

So the man asked me what I was doing and where I was heading. So I told him that I had just cooked for a party.

"So, you are a cook," he said.

"Now, look, I'm a Chef, not a cook."

"So, what's the difference?"

Now I tried to explain the difference between a cook and a chef that almost led into an argument right on the big highway.

Finally he said, "Get the hell out of here before I give you a ticket."

"Yes sir," I answered and I took off in my Studebaker.

The Chef

I am often asked about the function and work of a typical Chef. First of all, there are none alike. They are all professional individuals. It's like comparing great singers or players of Jazz, classical baroque, contemporary or hard rock music. Some pleasant and some unpleasant to our ears—in this case, to our stomach. Further, I will not conclude and draw a line of great importance that of a Diner cook doing a good job to please his early customers with an Executive Chef doing what he or she should do.

Francois Boeres, Chef de Cuisine

I say with much regret, large numbers of big hotels and other institutions are becoming more and more "hostile" working places with the camaraderie of the past infiltrated by indifference. In some places, the turnover in management and help is so bad, the food service from last week has been replaced by...who knows?

I have seen cooks and chefs, if you might call them that, burning sheets and sheets of bacon for breakfast and tons of dinner rolls. Some of these cooks or chefs wore dirty baseball caps, ran around in circles, knocking down coworkers and "charming" the boss.

On the other hand, we are fortunate and proud of so many who give their best to the profession. These people are working year in and year out in renowned institutions and restaurants, and it shows.

As a Chef, I worked in Country Club kitchens on different shifts staffed by a full brigade. Did I mention "kitchens?" Well, most clubs and hotels had two kitchens, one up front for the regular service and one in the back for large parties. The one for the parties had big steam kettles, used to make "stock," soups, stews and the like. Besides other "kitchen paraphernalia" we had huge storage bins with racks to keep the food warm. Her we served many elaborate buffets for big parties—the real thing, all from scratch: stuffed boneless turkeys, whole poached salmon, galantines, whole spiced pigs,' parsley' rack of lamb, prime rib, steamship rounds, gelatin wine aspic, heaps of shrimp, seafood Newburg in patty shells, ice sculptures, and big Cornucopias made out of hard dough and filled with fresh fruits.

In Country Clubs, we served every Saturday night a grand buffet attended by neatly dressed waiters wearing gloves. The party then was followed by dancing. Did I say dancing? Let me know where it is, I will be there!

A chef has to know how to "create" exciting and profitable menus so to keep the food cost in check, be responsible to support and keep a good morale in a congenial atmosphere, also to do the correct ordering and keep a clean and organized kitchen.

Now, we find all kinds of prepared and portion controlled frozen foods available. The old stock pots are long gone and replaced by concentrated bouillon paste. (some are not bad) Then we have frozen portions of fish, chicken, beef, veal steaks, stuffed manicotti and all kinds of breaded foods. This kind of stuff was schemed and cooked up for the demands of institutions like in-plant feeding: hospitals, airports, armed forces and the like. They can be heated up quickly in a convection oven and served by anyone working in a kitchen.

It makes me very upset to see some of this food served in high priced so-called "fine" restaurants.

> THE BEST TEST OF A NATION'S CULTURE
> STILL REMAINS WHAT IT HAS ALWAYS BEEN
> SINCE THE DAYS OF GUTTENBERG -
> ITS ATTITUDE TOWARD BOOKS
> *All. Nevins*

Our Own Restaurant

A great moment was at hand the day we opened our own French restaurant in a little provincial town. The menu had been carefully planned. The kitchen was "humming," the ice was filled in the bar and all the candles were lit in the dining room...and nobody came.

Did you ever had a nightmare like that? like being all dressed up and no place to go. This all changed soon, not for to long, we got so busy we had to send people away and Main Street ran out of parking places. The fare of drinks and wine soon eclipsed that of the food. This sunny highlight kept going for almost 14 years, excluding a few low "water marks" of floods, fires, break-ins and financial struggles, until I was nearly "burned out."

One thing I never forgot was the limelight of the pleasant crowds, many friends, and faithful customers, immeasurable at any price.

In retrospect, I hardly can think of a few items not being fresh, few ducks, shrimp or maybe peas came frozen. Most other stuff was fresh, like leg of veal, leg of lamb, whole fish. Dover soles came with the skin on. Scallops, blue fish, Pompano, Oysters, Fowl, so all other meats and Daily Specials.

Francois Boeres, Chef de Cuisine

Recently I found one of these old menus.

Soup du jour or Onion soup au Gratin
Appetizers: Clams casino, escargot Bourguignon, Pate Maison, Coquille St. Jaques, Oysters Rockefeller, Crabmeat St. Louis and Shrimp cocktail.
Entree: New York Shell strip steak Wine Merchant or au Poivre Vert. Veal Cordon Bleu, Wienerschnitzel, Veal Scaloppini-Francaise, Breast of Chicken Cumberland, Duckling a l'Orange, Sole Marguerite, Shrimp or Frog Legs Provencalle, Calves Liver "Anna" with apple rings and Veal Beaumont (Veal boiled in wine sauce with vegetables)
Desserts: Baba au Rhum, Creme Caramel, Parfaits and cafe glacee, crepe mandarin flambe, Isola Bella dessert and a list with all the cordials and many pastries.

Peeling onions once awhile makes me cry and think of Ibsen's "Peer Gynt", who went out to see the world of pleasure and suffering, richness and poverty, love and deprivation, power and defiance, finally to return home as an old disappointed man. Peeling the onion, he also started crying and noticed that the onion only had peels and no substantial core or kernel, just like the life he led.

ONION SOUP AU GRATIN
for 4 to 6 servings

Sauté: 8 thin sliced medium **onions in 4 TBS. butter and 1 TBS. oil** until golden brown. Add **1 TBS. flour**, stirring often, then pour in **7-1/2 cups of beef broth, 1/2 cup white wine, pepper, a little salt, a "filet" of Maggi or soy sauce**. Cover and simmer for 3/4 hour.

Optional: a dash of Kitchen Bouquet.

To Make the Croutons:
Toast slices of **French bread**, place each crouton on top of the individual soup bowls and top generously with slices of **Gruyere or Provolone**, sprinkle with **Parmesan cheese** and brown in the oven for about 8 to 10 minutes.
Serve piping hot.

HIS-STORY of Good Cooking

ESCARGOT BOURGIGNON IN RED WINE
4 dozen

As an entree for 2 people, serve a dozen each, so you need a can of 24 count. The same can of 24 can be served as an appetizer for 4 people, 1/2 dozen each. If served as an entree for 4 people, 2 cans of 24 are needed. Snail plates come in stainless, "Pyrex" or more affordable aluminum. I buy the shells in restaurant supply stores. Snail shells are a must and are reused by boiling them out. Also "tongs" and little forks are nice to have.

First: Prepare a quick red wine sauce: Sauté one small chopped **onion add 3/4 cups of beef bouillon, cup red wine, pepper and a squirt of "Maggi" or soy sauce**. Boil for 8 minutes and thicken lightly with **cornstarch**.

To make the snail butter: Soften **3/4 pound of butter**, chop **1/3 of a bunch of parsley**, separate, by hand. In a mixer or food processor (handy at this time) chop **5 shallots or one medium onions with 8 garlic cloves**.(Not to fine) Mix all this with the butter, parsley, a little **salt, pepper**, a few grains of **nutmeg** and the **juice from a lemon section**.

Now, place the snail shells on the escargot plates and fill them with the wine sauce. Best is to dip each shell into the sauce and scoop out enough to fill the bottom. Squeeze snails into the shells with it's shoe out, pluck and heap up the shells with the snail butter.

The snails are now ready to broil in a 450° preheated oven. Cook for about 15 minutes or until they bubble and the top is light brown. The very hot escargot plates are placed on serving platters and served with French bread (or Angel hair pasta). The connoisseur cleans out all the sauce with the bread or swirls the pasta in the sauce.

Wine: A Santa Clara or a Petit Sirah
Music: Violin concerto by Telemann

NEW YORK SHELL STEAK WITH GREEN PEPPERCORNS
4 servings
(Entrecote au Poivre Vert)

In **butter**, sauté 3 fine chopped **shallots or one medium onion** with one fine chopped **garlic clove** until glazed. Add pieces of fresh **mushrooms**,

Francois Boeres, Chef de Cuisine

little **salt, pepper** and cook until mushrooms are done. To this add **1 cup of dry white wine**. Boil for a minute, add 1/2 cup of **brown stock or beef broth**, then stir in 1/2 cup of **heavy cream**. Reduce by half.

Broil or pan-fry steaks with salt and crushed **pepper** and place on a serving platter.

Reheat the sauce, add 2 tsp. of soft **green peppers** and a jigger of **brandy**. Cook for over a minute and pour sauce over the steaks. Garnish with **parsley** sprigs, braised Belgium endive or celery.

Wine: California Barbera, Grignolino or Cabernet Sauvignon.
Music: Fat Kates Wedding by Philidor

COQUILLE ST. JAQUES
4 to 6 servings

Have a few natural **scallop-shells** ready.

Prepare: 3/4 cup of thick **béchamel** (white sauce), 3/4 cup of **hollandaise** (use only 1 egg yolk), 3/4 cup of **whipped heavy cream**.

Preheat oven to 450°. Broil 1 pound and 4 oz. of fresh **scallops** until tender, but still soft inside (don't overcook). Sprinkle with a **semi-dry sherry wine**, a squeeze of **lemon juice, salt, white pepper**. Add the béchamel and quickly bring to a boil, take from the fire and divide scallops into the required shells, top with the blend of the Hollandaise and whipped cream. Sprinkle with any **grated cheese** and place in the 450 degree preheated oven for about 8 minutes or until brown bubbles appear (this is called "gratinee").

Option: Fresh mushrooms or a few drops of Pernot.

Note: All menus are planned. Now, I know that there probably will be some cream left over. Use this to make some sweet whipped cream to top any dessert. This is called Creme Chantilly.

Whip cream to stiff peaks (for not too long or you make butter). Add sifted confectioners sugar and vanilla extract or a few drops of liqueur like Amaretto, Cointreau, etc.

Chef Cheng

TO PRESERVE OUR SENSES

It should be a great disturbance to anyone to lose his senses and sensibility. This often is demonstrated by people looking the whole day at things that make no sense or are so loud and noisy enough to wake up the dead. Then we have those who suppress their senses with drugs or intolerable amounts of alcohol....enough to make a trip to the moon.

People in control of their senses are indeed cultivated, especially in the preparation of food. Many people I have known over the years were seriously devoted to the art of cooking, especially vegetables. I can't think of any other group who take their vegetables so seriously than the Orientals. To them, vegetables are a way of life. Only the freshest and youngest are given great care to cook, with the quickest time possible so as to retain their virgin quality. Here all senses are savored, touch, smell, taste and even listening to the sound of cooking (you know when the fat is "quite" ready for cooking). Great care is taken in steaming or quick stir-frying in the wok.

Some years ago, I worked in a fine restaurant in Elmira, New York. Here we also had a separate Chinese kitchen run by Chef "Cheng". There I learned to cook with Napa cabbage, Bok-choy, Anise, Snow-peas, Bean-sprouts, baby corn, celery, bamboo shoots, Hearts of Palm, Daikon radish, water chestnuts, scallions and even collard greens, Swiss chard, Rabe-rappini and what have you. I will always remember Cheng as one of the funniest, most amusing and sensible persons I ever met. He called me "Franciosy."

On a good, sunny day, working in my garden, a dude came spelunking on our farm and wanted to know if we had any marketable standing timber. I did not look my best, dirty hands, muddy pants, sitting on my knees on the ground. "You don't have to work like that in the dirt if you are selling timber." (Now, I am annoyed.) "That is the stuff we are made of and return to," I replied. He mumbled something about going to heaven or what if he died. I said I did not give a damn if he went to Rotterdam or Amsterdam. After I finished my planting, I stood back to look at it and was well pleased with my work and hoped the good Lord gave good weather and a heavenly "recolt." One thing I didn't plant this year were radishes, I used to dip in salt and quaff down with a sip of beer. Gee, I wish I still had all my old teeth! One can do a lot with vegetables, a meal without them is like a frame-less picture, a song without words, or a woman without charm. So remember what Ma told you: Eat your vegetables, they're good for you!

CHEF CHENG'S SWEET AND PUNGENT PORK
for 6

Combine: **2 beaten eggs** with **1 cup of flour**, little **salt**, 1/4 cup water.

Slice 1-1/2 pounds of **pork shoulder** into 3/4 inch cubes and stir into flour mixture until coated, then fry the pork cubes in plenty of very hot **peanut oil** for 3 minutes or until golden brown. Take out of oil, drain and keep warm.

Combine 3 sliced **green peppers** with 2 cups of drained **pineapple chunks**. Add 3/4 cup of **brown sugar**, 1 cup of **vinegar**, 3 TBS. of **molasses, pepper** and 1-1/2 cups of water. Bring to a boil, stirring constantly. Add 3 peeled and cubed **tomatoes, soy sauce** and let simmer for 5 minutes, stirring often.

Combine 2 TBS. of **cornstarch**, dissolved in 1/4 cup of water and cook until thickened, stirring often.

Add all the pork and other ingredients and cook slowly for 15 minutes. I often serve this with transparent or homemade noodles.

Here tea is served.
Music: In a Chinese Temple Garden by Katelby

CHEF CHENG'S BEEF CHOP SUEY
for 6

Fry 1-1/2 pounds of diced tender **beef chunks** in 1/4 cup of hot **peanut oil** for 3 minutes, stirring constantly. Add 2 TBS of **Maggi or soy sauce, salt and pepper**. Remove meat from the pan and keep hot. To the remaining oil add 3 cups of "diamond" cut **celery**, 2 large sliced **onions**,* fry golden brown and add 1 TBS of **molasses**, 2 cups of **beef bouillon**. Boil for 10 minutes, stirring often. Add 2 cups of **bean sprouts** and cook 3 more minutes. Add all the beef cubes and 3 TBS. of **cornstarch** dissolved in 1/4 cup of water. Stir the boiling Chop Suey until thickened.

Serve with steamed short grain rice.

*Note: To slice onions for Oriental dishes, cut onions in half and lay with the flat side on the cutting board. Slice with the grain into a fan tail fashion so all the pieces look like little boats. Cook quickly til thin ends are soft and the middle is crunchy.

Wine: Rice-wine
Music: Hawaiian Melodies by Led Kaapano

CANTONESE ROAST DUCK
4 to 6 servings

Defrost **duck** and remove the package with the innards. Pat the duck dry and **salt** inside and out. Sew the "floppy" skin around the neck tight and leakproof.

> Bring to a boil: 1 cup of chicken broth
> 3 TBS of dry sherry, 1 TBS. of imported soy sauce
> 2 TBS. of sugar, 4 anise stars (from Oriental store)
> 2 chopped scallions, 1 crushed garlic clove,
> 1 peeled and minced ginger root.

Remove from heat and let cool for 5 minutes. Place duck in a tall pot and pour this sauce into the cavity, then sew this opening tight and leakproof.

Place duck on a rack in a roasting pan with 1 inch of water, make sure the duck does not touch the water. Roast duck in a 400 degree preheated oven for 30 minutes.

> For basting, combine.....
> 1 cup of water with 1/2 cup of honey,
> 1 TBS. white vinegar, 1 TBS. imported soy sauce.

Baste duck every 15 minutes for about 1-1/2 hours or until meat is soft and done. Place duck in a colander that is set into a bowl. Remove all

Francois Boeres, Chef de Cuisine

threads and let liquid drain into the bowl. Cut up and carve duck and place in a hot serving platter and cover with the liquid sauce.

Serve with wild rice and Hoisin sauce on the side.

STIR-FRIED SNOW PEAS WITH CHICKEN BREASTS

In a small skillet sauté 2 **chicken breasts** in light **vegetable oil** until slightly golden. Add little **salt**. Quench with 1/2 cup **Sherry** and 1/2 cup **light chicken broth**. Cover and cook slowly for about 15 minutes or until done. Set aside and keep hot.

In a wok or skillet, stir fry 3 finely sliced **scallions in peanut oil**, over high heat for a few seconds. Add 1 pound of stringed **snow-peas** and stir fry for 2 minutes.

Add 1/4 cup of **light chicken broth**, 2 TBS. of **semi-dry Sherry, 2 tsp. of Oyster sauce** (available in specialty stores) and a pinch of **salt**.

Toss snow peas around in the wok for about 2 minutes. They should be crisp and green, but not overcooked.

Place in a hot dish topped with sliced strips of chicken breast and sprinkle with a few fresh roasted matchstick cut **almonds**.

Serve immediately.

SUB GUM CHOW MEIN

Prepare: Shred 4 cooked **chicken breasts**, toast 3/4 cups sliced **almonds**, 3 cups of **chicken bouillon**, make a few thin **egg-crepes** and slice into thin noodles. Set aside.

Prepare the vegetables: **3 cups of diced celery, 1 diced green pepper, 1 cup thin sliced green beans, 8 chopped scallions, 1 cup of diced firm mushrooms, 2 cups of sliced Chinese cabbage, 2 minced garlic cloves**.

Fry all vegetables in 1/2 cup **peanut oil**, preferably using a wok, stir vegetables for 2 minutes.

Add: 2 cup of sliced, canned **water chestnuts**, 1-1/2 cups of diced, canned **bamboo-shoots**. Add the bouillon, cover and simmer for 10 minutes.

Combine 3 TBS. of **cornstarch** with 4 TBS. water and 1/4 cup of **soy sauce**. Add to the vegetables. Cook and stir until thickened.

Add chicken and cook for 5 minutes.

Serve in a round bowl and top with the sliced crepe noodles and sliced **almonds**.

Wine: Pina Paceta or a Solera

Venison And All Kinds Of Birds

THE WILD IN AMERICA

Early settlers in this young country never thought that such an abundance of game found here could possibly ever be exhausted, eliminated or even put on the danger list. Here in the Colonial Eastern States, where it all began, we had plentiful moose, elk, bear, deer and others now gone. (Sorry there were not many buffaloes around Buffalo, New York. The name of the city of Buffalo derives from the French word "Beau-falon" or pretty fallow) First, the immense never ending territory begged for trapping. Secondly, hunting. As the pressure rose from an ever growing population, hunting became a way of life.

Bountiful were: wild turkey, grouse, partridge, wood-cock, snipe and song birds, considered fair game at the time. The vast pristine wetland had a selective assortment of all kinds of water birds: different breeds of ducks, geese, mergansers, teals, rail birds and even bittern, at that time a delicacy. One of the greatest spectacles ever of birds in America were the Passenger Pigeons, about the size of a turtle-dove, except for its long, wedge-shaped tail. In colonial times, this multitude of birds caused threats to early agriculture. They were the most hated and cursed birds, especially after ravaging and destroying everything one had planted in his garden with great toil.

In the beginning of the 19th century, these pigeons were so plentiful that Ornithologist Wilson estimated them at over 220 million. For almost two weeks, swarms and swarms of never ending formations, over 150 miles long and a mile wide, came in a rapid and sustained flight from South Carolina to New York, from Kentucky, over Ohio, toward Canada. An unimaginable phenomena for us to comprehend. As soon as they were spotted, people dropped all work, went for their guns and the shooting started, far from what is called hunting, more of a wholesale slaughter, often killing over eight birds with one shot. That lead to heaps of bagged pigeons.

They were good tasting and they had a fine meat texture and supplied plenty of meat for the whole family. The whole country seemed to be infested with those cheap Belgian black powder Damascus shotguns that sold for four dollars and were used for hunting. They still can be found today in antique stores, leaving testimony of their past. In 1896 flocks of 50 to 100 pigeons were reported. The last one died in 1904 in an Ohio zoo.

In the past, as today, we had hunters with good ethics and standing. On the other hand, we also had the slinky, greedy market hunters that could be found everywhere game was aplenty. Their way of hunting was only for profit and was exercised in the most unorthodox manner, by using some awesome, six foot long, so-called pond or punt-guns, mounted on the "gun-wall" of a boat or shot from a blind. The waterfowl, like geese and ducks were indiscriminately eliminated by heavy charges of a pound of lead shot, often killing 30 birds with one shot. The "catch" was sold to hotels and game markets.

The same fate almost loomed over big game hunting from the Adirondacks to Maine. In the mid-nineteenth century, a great Naturalist movement became evident. It was back to nature. They were all over the country and their "works" were followed up with great compassion. Naturalists like John Burroughs, John Muir, Burke, Traubel, Thoreau and his friend Emerson, who believed that a man's spirit is related to nature. It was a force to be reckoned with. They came by train, boat, wagon and horse to build summer and hunting camps to recluse and wrap themselves in Mother Nature. They represented the average hunters, and accounted for taking 20 percent of deer. The greater part, 80 percent, was taken by determined market hunters, to shoot as many deer as possible for profit. Then we had these huge lumber jack camps that fed on the deer population, not to forget many resort hotels with an extensive game menu.

Tracking down deer was done almost all year round and often day and night. Hounding and floating were common methods. This was done by driving deer into a line of hunters or chasing them into the water where hunters were waiting to float and kill the deer.

Another way was "Jacking" a deer in the dark of the night. This was done from a boat equipped with a Kerosene or Carbide reflector lantern. Deer that gathered near the water were blinded and confused and so became an easy target. This enormous hunting pressure was felt. By 1890, deer became very scarce in the Adirondacks and most other places, non-existent.

HIS-STORY of Good Cooking

The moose had disappeared around the time of the Civil War. Attempts were made to reinstate the moose, but failed, forever. These did not fail in Maine. In the years of 1896 to 1900, the white tail deer was practically gone. In 1895, the sale of venison was prohibited and followed with a ban on hounding and jacking deer. In 1912, it was one buck per season.

Conservation laws and their measures could hardly be enforced because there were just not enough game wardens. Besides, it was a hard thing to bring down an old tradition. In the woods of Maine, we had a game warden named Cash (Cassius). His perseverance and commitment to catch and track down poachers and offenders in their act was the "take them from behind" approach. this man was mean and unyielding to any law breakers and hunted them down until he "got them". Soon his reputation demanded attention and great respect for the law. This made many law enforcement worth looking into. His method was later copied and other game wardens did it his way. The successful introduction of deer in many states also called for new laws. Now, there are so many deer around every day that some of them are hit by cars. One of them even ran into my barn (that was not moving) and put a big dent in the metal.

If you happen to be not partial to hunting and get mad if a deer runs into your nice car or eats up all your plants, maybe you would like to take a shot at those hunters who made the return of a healthy deer population possible by their support and hard work. And if you think you don't like deer or any other game, think twice. It is very good tasting, and of low cholesterol and free of any bio-chemicals. So if you hunt or a neighbor brings you some venison, be thankful and do yourself a big favor: cook up a storm.

Here are some delicious recipes from the Wilds of America.

A "WILD" EXPERIENCE

As young lads in my hometown, we often hit for the hills and endless woods. There we became adventurers and pioneers, rediscovering "new frontiers". Our names changed to Buffalo Bill, Jim Badge, Hawkeye, Dan Boone, Humple Bill and Rusty Jack. Some of us carried old double muzzle loaders, one of us had a more "modern" le Faucheux Pinfire gun that shot old copper shell, still available at that time. There was a dusky place near, called "Kayler Potto" with Larch and towering Fir trees. Here we made camp and built fires to keep us comfortable at night and mainly to get ready to do some cooking. This was the place where the crows gathered at dusk to roost overnight and was known as the "Crow's Woods." It started to get dark and chilly, and suddenly here they came, thousands of crows. Crowing and circling around finally to fall in. There must have been hundreds sitting on a tree. All we had to do was take a couple of thunderous shots that broke the dark and spooky silence of the woods and there we had 12 crows lying at our feet. As we plugged them, we noticed that their legs were kind of small, but nevertheless, we promptly cooked them in a big aluminum pot that was hanging over the fire, supported by a tripod. We seasoned them with salt, pepper, onions and knob celery. We had the "bakers" already in the fire and soon had crow "a la Humple Bill" with baked potatoes so black that eating them made our faces just as black, ready to attack Indians at night.

We slept there that night and took our memories home next morning. Now, I don't expect people to eat crow. I just want to say, it sure was not bad tasting, considering all the circumstances. Imagine what real good conventional game can be, just naturally gratifying.

Gee I wish to be a kid again!

Preparing, Larding and Marinating Game

Dressing and cleaning fowls and other game like rabbits or hares is not that complicated and can be done easily once you have mastered that art. Or ask a hunting buddy to show you or let a local butcher do it. Skinning and cleaning hares and rabbits - start with tying and hanging up the animal by its rear feet and cutting loose the pelt around both ankles. Gradually loosen and pull down the pelt with the aid of a few relief cuts along the inner side until you get to the front legs that have to be pulled out of the pelt and cut off at the "paws". If the head is to be saved or processed further, cut the ears loose, ending up right at the snout. To eviscerate and clean, cut open the belly and split open the bone near the anus so all guts can be taken out easily. Discard them with the lungs. Next, carefully take out the liver, heart and kidneys. Remove the "esophagus" from the throat and discard. Clean the liver, rinse, wash and dry meat with a paper towel and hang in a cool dry place for at least a day.

The cleaning process for big game is pretty much the same, except big game is aged much longer. Most game and venison have little fat, therefore, fowl is often braided with bacon slices and covered with young grape leaves. Others like rabbits, hares and deer saddles are often "spiked" or larded with pork fat-back slices. This is done by pulling thin slices of fat-back through the meat with a "hollow" larding needle. If no larding needle is available, just stab some holes into the meat to be roasted with a thin boning knife and plug them up with one inch long larding strips. A larded roast resembles a porcupine with all this larding sticking out. This larding procedure will be rewarding by creating a nice, tender and not too dry roast. Occasional basting is also highly recommended. We all know that hinds, ribs, saddles, steaks and chops are the most tender. Whatever, they should not be overdone!

Other cuts, like front legs, necks and end-cuts are usually boned out, cut into cubes for stews and marinated for at least two days.

This **MARINADE** can be used for ragouts, venison stews and beef a la mode:

Mix **1/2 red wine and 1/2 red wine vinegar**, crushed **garlic cloves** and crushed **peppercorns, salt (preferably Kosher), thyme, bay leaves, coriander, a few juniper berries, some brown sugar, cut up celery, onions and carrots**. Marinade meat for at least two days in the refrigerator, turning often.

HASENPFEFFER AND RABBITS

An average hare weighs about four pounds and can serve four to six people. "Hase" means "Hare" in German. If hare is not to be had, use two rabbits. Clean and prepare as described above, except save the **blood** if you can, and mix with a little **vinegar** to prevent clotting. This is later to be added to the sauce.

Start by cutting it all into serving pieces, the whole back should be cut across into 1-1/4 inch pieces. Soak and cover meats with the marinade. Refrigerate, cover and turn meat over four times for two days.

Render thick cut pieces of **bacon** in a little **oil or shortening** until brown. Take out the bacon and save the fat. Remove the pieces of meat from the marinade and dry them on a paper towel. Dip them into **flour** and sauté in the fat until light brown. Add some sifted flour, mix well, and add the marinade until covered. Add some **salt, pepper**, a little **garlic powder**, all the innards, the bacon bits and a trace of **brown sugar**. Cook slowly

Francois Boeres, Chef de Cuisine

until done (about 50 minutes). Take out all the pieces of meat and place in a tureen. Add some **sour cream** and the blood (if any) to the pan. Boil and pour the sauce over the meat. This can be served with noodles, new or riced potatoes, virgin or red cabbage.

Wine: Cabernet Sauvignon, Spanish Rioja or Amarone
Music: The Surprise and the Miracle, by Hayden.

RABBIT RAGOUT

Cut **rabbit** into serving pieces (save innards). Render thick pieces of **bacon**. Add **butter** and sauté rabbit pieces light brown. Add some **shallots or small onions, a clove of garlic, salt and pepper, summer savory**. Sift in some flour, mix well and quench with **dry wine** and **chicken bouillon stock** until covered. Add heart and liver pieces and bacon. Cover and cook until done (about 50 minutes). Before serving, place rabbit in a tureen. Reduce the sauce and add some **Dijon mustard**.

Serve with small boiled potatoes, Brussel sprouts and glazed onions.

GLAZED ONIONS

The boiled **onions** are sautéed in **butter** with a little **sugar** added. Swirl around in the pan until golden brown (caramelized).

Serve rabbit with a California Pinot Gris or a Sauvignon Blanc.

Dad often took me to town to buy quails and snipes for a home-party. This store, called Comestibles, sold all kinds of game and was owned by a friend, Mr. Decker, who was an ardent hunter and acquired all kinds of game from hunting parties. Hunting in Europe is strictly regulated to all game sold. His business primarily was catering. In colder days in the fall, most game was on display on racks in front of the store. Deer, roe-bucks, wild boar, rows of hares, rabbits, Hungarian partridges, snipes and many I don't remember.

But I still remember the French song, "Alouette, je te plumerai" (plucking the lark). Long before my time, many other birds like Bob-O-Links, larks and ortelons were sold. Today, in many states in America, it still is possible to hunt and cook pigeons, doves, quail and wood-cock .

HIS-STORY of Good Cooking

Pigeons, Pigeons. . . Pigeons had been raised in coops. Now there are still plenty circling around barns and city squares. There was a time when everyone liked to eat pigeons. In sweet dreams they flew roasted in Lubber-land. From horses to man's best friend, the connection between men and animals had been invaluable and inexorably (and probably still is) linked. Great battles fought with horses often detoured and changed the course of history by last minute decisions and plans through messages and information carried out in rapid flights by. . . pigeons. Oh well. We also had stool pigeons to lure more pigeons into the pot. Pigeons can be prepared like chicken or Cornish hens, except older ones take twice as long to cook and are used for soups. Young pigeons have pinkish legs and softer beaks, not ground off yet. Pigeons have more pin feathers and no bile, often seen picking up small pebbles to digest their food.

SHOOT AT BIRDS, NOT AT FLOCKS
Old Proverb

ROASTING GROUSE OR PARTRIDGE

The birds are to be hung for two days before plucking, cleaning and cooking. Also, all pin feathers are pulled out and the fine down feathers scorched and rubbed out with a towel, then the crop and windpipe is removed. Most recipes call for a pair of birds. Save the liver for the sauce.

Rub **birds** inside with ground **sage, celery salt, pepper and ginger**. Roast birds in a 425 degree preheated oven for 35 minutes with a 'mirepois' of vegetables added. Baste often and sprinkle with **white wine** until done. Split the birds in half, dress on a plate and keep warm.

Deglaze the pan with **light chicken stock**. Strain the sauce, add the **chopped liver** and boil for 5 minutes. Add Cumberland sauce with **sour cream**. Serve the sauce separately. The birds can be dressed on braised virgin cabbage. The grouse has a fine texture and delicate flavor.

My wife likes to braise them, cut up into pieces, mixed in a white wine and mushroom sauce and serve them in a patty shell sprinkled with cilantro and capers.

Wine: A Pinot Noir or a Ermitage Blanc
Music: Mozart's Horn Concerto by Baumann.

Francois Boeres, Chef de Cuisine

ROAST LEG OF VENISON or Leg of Lamb.

Prepare **leg of venison** (deer) with larding. Cut out the small lover muscle from the bone and cover with aluminum foil so you have a nice "handle" for cutting the meat when serving. Stab three holes around the leg and insert fresh **garlic** .Sprinkle with; oregano ,marjoram, chervil ,thyme, pepper and celery salt. Roast the leg as you do the saddle, observing the same temperatures. It should be pink inside. Deglaze the pan to make the jus. This roast is to be carved at the table and sauce served on the side.

Note: This also can be made with a leg of lamb.

Wine: A Medoc or a fine St. Emilion
Music: Der Freischutz von....Karl-Maria von Weber

TO ROAST WILD DUCKLINGS

Sprinkle **duck** cavity with **sherry wine, celery salt, pepper, sage and ginger**. Stuff ducks with a few **bread crumbs** sautéed in **garlic butter** and add a few **juniper berries**. Place ducks in a roasting pan. Add a few pieces of **onion, celery and orange peel**. Roast in 350 degree oven for about 45 minutes, or until soft and done. Split ducks, remove breast bones and return the stuffing. Before preparing the sauce, discard all fat and replace with butter. Deglaze the pan with **sweet apple cider** and add some **brown sugar** and the **juice of the peeled orange**. Reduce the sauce and thicken with **pear puree**.

Place split ducks, with the dressing, on a hot platter, then pour some of the sauce over and serve the rest on the side. Serve with steamed Chinese cabbage and baked pears. This preparation can also be used for other domestic water fowl. A wild goose should be cooked quick with chicken broth added.. They should be soaked a while in salt and vinegar water before cooking.

Note: Wild rice is nice to serve with any duckling or other 'wild' fowl.

Wine: California Semillon or a Cote de Nuits.

Music: Purcells, Roy Arthur or Scherzi - Ballad or a prelude by Chopin.

How to Cook (Steam) WILD RICE

Some cooks only boil this kind of rice until done and that's it. Now, remember Epicure's quotation.... "The more attention given, the better things turn out!" This often can be the difference of a meal or an Epicurean delight.

Pour a package of **wild rice** into a pot and place it under slow running water for 2 minutes. Drain rice entirely and let stand for 5 minutes. In a large pot (the volume of the rice will triple), bring enough water, **salt** added, to a boil. Add rice so it's covered with 3 inches of water.

Cook for 30 minutes or until tender. Drain rice into a sieve large enough to place into the pot with 2 inches of water without touching the rice.

Place a wet towel or napkin between the pot and the cover to seal it good, without letting too much steam escape. Steam for about 15 minutes, or until fluffy.

GREAT TASTING QUAILS

We served this quail many times in a fine Albanian restaurant in New York. Can't remember the name. I should call them "a la Robespiere", because, first we chopped off their heads and.... oh well.... most important, they are delicious. The **quails** are marinated for 3 hours in **red wine, brandy** added, then taken out, dried and filled with mushroom stuffing, made by sautéed chopped **shallots or onions**, adding fresh cut **mushrooms** and stirring until soft. Add a little **salt, pepper, thyme, a pinch of celery seeds** and a few fresh **bread crumbs** to hold the stuffing firm.

In a preheated 450 degree oven, roast the birds in **margarine or olive oil** for 25 to 30 minutes or until done, basting occasionally and brushing with **butter**.

Take the quails out, dress them on a hot serving platter....keep warm. Deglaze the pan with the wine marinade, add a few **red grapes, some apple jelly** and a few chips of **butter**. Cook the sauce for 8 minutes, bind slightly with **cornstarch**.

Francois Boeres, Chef de Cuisine

The birds, if served very hot, can be flambeed and cut in half with a poultry shear.

Wine: a New York Chelois or Gold Seal Champagne.

RAGOUT OF VENISON

Cut up pieces of shoulder, neck or other secondary cuts of **deer meat** into cubes, marinade them for 2 to 3 days in the afore mentioned marinade of wine and vinegar.

Heat some **oil or pork fat** in a big pan. Stir in a small amount of the meat at a time, then transfer them into a big heavy pot. Add sautéed, cut up **onions, celery** and crushed **garlic**. Sauté and sprinkle with some **flour**. Stir and add **salt, pepper, a dash of paprika, savory, some brown sugar**. Cover with the marinade, water added. Stir well, cover and cook slowly until done, stirring occasionally.

Serve with Pennsylvania Dutch noodles, red cabbage or baked apples. Some chefs add some dark caramelized sugar to the stew.

Wine: A red California or a red Sonoma.

Of Pheasants

The game pheasants we know are of eastern Chinese and Caucasian origin. They became a very popular dish in the Victorian era. These birds, of fine texture and distinctive taste are still used in refined and "polished" kitchens today. Naturally, game birds of this kind have been "crowded out" by Cornish hens and inexpensive and plentiful "supermarket" chickens for every pot, rather than the more cosmopolitan pheasant under glass. Contrary to waterfowl that are prepared fresh, pheasants should be "ripe" in a few days.

OVEN ROASTED PHEASANT "BALTIMORE"
2 birds for 2-4 people

The preparation: Before preparing the birds, cut off a pair of wings and save some tail feathers for decoration or as a centerpiece. Place the cut off side of feathers in salt water for 6 hours. Dry, wire or fasten wings and feathers in a nice fashion to a wooden block so this nice display can be reused.

Cut one **acorn squash** in half. Add **brown sugar** and **butter** and cook(with the pheasants) in the oven until done.

The cooking: Separate and bone out the legs. Grind all with the heart and clean liver. Mix with chopped **onions, celery, sage and savory**. **Salt and pepper** the cavity of the birds and fill with the 'stuffing'. Cover breasts with **bacon** and place, in a pan with **butter** added, in the oven at 375 degrees for 30 minutes. Add a little **chicken stock** and baste occasionally. Cook for the next 15 minutes at 330 degrees, or until done. Take out the pheasants and split them in half. Remove the back and breast bones and keep breasts in a warm place until serving. Add all the bones to the roasting pan and de glaze with a cup of **wine**, like Port or Manichevitz. Add **1-1/2 cups of chicken stock** and a pinch of **ginger**. Reduce the sauce and strain. Add half of a small can of sliced **apricots** with it's juice (save the other half for decor). Reduce, squeeze in some **lemon juice**, cook for 5 minutes and thicken slightly with starch.

The serving: Scoop out meat from the acorn squash, dress on a serving platter topped with the stuffing and breasts. Pour half the sauce over the meat. Serve the rest in a boat. Heat the remaining apricots and decorate the dish with a few slightly roasted **pinadas** and chopped **parsley**. Now use the colorful wings for decoration or as centerpieces.

TO ROAST SNIPES OR WOOD COCK (Becassines)
For a party, 3 - 4 birds for 2 or 6 - 8 for 4 people

Hang birds at least two days in a cool place with the innards, crop and windpipe removed as soon as possible. **Salt and pepper** the inside. Add **juniper berries**, sliced **apples,** a piece of **butter and sage**. Cover with a piece of **bacon** and a **grape leaf**. Fasten with toothpicks. Its customary to punch the beak through the left drum of the cleaned head with its eyes removed. The feet declawed and turned backwards.

In a roasting pan, roast the snipes with butter for a few minutes, then place in the oven for 18 to 20 minutes at 400 degrees, basting occasionally with **white wine**. The birds are to be served crisp, but not too dry inside. (Some people prefer a pinkish color around the bones.)

Francois Boeres, Chef de Cuisine

Deglaze the roasting pan with some **white wine and fresh butter** and pour over the birds that are served with triangle shaped liver canapés. Serve with new potatoes with dill weed and Boston lettuce.

How about a nice Riesling or Montrachet?

TO MAKE LIVER CANAPES

Add **chicken livers** to the **game livers** to make enough. Sauté clean livers in **butter or margarine**. Add **salt and pepper**, fine cut **shallots (or onions), sage and sherry wine**. Don't overcook. It should be almost pink inside. Cool off, grind and mix with fresh butter.

Quails can be served the same way. Quails are roasted at 400° for about 20 - 25 minutes.

BROILED QUAILS

A custom brought over by early German settlers was to dress and flatten the **fowl** on the kitchen table with a mallet. Some hit or rolled the bird flat with a rolling pin and broiled them in the fire place on a gridiron. Today we can do this on the grill. **Season and butter** well, beginning with the bony side down. Brush often. It should be served crisp and brown.

Wine: A California Barbera

ROASTING A WHOLE SADDLE OF DEER

Most deer I prepared were quite young animals. With all the eager "bucks" hunting deer today, old and tough meat is seldom found.

Again, I like to emphasize the importance of trimming and larding the deer saddle. In a big roasting pan, place saddle side up.

Prepare a dry mix of crushed **sage, chervil, rosemary, marjoram, chopped parsley, crushed peppercorns and salt**, preferably sea or kosher salt. Spread this mixture over the saddle. Lard and roast in a preheated 450 degree oven for 30 minutes. Add a few pieces of cut **celery and onion**. Reduce heat to 350° and, according to size, cook until done. It still should be rare or pink inside or until the thermometer registers 135 degrees. Dress saddle on a huge silver or stainless steel platter and keep warm. Cut the meat along the ridge bone loose before slicing.

Deglaze the pan and carefully strain the jus over the saddle. Serve with Cumberland or Bordelaise sauce.

Wine: A Traminer or a Chateau Neuf-du-Pape.

ANOTHER METHOD FOR SADDLE OF DEER

For the novice or old hand, best, use a thermometer and insert in the fleshiest part. Roast at 450° for 30 minutes, then reduce to 350°. Baste often with **beef bouillon** until thermometer is at 135. This is on the rare side. If medium is preferred, go to 150. Remember that a roast taken out of the oven still be cooking and should rest for 15 minutes. It would be a shame to overcook such a beautiful roast. The saddle is carved by loosening the loin along side of the spinal column and slicing diagonally from the spine with a sharp knife. Before slicing, any filet under the saddle is to be carved out, slice and place along side the roast.

To make the sauce, de glaze the roasting pan with two cups of **beef stock and one cup of light white wine**. Cook for 5 minutes. Add **2 TBS. of honey, 1/2 cup sour cream, 1 TBS. Dijon mustard**. Reduce and bind sauce with **starch**.

To enjoy time sitting with your guests, cut the whole loin in slices and reassemble the saddle (reheat quickly before serving).

Serve the sauce on the side. I recommend blanched **chestnuts**, browned in **butter** and swirled around in **caramel sugar**, half cut, broiled "parsley" tomatoes, whole fresh green beans "amondine", croquette or little roasted potatoes.

Serve with a heavy Bordeaux....Pommard or St'Julien

Note: This also can be made with a saddle of lamb without larding

Francois Boeres, Chef de Cuisine

CHAPTER 9 . . . .DEVILED FARE, SUCCULENT INNARDS PLUS INDIAN AND SAFFRON DISHES

Meet Some Deviled Fare

Ah, that Devil, that notorious unpredictable figure of all evil, damnation and vices, where is he going to strike next? Often, we say, "Go to the Devil," "To Hell with it," and all that. Now, how many people today believe in the Devil? But then, on the other side, the more things change, the more they stay the same. If no attention is given to this symbol of darkness, then we can not define or draw the line between good and bad.

Goethe's play *Faust*, he mentioned a stray dog had followed him right into his home. There the dog suddenly turned into a mean monster. Faust immediately recognized a demonic villain had followed him. Several attempts of banishment failed, so he asked the beast, "Are you the Devil himself?" Once the Devil was aware he had been identified, his spell and power were broken and he disappeared at once.

Another reason to mention Faust in this book is, it all started with a book, for that matter, the first book ever printed: *The Guttenberg Bible*. Guttenberg or Guttemberg also known as Gensfleich, printed his 42 line book between 1450 and 1452 with the help of his new partner, a goldsmith named Johan Faust also known as Fust. By 1455 the partnership had dissolved, but Faust understood the printing business and kept on printing books with help from his journeyman Peter Schoeffer, who later became his partner.

HIS-STORY of Good Cooking

It was here that Schoeffer invented a revolutionary process and method of casting metal letters mostly made out of lead and bismuth, using a matrix or mold. This replaced the cumbersome and painstaking engraving of wooden letters by movable type printing.

In 1452, Faust came to Paris to sell a few "manuscripts" of the bible for good money, but when he kept selling them in numbers, for less and less money, people became suspicious because it seemed incredible and astonishing that some one could "write" so many "manuscripts" in such a short time. Normally, they required months and years to write and execute. surely, he (Faust) must have a contract with the Devil himself. It was clear, so they believed, that the first letters, the *insipid* that started the text, embellished with fancy scrolls all in red, surely came from his blood. This started the saga and the rise of the Devil and Dr. Faust. The fascinating story had been employed in Gunod's Opera *Faust* and Liszt's *Faust Symphony*. Paganini was called "the Devil" with his violin and the violinist Tartini loved to play *The Devil's Sonata*.

> *THE ONLY THING NECESSARY FOR EVIL TO*
> *TRIUMPH IS FOR GOOD MEN TO DO NOTHING.*
> *Edmund Burke*

Note: Who really was that mysterious Dr. Faust? The history of Faust often is credited to George Sabellicus, known around 1507. It is said that the "real" Faustus died in 1540 and his legacy supposed to be carried on by the self acclaimed George and Johann "Faust". All these people were wicked charlatans and Devil wor' shippers. Many a book appeared after the TRAGIC HISTORY OF DR. FAUST....but the most acclaimed book of all was the first printed book itself....THE BIBLE.

Soon, scores of people started to write about Faustus and Dr. Faust.

The story of Faust (Fust) became more known and intriguing. Soon it was like most politicians - jumping on the band wagon if they see opportunities. All sorts of self-proclaimed Faust stories emerged.

Francois Boeres, Chef de Cuisine

DEVILED BEEF RIBS au diable
for 4 to 6

Fresh ribs often are sold "on the rack" to be cut into portions. Precook **ribs** in oven or on B.B.Q. grill on medium fire for 20 minutes, preferably on aluminum foil with a little **oil, salt and pepper,** till light brown.

Make a basting mixture of:
    1/2 cup spicy mustard
    2 tsp. dry mustard
    3 TBS. of molasses
    2 TBS. of vinegar
    1 tsp. ginger, 1 tsp. Tabasco,
    2 TBS Worcestershire sauce,
    pepper and salt.

Brush and baste beef ribs often with the sauce. Broil on the B.B.Q. grill or in the oven at 400° for 25 minutes or until done.

Wine: Rioga Santiago or Merlot
Music: Dardanus suite by Rameau.

CAFE DIABLO

Cafe Diablo is a great finale to any fine dinner. In a coffee pot, make 4 cups of strong premium **coffee**. If possible, choose a chafing dish....to heat on low fire:
    1/2 cup brandy
    1/2 cup rum
    3 TBS sugar
    1 stick cinnamon
    4 cloves

With a potato peeler, cut and add **peel from 1 orange and 1 lemon**. Stir the mixture occasionally until the sugar is dissolved. Light with a long match. While the alcohol is flaming, pour in the coffee and take out the cloves before serving. Preferably serve in a demitasse.

DEVILED CLAMS
for 4 appetizers, 6 clams per person

Open 24 medium size **clams**, remove clams and save the juice. Mince the clams and add the juice. In a pan, simmer clams with the juice for 1 minute and set aside.

In **butter**, sauté 1 small chopped **onion**, 1 minced half **green pepper, 1/4 stalk chopped celery**, till done, then add the clam mixture with 1/2 cup **cracker crumbs** and 1/2 cup homemade **bread crumbs**, mix in **2 beaten eggs**, fresh minced **parsley, thyme, a dash of cayenne and a dash of Tabasco, 1 TBS. Dijon mustard, salt and pepper** to taste.

Mix well and divide into 24 shells. Top slightly with melted **butter** and bake in a preheated 350 degree oven for approximately 15 minutes or until light golden.

Wine: a light Gamay or Granache Rose
Music: Norwegian dances or 'Peer Gynt', by Grieg.

DEVILED BASS
for 6

Cut 2 pounds of striped **bass** into 6 portions and place in a broiler pan.

Combine: **1/4 cup chili sauce, 1/4 cup melted butter, 2 finely sliced scallions, 1 TBS. spicy mustard, a pinch of cayenne powder, 1 TBS. crushed green peppercorns.**

Brush the sauce over the filets and broil in a 380° oven for 15 minutes or until flaky. Garnish with fresh **parsley, lemon wedges and Tabasco** on the side.

Wine: A Sauterne or a Clos de Vougeot

DEVILED CRAB
for 4 to 6 servings

Take 1 pound of **crabmeat** and pick out any tendons or pieces of soft shell.

Francois Boeres, Chef de Cuisine

Sauté: 1/2 cup of minced **onions, 1 stalk of minced celery, 1/2 minced green pepper and a finely chopped garlic clove**. Cool the mixture and add to the crabmeat with 1 cup of **heavy cream, 2 beaten eggs and 1 chopped hard boiled egg. 1 TBS. of vinegar, 1 tsp. of Worcestershire sauce, a pinch of thyme, salt and pepper, 2 TBS melted butter, Tabasco** sauce to taste.

Divide crabmeat into Quahog or scallop shells, top with **bread crumbs** mixed with **butter and chopped parsley**. Bake in 450 degree oven for 10 minutes or until done.

Wine: Sangria or Rose
Music: "A Potpourri" by Duke Ellington

GRILLED CHICKEN DIABLO
for 6

Split 3 - 2-1/2 pound **broilers** in half, separated at the back bone, breast attached. In plastic wrap or wax paper, pound them as flat as possible (using a clever or tenderizer). Tuck in the wings. Lay out chicken on aluminum foil with the edge crimped over, skin side up, **salt** added.

For the basting sauce, mix:
1 TBS. of **brown sugar** dissolved with 1 TBS. of **white vinegar**, 3 tsp. of **Dijon mustard, 1 tsp. of Tabasco, thyme, tarragon, pepper and 1/2 cup of melted butter**.

Brush and spread mixture over the chickens and top with homemade **bread crumbs** covered with more **butter**. Broil slowly on the grill on medium fire, cover closed, baste often, or in a 375 degree oven for 20 minutes, then cover with foil and broil for another 15 minutes or until done.

When chickens are almost ready, prepare the Sauce:
In a pan, sauté with 2 TBS. of **butter, 2 chopped shallots or a small onion** and add all the de-glazed pan juice to it with. 1/2 cup of **white wine**, 1 medium peeled and chopped **tomato**. Cook and reduce the sauce and add 1 jigger of **brandy**. Boil and strain trough a fine strainer, serve in a gravy boat. Cut chickens into servings and dress on a hot platter. Serve sauce on the side.

Garnish with broiled tomatoes and garlic (Provencale), artichoke bottoms and a good salad.

Wine: New York Gray Riesling or a Gamay
Music: Sonatas by Corelli or Chopin Polonaise.

DEVILED PUFF BALLS

First, prepare the "Cream" Puff Pastry (Pate a Choux).

In a casserole boil 1 cup of water with 1/2 cup of **butter**. On a low fire, add 1 cup of sifted **flour** by stirring vigorously with a wooden spoon until dough 'leaves' the side of the casserole and spoon to form a ball.

Remove from heat and mix in **4 eggs**, 1 at a time until incorporated firm and glossy.

With a teaspoon, form little balls, and place them in a sheet pan. Bake in a preheated 400 degree oven for 25 minutes or until puffed and golden.

To Make the Deviled Mixture:

Blend 2 cups of chopped **ham** with 1 TBS. of **horseradish, 1/2 cup sour cream, salt, pepper, 1 finely chopped celery stalk and a pinch of cayenne or Tabasco.**

Place stuffing in to a pastry bag with a #4 tip. Squeeze and fill (trough a small opening) in to the puff balls..

Wine: North Italian "Inferno" or a Pinot Noir.

BRAZIL QUIBEBE DIABLO
(served like a thick soup)

In a casserole, sauté 1 and 1/2 inch cut up **onion in 1/2 stick butter** until glazed. Add 1 peeled, chopped **tomato, 2 chopped red hot peppers, 1 minced garlic clove.**

Sauté for 5 minutes and add 2 pounds of 1/2 inch cut up **winter squash** (Calabazo preferred). Pour in 2 cups of **beef stock, add salt and pepper**, cover and simmer for about 20 minutes or until squash is soft and has thickened the soup. Season with **pepper**, a pinch of **sugar, a dash of cayenne.**

Francois Boeres, Chef de Cuisine

Can also be served with Parmesan cheese.

DEVILED DENVER CLUB SANDWICH

In a big pan ,brown on both sides; 8 slices of **Pullman or white bread** in **butter or margarine** until crisp and golden.

In another pan sauté 1 fine chopped **onion, 1/2 fine chopped green pepper, 1 cup of chopped ham**. Add 4 slightly beaten **eggs**, cook til done, but not overdone.

Divide on 4 toasts and cover with lettuce.

Add some **Tabasco** and some **Worcestershire sauce**. Place the other 4 toasts on top and cut each into two triangles. Secure each triangle with a toothpick.

Wine: Sauterne or Colorado Beer
Music: "Have you seen my Sweet Gypsy Rose?"

Serving Innards, Respectfully

In nature, predators first eat the innards of their prey. I have seen an owl eat first the head of a duck and leave the rest. Prairie buffalo hunters ate first the raw liver of buffaloes and deer hunters first feast on deer liver before even cutting up the deer. A respectable amount of innards could be found on menus from French restaurants mentioned here, besides Ducks' Bigarade or Montmerancy, beef bordelaise, filet mignon, béarnaise, coque au vin, escallop of veal and fish, they all served meticulously prepared innards like:

Cervelle au beurre noisette
Veal brains with brown butter

Foie de veau meuniere or English Style
Calf's liver sautéed in butter or served with bacon.

Rognon sauté Madera au champignon
Veal kidneys in Madeira wine and mushrooms

Lange de Boeuf in piquant or deviled sauce
Boiled beef tongue in sauce

Ris de veau au gratin (with mushroom puree)
Sweet breads, any style
Tete de veau vinaigrette or espangnole
Calf's head

Personally, I am not partial to hearts, or lungs. Speaking of lungs, Grandpa often cooked lung stew with prunes during the Great War. Now, I don't like this anymore. It is appalling what people throw away these days. In food processing plants, nothing is thrown away. The heart and cleaned gut-skins are used for sausages. Liver in liverwurst, pork and veal heads cleaned and used in scrapple.* Headcheese and tongues pickled or used in cold cuts or charcuteries. Lamb and pork kidneys served for breakfast or lunch. In comparison to other continents, America almost has acquired an ignorant prejudice against serving "innards". Although, served in fine restaurants, the almost dwindling ethnic communities have thinned them out from home. So, be adventurous and do yourself a favor to a higher order in cooking great meals and be "on guard" for pleasant surprises.

* A patty made out of cooked pork ,bacon fat, sage and cornmeal and other trimmings.

RECIPES FOR INNARDS

TRIPE A LA MODE

In the past directions for cleaning tripe were included in the recipes. Today, they come cleaned and pre-blanched. This is a very tasty dish not to be passed by.

For 2 pounds of tripe....Take 1 **calves foot** cut in half (or substitute 2 pork feet). Place in cold water and cook for 1/4 hour. Drain and cool. Cut **tripe** into 1/2 inch slices. Place all in a casserole and cover with water. Add 2 cut up **onions, 3 crushed garlic cloves, 2 carrots, sprigs of parsley, 2 bay leaves, 2 cloves, crushed pepper, thyme, marjoram, a pinch of cayenne, little salt** (because the sauce is going to be reduced). Cook slowly in a casserole, or in the oven, for 4 hours ,half way trough, add 2 glasses of

Francois Boeres, Chef de Cuisine

dry wine. Before serving, pick out the bones from the feet and discard the parsley sprigs. The sauce should be glutinous. Some prefer to add a little **tomato paste and apple brandy** (Calvados).

Wine: Chenin Blanc

VEAL SWEETBREADS
(Ris de veau)

Soak **sweetbreads** in cold water for 2 hours. Clean out all unwanted pieces and tubes. Blanch for 15 minutes in fresh water with **salt, 1 bay leaf, a few juniper berries** and some **white vinegar**. Drain, cool off and slice into scaloppine like portions (so they can be smartly dressed on the plate). Dip in **flour** and sauté light brown in **butter**. Adding **pepper, salt and thyme**. Quench with **white wine**. Add 2 cups of **béchamel sauce** (a white sauce prepared in advance). Add 1 tsp. of **Dijon mustard**. Cook for 15 minutes. Before serving, bind the sauce with 2 TBS. of **heavy cream**. Serve with half moon **pastry** (croissant type) or **buttered toasts and parsley**.

Sweetbreads can be sliced and added to 'salpicon', chicken fricassee or Bouchee a la reine.

The white wine and white sauce can be replaced by a brown sauce with red wine added (espagnole).

Wine: Frascati or Riesling-Sylvaner
Music: Dave Douglas: "Soul on Soul"

FRESH VEAL KIDNEYS
(Rognon de veau)

Veal kidneys can be ordered ahead from the butcher. They come enclosed in white suet. Cut the fresh **kidneys** in half, remove from the fat, clean out the white core and slice the kidneys into morsels. Sauté quickly (for over 1 minute) in a hot pan with a little **oil**. Pour kidneys into a strainer with a bowl and let them stand for 10 minutes (now, all impurities are squeezed out). Discard the drippings.

Next, sauté the morsels in **butter or margarine**. Add minced **onions, pepper and salt**. Cook on moderate heat for 4 minutes. Quench with

port or light sherry wine and a cup of **brown sauce** (made from beef bouillon). Reduce sauce for a few minutes. It can be thickened with **potato or cornstarch** (I prefer potato starch, it lasts longer). **Mushrooms** can be added. It is served with a border of duchess potatoes and buttered spinach leaves. It can also be flamed at the table.

Wine: Gamay Beaujolais or a Moulin a Vent

VEAL OR BEEF LIVER
(Foie de veau) I prefer veal

Best served the same day brought from the butcher. Clean **liver** by removing the thin skin and arteries, if any. Sprinkle with **pepper and salt**. Dip in **flour** and fry in **butter or margarine** till rare. Reduce heat, add more butter, sauté until little blood appears. Now, take out the liver, deglaze the pan with a little water and pour the juice over the liver. It should be soft and pink inside. Top with fresh **parsley, bacon or smothered onions** (prepared in advance). Serve with mashed potatoes. Remember, keep it 'medium' or it will be a dry proposition.

Wine: A dazzling Anjou

FRESH CALVES BRAIN
(Cervelle au beurre noisette)

Soak **calves brain** in cold water for 1 hour. Pluck off the membrane under fresh running water (this is easy). Blanch for 20 minutes in water with a little **vinegar, salt, bay leaf and chervil**, if available. Strain and serve with light brown **butter, white pepper, a few capers and parsley**. This is to be served with French bread or toast and Boston lettuce. Extremely gratifying! Now and then, I love brains fried in butter and onions on toast.

Wine: Monterey Riesling
Music: Dreams by Schuman

Francois Boeres, Chef de Cuisine

SMOKED BEEF TONGUE
(Average 2 - 3 lbs.)

Boil **tongue** for about 2-1/2 hours with **peppercorns, mustard corns, 2 bay leaves and a dash of vinegar**. After done, turn off the heat and let it rest for 15 minutes. Take out the tongue (discard water) and peel under running water. In big kitchens it was customary to cut off and discard the tips of both ends of the tongue. The slices should be cut diagonally (at an angle) so that they are bigger and can be smartly presented on the plate. I recommend a border of duchess potatoes (mashed potatoes with eggs and butter) that can be dressed with a pastry bag with a large star tip. The tongue usually is served with a sauce espagnole* or Madeira sauce. Garnish with fresh watercress or whole green beans. (Look for Madeira sauce)
This was served in the Cafe "Hindenburg" on 86th St.

Wine: A good California Sonoma or a Lambrusco
Music: "Lady be Good" by Charlie Porter

*A basic kitchen sauce made out of reduced meat stock, vegetables, spices, white wine and tomato paste.

The Other Kitchen

To a Westerner, India always had been a strange, mysterious, diverse and far away place of many cultures and faiths. A World by itself. If one is fortunate enough to visit there, the best thing is to take time. Here, to us, time is money, and for them, they have a lot of time and not too much money. Our standard of poverty is their way of life. India has about three times the population of the United States and of such a variety of food it can eclipse any kitchen I can think of.
Curry is generously used, however, it is only the tip of the iceberg.
Curry in India is on the sharper side and consists of a mixture with a good deal of coriander, followed by turmeric, cumin, black pepper, chili powder, fenugreek and cayenne.
Other spices are added to the curry powder, mostly used in sweets. Some are caraway, ginger, mace, cloves, cardamom and cinnamon. Most spices

HIS-STORY of Good Cooking

in Indian dishes are lively, aromatic and complementary. Not overpowering and severe to paralyze the palate. (Sambal Oelek is hot!)

As one suspects, most Hindus don't even think of eating beef and devoted Muslims shun pork and alcoholic beverages. Besides, most Indian people are vegetarians. There are religious doctrines that shy away from all kinds of meats or killing animals. Some people even brush clean the place they are going to sit, so not to disturb any crawling critters on the floor.

In America, we had the Hudson Bay Company. In India, it was the flourishing East India Company (The one that delivered the tea to Boston). The sun never went down on the British Empire and so Indian dishes in England are still very popular. An English woman of good standing would never be left in her kitchen without a good curry powder or Madras style chutney.

It all started with the East India Company that seized the moment of opportunity from this turmoil and unrest from a disorganized "coup". Most of the upheaval was supported by Mongol "Bahadur Shah II". Eventually, his dispersed and subdued forces surrendered and Bahadur exiled. The British celebrated a great victory and in the year of our Lord 1858 Britain presided over this great land of India under Queen Victoria and in 1877 officially became Empress of India. Many islands from the Indian Ocean to Indonesia through the China Sea changed hands from the Mongols, Portuguese, Hollanders, Englanders and French in Indo-China. This is where Uncle Victor comes in . . . the one who had been in the Foreign Legion.

Vic was a very interesting man and a real Maverick. As a boy, he often took me hiking or fishing and always treated me like a grown-up. You listened when he talked, because he had a lot to say. In the Legion, he was a real Daredevil. Wherever stationed, Vic went out to mingle with the natives and walked around where no other Legionnaire in his right mind would go. So, the natives took a liking to him because he was an open and sincere man. He told me, "If you visit a country, treat the people with respect and then you can learn a lot from them. You will be judged on how you treat others. In other words, we all are Diplomats, representing our Country!"

Victor frequently visited and took pictures of very old Temples overgrown with trees, hardly known to the world that time. When Victor passed away, he left behind him a five by six foot room full of Indian, Indonesian and Oriental spices. No one knew what to do with them.

Francois Boeres, Chef de Cuisine

Here is one of Vic's:

LAMB STUFFED TOMATOES

Cut off the top of the **tomatoes** and spoon out the seedy soft innards. Sprinkle a little **salt and pepper** inside, turn over and drain for 20 minutes. Sauté 2 medium chopped **onions in oil** until "glazed". Add 1 chopped **garlic clove**. Stir in 1-1/2 pounds of ground **lamb shoulder**, 1-1/2 tsp. grated **ginger root, 1 tsp. turmeric**, 1 small, finely chopped **chili pepper**. Sauté and stir for a few minutes. Add 1 cup of hot water. Boil and stir occasionally for 20 minutes. Cool mixture and add 3 tsp. of fresh **coriander**, 2 tsp. **lemon juice**, 1-1/2 tsp. **"Goram Masala"** and **salt** to taste. Divide mixture into the tomatoes and bake them in a preheated 375 degree oven for 20 minutes or until done.

Serve with

PARSI WHITE CHEESE

In a pot bring 6 cups of good **cream milk** to a boil. Add 1/3 cup **lemon juice** and boil, stirring for a few minutes. Remove from heat and let the mixture cool.

Aunt Suzette Hipp never married; instead she went to London and studied Podiatry in Dr. Scholl's Institute. To pay for this, she worked as a housekeeper in a prestigious household. There she learned how to prepare English and Indian dishes. In a few years she owned a high-rise apartment in London. Not included was the land where the building stood—that was Royal property. Later, she opened a practice in Luxembourg where she joined the Bah'ai Faith and met a lot of wonderful friends from all over the world: from England, Canada, Australia and India. Her "savvy" of international cuisine was equally admirable.

Here is one of her recipes for:

MANGO AND DATE RELISH

Clean and cut up 5 fresh **mangoes**. Add a little **salt**. Place them in a cheesecloth and tie them into a bag. Hang up the bag and drain for 1 hour. Boil and dissolve 1-1/2 cups **sugar with 1 cup of cider vinegar**. Add 3 TBS. of **chili powder**, 1 finely chopped fresh **ginger root** and 1 finely chopped **garlic clove**. Cook and stir the mixture on moderate
heat for about 10 minutes. Add the mango mixture to 2 cups chopped (not too dry) **dates** and 1-1/2 cups of quickly blanched **raisins**. Cook slowly for about 15 minutes, stirring often. Sterilize in a jar or refrigerate.

Another recipe to make:

RED ONION RELISH

Heat 1/2 cup **coconut or peanut oil** and sauté a big fine chopped **red onion**, 4 fine chopped **garlic cloves**, 1 tsp. fresh minced **ginger root** and cook until glazed. Add **4 cloves, 4 curry leaves, 3 bay leaves 1 tsp. salt, 1 TBS. cinnamon, 1 tsp. cayenne, 1/2 tsp. cardamom and stir in 1/2 cup coconut milk**. Cook over moderate heat for 15 minutes. Stir occasionally. At the end mix in 1/2 cup **lime juice** and 1 TBS. of **sugar**. Keep in a cool place.

—

It is said that Truffles are the black diamonds of the Kitchen and that Saffron is the gold and the most expensive of all seasoning. Saffron is often sold in drams. It takes more than 130,000 Crocus blossoms to make a pound of Saffron.

At the time of harvest, all the family members are engaged in collecting the crocus flowers and plucking out the orange colored stamen (3 per crocus) to be used in cooking, baking, medicine and for dye. That gives the beautiful golden yellow color to the garments worn by Buddhist monks. Saffron in food should be used with great respect and reverence as so little is needed.

Francois Boeres, Chef de Cuisine

In some parts of the world, a Pilaf, Paella or even a Bouillabaisse without saffron is unthinkable.

Here is Suzette's recipe for

BOMBAY SAFFRON RICE
Serves 4.

Rinse a cup of **long grain rice**. Sauté 1 medium chopped **onion** in **clarified butter**. Add 2 **bay leaves**, 1 tsp. fresh, finely chopped **ginger root**. Stir into the rice. Add a little **salt**, 2-1/2 cups of **coconut milk (or canned evaporated milk)**, a pinch of **cardamom**, a pinch of **cloves** and 1/2 tsp. of **saffron**. Cover and slowly simmer for about 30 minutes or until tender and done. Let it rest awhile, loosen the rice with a fork and garnish with chopped **pistachios** and **parsley**.

SUZETTE'S PLUM PUDDING

Now, how did this plum pudding get into Indian dishes? Well, the Indian people were just as fond of some English dishes as we are of theirs and if you visit India today, there you will find a lot of English tradition.

In a large bowl, beat 3 **eggs** with 1 cup of **sugar** until they are white and smooth. Add 2 cups of sifted **flour**, 1 at a time. Add 2 cups of blanched **raisins**, 6 oz. of **white beef suet**, chopped fine, 1/2 cup of chopped **pecans or walnuts**, a whole **lemon** without the seeds, ground up. 1/2 tsp. of **cinnamon**, a dash of ground **cloves**, a dash of **nutmeg** and some **salt**. Mix all together and place in the refrigerator overnight.

The next day dip a piece of muslin or cheesecloth in flour, enough to wrap the dough in completely, then, tip over and place on a rack that fits in a big pot. Add 3/4 cup of water, cover and simmer for about 4 hours, add water if needed.* Take out the pudding and cool overnight in the refrigerator. The following day steam the pudding on a rack placed in a pot with a little water for one more hour. Take out the pudding, remove the cheesecloth and place on a warm serving tray. Pour 1/2 cup of hot **brandy** over the pudding and ignite. Serve with brandy sauce on the side.

*Occasionally, some water might be added.

BRANDY SAUCE

1-1/2 cups of soft **butter** beaten creamy, add 2 cups of **confectioners sugar** one at a time. Beat vigorously and mix with 2 jiggers of **brandy**. Serve cold and pour over the pudding.

As one can see, prepare ahead. I miss our "Suss" and her great cooking.

SUZETTE'S BOMBAY CHUTNEY

Mix 1 quart of small cubed **mangoes and kumquats**, 1/2 cup **sugar**, 1 cup **brown sugar** and **1/2 cup cider vinegar 1 tsp. chili powder, 1 tsp. cumin, 1 tsp. mustard seeds, 2 tsp. shredded fresh ginger root, 1 medium chopped onion, 1 fine chopped garlic clove, 1-1/2 cup peeled and diced tart apples, 1 cup of blanched raisins, grated rind from 1 lemon and it's juice**. In a heavy pot, cook the mangoes and kumquats slowly. Stir in all the rest and keep on stirring until all is thickened and well blended. Sterilize in jars while still hot and keep some in the refrigerator for immediate use. This chutney is served with many dishes.

ROGEN DSCHAUSCH (CURRIED LAMB)

Prepare 1/2 cup **drawn butter (Ghee)**[5], 6 small chopped **onions**, 2 lbs. of cubed **lamb (neck or shoulder)**, 3 ripe cut up **tomatoes**, 3/4 cup of **yogurt**.
To make the Curry powder mix **1 TBS. of coriander, 1 TBS. cardamom, 1 TBS. ground ginger, 1 tsp. ground caraway, 1 tsp. red chili powder and some salt**.
With a wooden spatula, stir chopped **onions** in a pan with butter until golden. Add all the meat and stir continuously. Add all the spices (curry), yogurt and tomatoes. The most important thing is to keep stirring so the meat doesn't stick or brown. If too dry, add more water, but keep stirring

---
5. Ghee: A reduced, clarified butter.

Francois Boeres, Chef de Cuisine

until the meat is done. The last 5 minutes, cook on slow fire until sauce sticks to the meat. Best...stir constantly so the meat doesn't burn or get messed up. This is one of the finer Indian dishes.

Serve with rice without salt.

Recipe from Uncle Victor

INDONESIAN NOUHGEN NIAM
(Roast Chicken or Cornish Hen)

Clean **chicken** throughout, dry and rub in and outside with a crushed **ginger root**. Sprinkle with **salt, paprika** and roast in **butter** till golden. Take out chicken and keep warm. Pan fry on moderate heat; fine chopped **livers, stomach and heart** in **chicken fat** and butter, adding 1 clove of ground **garlic** and 2 peeled and cubed ripe **tomatoes**. Stir and cook until meat and tomatoes are done, add some red **paprika** and **cream** and cook all together into a smooth sauce.

Pour sauce over the chicken and sprinkle with **Gruyere cheese** (the original calls for some kind of Buffalo cheese) and broil in oven till done. Serve with "sea tang" noodles or rice.

Recipe from Uncle Victor

Wine: A fine Macon or a Ruedesheimer.

INDIAN CURRIED EGGS
(ANDA KABAB)

Needed are **6 eggs, 1 tsp. green or conventional Ginger, 1 tsp. coriander, 1 chopped medium onion, 1 TBS. of ground yellow Kurkuma root, 1/2 TBS. cardamom, black pepper and salt, 1/2 cup of ground almonds and a trace of cayenne.**

Carefully, with a pointed knife, puncture a small hole on top of a fresh egg. With a bent skewer or a small 'forked' split wooden stick, twirl the egg's contents inside and empty the egg. Beat the egg mass and strain. Mix well with very fine chopped onion and all the spices above.

Fill egg shells with a small funnel or one made out of aluminum foil. Close the cap with a hard dough mixture of flour and water and enclose all openings with aluminum foil.

Boil for 15 minutes, cool off and peel.

Puncture eggs carefully all around with a fork and rub in the Kurkuma or Cardamom. Roast eggs in the oven for 15 minutes and keep warm.

To make the sauce:

Incorporate **melted butter, yogurt, ground Kurkuma (or cardamom), pepper and ground almonds.** Add some **cayenne** to the sauce and pour over the hot eggs.

Recipe from Uncle Victor

How to Make. "GORAM MASALA"
(Indian Mixed Spice)

This is mostly applied to chicken and lamb. Use spice ginger available in special stores.

1 TBS. of spice Ginger
1 TBS. of pulverized cardamom seed
Cinnamon stick crushed into small pieces
1 tsp. of cumin seed
1 tsp. of ground pepper and
1 big pinch of nutmeg.

Store in a small 'marked' pillbox.

CURRIED CHICKEN OR CORNISH HEN "BOMBAY"

Use a 1 pound **chicken or a Cornish hen**. Rinse and clean chicken, dry and cut into 4 pieces, **salt, pepper** and fry golden brown. Then add chopped **onions** and stir for 2 minutes. Add 1-1/2 cups **chicken broth** and simmer for 30 minutes. Add peeled, cut up **apples and curry powder**. Cook 10 more minutes on medium fire. Take out chicken, debone as much as possible and keep in a warm spot. Make a **béchamel (white sauce)**, add **honey, pepper and salt.** Place chicken in sauce, heat up and add **cream,**

Francois Boeres, Chef de Cuisine

blanched raisins and sliced roasted **almonds**. Cook all together with the chicken and garnish with **fried bananas**.

BEEF CURRY

Cut 2 lbs. of **beef chuck** into cubes. Prick cubes with a fork and sprinkle with **lime juice**. Marinate for 1 hours. Add 1 cup of **yogurt**.

In a frying pan, heat **coconut or peanut oil** to sauté 1 medium chopped **onion** till glazed.

Add: 6 curry leaves, 4 bay leaves,
    2 cinnamon sticks, 2 crushed garlic cloves,
    3 TBS dry mustard, 2 tsp. coriander,
    2 TBS. minced fresh ginger root
    2 tsp. ground cumin, 1/2 tsp. turmeric

Saute beef in the mixture until light brown, about 3 minutes. Add the yogurt and the juice from the marinade, 1 cup of **coconut milk** and simmer for 1 hour. Salt to taste. Remove cinnamon and serve in a heated dish.

Wine: A Merlot or a Semillion
Music: Global Fusion by Sub'ramaniam

INDIAN NASI GORENG

This can be made with **chicken livers**, cubed **chicken or pork** and deveined **shrimp**.

Needed are: **Ketchup Benteng and sesate bamboee**.

Ketchup Benteng can be replaced with a homemade concoction that consists of: sauteed dark brown onions with sugar and a dash of vinegar, chopped kumquats, raisins and little chili powder.

Sauté meats golden brown in **vegetable oil**, add **chopped onions**, 1-1/2 cup **long grain rice, curry powder** and a pinch of **chili powder**. Add the "sesate bamboee' and the homemade or bottled ketchup Benteng. Stir often and pour in 2-1/2 cups **light chicken broth**, cover, place in the oven or on a slow fire until done (35 to 40 minutes). Just before serving add all the shrimps.

Garnish with **fried bananas**, cut lengthwise, little fried **zucchini** and top with small pieces of 'shirred' **egg**.

Option: Saffron, crisp fried Agar-Agar gelatin, or ketchup Benteng served on the side.

Recipe from Uncle Victor

Wine: Sylvaner or a Pinot Blanc
Music: Sounds of India by Ravi Sharavis

PACHADI OR YOGURT SALAD
4 to 6 servings

This salad is a real 'humdinger' on hot days, it can be eaten with a spoon.

Mix together: 1 pint **yogurt**, 1 peeled diced ripe **tomato**, 1 minced small **white onion**, 1 tsp. minced hot **chili pepper**, 2 TBS. chopped **celery greens or cilantro**, trace of **coriander** and 1/2 tsp. **cumin seed**, 1 tsp. **mustard seed** and some **salt**.

Prepare and cool in the refrigerator.

GAJAR HALVA (CARROT DESSERT)
4 to 6 servings

Delightful and different. . . . In India, they use cream or milk from the Brahma cows.

In a deep bowl add 1 - 14 oz. thick **sweet condensed milk** with the same amount of water, boil and add 2 cups of fine **grated carrots** and cook on low fire for about 45 minutes, stirring occasionally. Add 1 cup of good **oil or butter** at a time until fat separates, then add: 2 TBS. Blanched **raisins**, 2 TBS. blanched **almonds**, 1/4 tsp. **saffron**, 1 TBS. fresh **lime juice**.

Let stand for 1 hour. . . . serve hot or cold.

Francois Boeres, Chef de Cuisine

LAMB STEW "MADRAS"

Cut 1-1/2 lbs. **lamb shoulder or neck** into cubes. In a glass bowl, mix meat with 1 cup of **vegetable oil**. Add 2 **garlic cloves** crushed in **salt**, 2 **onions**, cut into small cubes.

Marinate meat in this for 20 minutes.

In a big pot, sauté the meat with the marinade, stirring often. Add: the grated rind of a **lemon**, 3 TBS. **curry**, a dash of **cinnamon**, chopped **parsley**.

Stir the meat for 10 minutes and cover the meat with water. Cook for 1 hour or until done.

Then add: 2 tsp. spicy **Chinese mustard, salt, pepper** and 2 tsp. **grated coconut**.

Serve with short grain rice and Mango Chutney.

Beef can also be used to make **BEEF MADRAS**.

STUFFED INDIAN SQUASH

Take any **squash**, I prefer acorn, cut squash in half, clean out the pulp and scoop out most of the center, leaving 1/2 inch thick wall.

Chop fine and add 1 minced **onion** and a pinch of **saffron.** Sauté in 1 cup of **butter** for 5 minutes. Add: 1/4 cup **yogurt** and simmer for 10 minutes. Add 1 cup **heavy cream**, a pinch of **cardamom** and 1/2 cup of blanched and ground **almonds**, 2 tsp. **lemon juice and salt**. Simmer for 5 minutes and place mixture into the shells.

Top with **melted butter, coriander seeds and fresh ground pepper**. Bake in preheated 350 degree oven for 20 minutes.

Here are some of the best SAFFRON DISHES:

PAELLA
3 to 4 portions

Needed are 2 dozen **clams**, 1 lb. of medium **shrimp**, cleaned and a fryer **chicken**, washed, breast bones removed and cut into 12 pieces.

Prepare: 1 cut up **onion**, 2 crushed **garlic cloves**, 1 fresh cubed **pimento**, 1 tsp. **saffron**, a pinch of **cayenne**, 1-1/2 cups **short grained rice** (rinsed),

3 cups **light chicken stock** (can be made from bouillon), **salt, pepper and 2 scallions**.

In a heavy "Creuset" type pot sauté chicken pieces in 1/4 cup preferred **oil** until golden. Add onions, garlic and the fresh pimento until glazed. Mix in the rice, the saffron, salt, pepper and the chopped white ends of the scallions. Stir and pour in the chicken stock. Cover and cook on slow fire for 25 minutes or til done. Last add all the shrimp and clams, cover tightly and cook for 4 minutes or until about done. Shrimp and clams should be soft inside!

Serve in a big bowl, family style (we bought ours from an Italian food store). Top Paella with the left over sliced green scallions and some blanched **green peas**. Arrange the clams around the border.

Optional: Cut up cooked ham, scallops, Tabasco and lemon wedges.

Wine: Soave or Rosé or Verdicchio
Music: Chopin...Impromptus and Valses.

—

The Mediterranean BOUILLABAISSE is known as a feisty meal, greatly appreciated by fish lovers everywhere. It can be proudly served at any special occasion. The unsold and not so popular fish, so the story, at last found a market in local restaurants that use them in the Bouillabaisse. (The name means "boil-low"). They come in many versions. Some Mediterranean species of fish like the "Rascasse" can hardly be found in the States, but here we can use sea bass, grouper, hake, halibut, red snapper. Even mackerel, once used as bait fish, also found it's place in this recipe. (I use only three different fish). The choice of clams here in New England, is limited to little round neck or the long necked soft shell clam with its trunk. Chef Hector called these "piss" clams, but they are really good. The Maine lobster, known as "Homard", and the spiny rock-lobsters are used in Bouillabaisse. These are known in the United States as lobster tails. In Europe, this kind of claw-less lobster is sold whole and alive and known as "Langouste", occasionally used in Bouillabaisse. The real connoisseur eats everything in a lobster that can be eaten by chewing and squeezing out any meats found in the legs or the cavities.

Francois Boeres, Chef de Cuisine

COOKING A BOUILLABAISSE
for 6

Fetch 3 - 1 lb. **"Maine" lobsters**, if they are served in halves, or 6 under 1 lb. lobsters (called chicks) or 6 - 6 oz. lobster tails, 3 lbs. of assorted **fish**, 2 dozen **clams**, 2 dozen **mussels**, etc.

Needed for the sauce are: 1/2 cup preferred **oil**, 3 crushed **garlic cloves**, 3 fresh **tomatoes**, cubed, 1/2 tsp. **thyme**, a few **fennel kernels**, 1 cut **leek**, 1 big **onion**, chopped, 1 tsp. **grated lemon peels**, 1/2 tsp. **saffron**, **1 bay leaf, chopped parsley or cilantro, salt and pepper** to taste.

Cook onions and leek in oil for a few minutes. Add the crushed garlic and stir in the tomato cubes. Use slightly over 2 qts. of water and all the herbs and seasonings. Cook for 20 minutes and set aside.

Before dinnertime, bring this all to a boil and add the lobsters and cut up fish portions, so all guests can have at least 1 piece of each. Boil for 10 minutes. Now add all the rest: clams, shrimp, mussels, etc. and boil for another 4 to 5 minutes or until done. Do not overcook!

To serve, carefully take out all the fish. Dress them smartly in a deep platter or big bowl. Strain the sauce (soup) and serve in a soup bowl. Each guest can help himself, filling his soup bowl with the seafood.

Serve with French bread or water rolls. To make it right, use a "bib", a finger bowl and a pot (pubelle) for the scraps.

Wine: A nice Mersault, Pouilly Fume or a California Sauvignon Blanc
Music: *Dreams* by Schuman or *LaMer* by Maurice Chevalier

RISOTTO MILANESE
(with Saffron)

With a wooden spoon, crush 1/2 tsp. of **saffron** in a glass and add one cup hot **chicken stock** and let rest for 1 hour.

In a pot, sauté a small chopped **onion in oil** or olive oil until glazed. Stir in 3/4 cup **Italian short grain rice**, add some oil and 2/3 cup **dry white wine**. Boil till liquid is absorbed. Stir and add 3/4 light chicken bouillon and the stock with the saffron. After 35 minutes on a very slow fire, remove and let rest for 10 minutes. Loosen the rice with a fork, add **Parmesan cheese** and some **butter**.

Note: If small pieces of tender meats are added with the onions before cooking, this will turn into a really nice main dish.

It is remarkable what people can do to support the cult of gastronomy. Nothing is spared in the hustle and bustle of hours chopping, manipulating and preparing delectable creations out of kitchens often bigger than dining rooms. Then looking forward with great anticipation to treat guests and friends to an enjoyable meal. The efforts are immeasurable and the memories cast in time. On an unforgettable West Coast vacation, we had a great Cioppino in a fine restaurant. Cooking this at home takes about 2 hours to prepare. It's not a soup, but more a fish stew, very complimentary to any table, and a kin to the Bouillabaisse. While one is devouring this, smacking and grunting is permitted.

So here it is:

THE REAL CIOPPINO
for 4 to 6 people

Get 1/2 lb. of **scallops**, 1/2 lb. of **shrimp** (cleaned), 4 Dungeness or Alaskan cracked **crab legs**, 24 **clams** and 1 lb. cut up **snapper filets**.

In a pan with 1/3 cup **olive oil**, sauté 6 chopped up **scallions**, 1 chopped **green pepper**, the white part of 2 cut up **leeks** and 2 chopped **garlic cloves**. Add 1/2 tsp. **saffron**, 1 chopped **onion** and cook for 5 minutes. Then add 2 **bay leaves, rosemary, thyme, salt, pepper and 1 lb. "Pomo doro" canned tomatoes, 1 lb. canned tomato sauce and 1 small can of tomato paste**. Mix with 2 cups **red wine**. Bring to a boil and simmer for 1-1/2 hours.

In a large pot or deep casserole, lay out all the fish. Pour over the sauce, cover and cook slowly for 8 minutes or until just done. Dress and serve in a big bowl placed in the center of the table.

Serve French bread on the side.

Wine: A Grave or Chambertin
Music: A Madrigal or Andaluz Concerto by Rodrigo

Francois Boeres, Chef de Cuisine

ITALIAN CACCIUCCO (fish stew)
for 6 - 8 people

A real cacciucco should include **'larger' pasta shells**. Boil them soft, drain, add some oil, cool and set aside.

To make the stuffing for the shells:
Take 1 cup of cleaned **crabmeat**, mix in 1 beaten **egg**, chopped **parsley, 1 chopped scallion, 1 TBS. of white bread crumbs, pepper, a trace of salt, a trace of cayenne and a little lemon juice**. Steam stuffed Shells in a Chinese Steamer or in a pot with little water, and a plate sett at the bottom, cover and steam for 10 minutes.

To make the stew:
Sauté in 1/2 cup of **olive oil**: 1 chopped **onion**, 1 clove chopped **garlic**, until glazed. Add **basil, 1/2 tsp. crushed red pepper, 3/4 cup dry wine, 1 2 lb. can of crushed tomatoes, 2 TBS. tomato paste**, 1 - 8 oz. bottle or can of **clam juice, salt pepper, 1 TBS. grated lemon rind, trace of saffron**. Simmer all for about 25 minutes.

Then add, 1 lb. thick slices of **cod**, 1 lb. cut up **halibut**, 1 lb. cut up **haddock**, 1/2 lb. **deep sea scallops**, cut in half if too big, 1/2 lb. medium size **shrimp**. Cook fish in sauce for about 8 to 10 minutes or until done. Scallops and Shrimps should be cooked last.

Take out all the fish and dress on a warm flat bowl and keep in a warm place.

Cook sauce for a few minutes and pour over the fish and place previously prepared stuffed pasta shells around and garnish with parsley. Serve with French or Italian bread.

Wine: Lambrusco or Valpolicella
Music: Sonatas by Scarlatti

Economics and Unexpected Guests

So, I thought, Oh, I know it all, and then some judge in a culinary concourse took many points away because I had thrown too much 'trimmings' away. Yes! They had checked out the garbage can. So, it's not how much you have, it's what you can do very well with so little and that's what counts. I have seen important people spending great amounts of money for late planned parties, just to be on the safe side, while others had great success with trifles.

Mom's pantry always had a supply of tuna, asparagus, whole green beans, pimentos, olives, artichokes, anchovies, capers, and good sardines (popular at that time). The coolest place was under the cellar stairs where we had a few shelves enclosed with fine screen wire. There we usually kept Gruyere cheese wrapped in a moist towel, smoked ham and sausages, eggs, cream and occasionally some pies.

Since then, times have changed and so have the trends in food. Whatever, your guests will be pleasantly surprised when you serve them great bits and morsels like Swiss Fondue or Crab Louis, once so popular. Now, if you feel kind of short changed serving unexpected guests, don't despair. Here are a few things Mom did and we can do in a jiffy.

Often we serve:

QUICK MADE PIZZA
(kids love them)

Preheat oven to 420 degrees.
Take 6 **English muffins**. Split them so there will be 12 portions. Toast them and sprinkle them with **oil**. Dust with a little **garlic salt, oregano and basil**. Spread the contents of an 8 ounce can of **tomato sauce** over the muffins. Top with either **Mozzarella or Provolone cheese**. Sprinkle with a little **oil** and **Parmesan cheese**. Bake for about 15 minutes or until done.

Francois Boeres, Chef de Cuisine

ENCHILADAS

...are Tortillas stuffed with all kinds of foods, like chopped or ground chicken, seafood, beef, pork or chorizo. (In Spain they serve you an omelet if you ask for a tortilla). Tacos are a sort of stuffed fried Tortilla. Enchiladas are also 'cemented' together with cheese, but just as messy, leaving fragments of food on your face and sticky Mexican 'debris' on your hands.

"Hey Sam!... How do you like my Tortilla", I asked my Grandson. I got no reply, he was too preoccupied ripping his teeth into the Enchilada, like an alligator trying to get into the meat of his prey....Aaah, what a delicious mess!

FRANCESCO'S ENCHILADA
for 8 Tortillas and some...

To prevent the tortillas from drying out too much, keep them wrapped up good. The best **tortillas** come fresh in a package.

Start with 1-1/2 to 2 lbs. of **#85 ground beef**, 12 oz. of preferred **salsa**, medium, hot or mild, 1/2 lb. of **cheddar cheese**, 1 medium chopped **green pepper**, 1 medium chopped **onion, butter and oil, garlic salt, oregano, Tabasco**, 1/2 head of shredded **Iceberg lettuce**.

Sauté onions and peppers in half butter and half oil until half done and still crisp inside. Remove from pan and set aside. In a big pan on a hot fire, with half butter and half oil, fry on high: broken up chunks of ground beef. With a wooden spoon, stir until all meat is fried into loose brown tiny morsels (like making Chili Con Carne), now it's time to add the salsa. Taste with garlic salt, oregano and Tabasco or hot sauce. Reheat for a minute and remove from the fire, then add all the onions and green peppers. To make the tortillas 'pliable', turn them quickly, for a few moments, in a hot pan with a little oil added. Also quickly mix the beef mixture with the cheddar and stuff in the tortillas, top with shredded lettuce.

STUFFED CELERY

Use only tender and nice looking **celery stalks** and cut into 4 to 5 inch pieces

Mix: 4 oz. of **cream cheese**, 1/2 cup **sour cream**, 1/2 cup **soft butter**, 1/2 cup chopped **pimentos, 1 tsp. dry mustard, 1/2 tsp. onion powder, white pepper and salt.**

Blend well and stuff celery with a pastry bag, using a star-tip.

Preparing Quick Finger Food
(Also known as sticky, messy, "Nosh's)

MAKING A B.L.T.

Ever tried to eat a bacon, lettuce and tomato toasted sandwich.....without the mayonnaise? The first bite will dribble lettuce on your table, littering the floor, tomatoes trying to creep up into your nose and the bacon will be in your hands...not in the sandwich. So, now you've found out that the most important building material for the sandwich is the 'cement'....the mayonnaise. Well, it will still be messy with the mayonnaise, unless it's cut into 4 triangles and fastened with tooth picks.

QUICK "BUFFALO" WINGS

Ever seen a guy bending over a plate devouring hot chicken wings like doing important precision work until all meats are gnawed away to the bare bones, now the fingers look like saucy wings worth licking.

Chicken wings are not expensive, they can be deep fried in very hot fat until they float. Fry no more than a dozen at a time. Take them out of the fat and rinse them in a **'Hot Sauce'** mixed with **oil** and melted **margarine**.

Serve with raw vegetables and dressings.

GREEK MUSHROOMS

Blanch small or medium size fresh **mushrooms** for 1 minute adding a little **lemon juice**. Cool off and mix with **salt, pepper, vinegar, a dash of lemon juice, olive oil, thyme**. Place in the refrigerator for a few hours. Black olives can be added.

Francois Boeres, Chef de Cuisine

FRESH MUSHROOM CAPS

Stuff **caps** with a mixture of sauté d chopped up **stems, onions and crabmeat.** Top with **melted butter, Parmesan** and broil in 350° oven until done (15 minutes).

CARROT SALAD

Use firm and crisp **carrots,** peel and shred through medium size holes so they don't lose too much juice. Mix with 1/2 **sour cream** and 1/2 **mayonnaise.** Add a few 'puffed' **raisins, salt** and mix well. The salad should be firm and not 'runny'.

MACARONI SALAD

Cook **macaroni** soft and cool under cold running water. Drain for 1/2 hour and cool off in the refrigerator. Mix with **mayonnaise**, a dash of common **mustard**, a little **lemon juice**, some chopped **onions**, blanched, chopped **celery, pimentos, green peppers, salt, pepper.** Mix well and place into a bowl on top of **leaves of lettuce.**

FRIEDE'S CUCUMBER SALAD

This is my wife Friederun's favorite salad.
Peel firm and medium size **cucumbers** and shred through the biggest shredding holes. Add a little **salt** and drain for 15 minutes. Add some **vinegar, preferred oil, finely chopped onions, parsley, dill weed and a pinch of sugar.** Mix with a little **sour cream**.

SERVE OLD BREAD AS CROUTONS

Cut **older bread** into cubes. Sauté in **butter or margarine, garlic, salt, onion powder, trace of paprika, rubbed sage and oregano.** Serve in a bowl lined with a napkin.

POTATO SALAD

Boil **potatoes** in the jacket until done. Peel while still warm. Cut into slices, add a good amount of **vinegar** (potatoes are very absorbent). Mix with **pepper, little salt, fresh chopped parsley, some mild mustard and plenty of mayonnaise.**

Optional: chopped eggs, green peppers and celery.

GERMAN POTATO SALAD

As above, except replace mayonnaise with **oil, vinegar** and top with crisp rendered small pieces of **bacon**.

Also serve hot rigatoni stuffed with ricotta, cream and Parmesan.

Broiled cut up fresh sausages (or breakfast sausage) with mustard and sour cream.

Or link-sausages wrapped and baked in a phyllo-dough blanket.

SWEDISH MEATBALLS

use; Hamburger or chopped beef, roll in little balls and fry light brown in a pan, mix with sour cream, add a small amount of mustard and a few tarragon leaves.

WELSH RAREBIT
for 2 to 4 servings

Cut 1 lb. of medium **cheddar** into cubes, place into a chafing dish with 2 tsp. of **butter, 1/2 cup of ale, pinch of cayenne and some English mustard**. Cook slowly until cheese is melted into a creamy texture. Keep stirring and serve with toasts or large croutons.

This can be served with a Mersault or Chardonay.

Francois Boeres, Chef de Cuisine

#2 GUACAMOLE SALAD

Remove and 'mash' meats from 3 ripe **Avocados**. Blanch 1 small chopped up **onion** in **white vinegar**. Cool and add to the avocados 2 cloves of minced **garlic, 1/2 tsp. cayenne, pepper, salt, a dash of good oil and 7 oz. of Ortega green peppers**. Place the mixture of 'Guacamole' on a bed of **Boston or Romaine lettuce**. Sprinkle with sharp shredded **cheddar cheese**.

STUFFED TOMATOES

Cut off the tops of medium size round **tomatoes**. Spoon out the meat and dice into small pieces. Drain and mix with imitation **crabmeat (or popcorn shrimp)**, finely chopped **celery, salt, pepper, rosemary and pinch of tarragon and mix with mayonnaise**. Stuff tomato shells and top with the lid. Dot with a few tiny tips of mayonnaise so to give it that 'mushroom' look.

Optional: capers and parsley.

CRAB LOUIS SALAD

Use real **crab meat or imitation**. Dress crabmeat on top of a platter laid out with **lettuce leaves** with the edges dipped in **red paprika** and topped with **shredded lettuce**. Cover with **Thousand Island dressing** and garnish with **Belgian endive leaves, black ripe olives, eggs and tomato wedges**.

Optional: Artichokes.

THOUSAND ISLAND DRESSING
for 2

1/2 cup **mayonnaise**, 2 tsp. **chili sauce**, 1 tsp. chopped **pimentos, green olives, 1 tsp. chopped onion, 1 chopped hard boiled egg, dash of paprika, pepper and salt**. Mix well.

Wine: Cold Rose, blush or a chilled Sauterne
Music: Frank Zappa, Eric Clapton or Frank Sinatra.

1 GUACAMOLE SALAD
for 6 portions

Peel, chop and mash up 2 ripe **avocados** to a pulp. Add 2 peeled, seeded and chopped up ripe **tomatoes**. Puree the mixture and add: 1/2 minced **onion** cooked in a little **wine vinegar**. Cool off then add: 1/2 tsp. fresh minced **coriander or coriander powder, 1 tsp. of chili powder, 1/4 tsp. of minced garlic, salt and pepper, 1 TBS. of good oil**

Combine all and chill. Dress on **lettuce with olives and tomato wedges**.

MEDITERRANEAN "SALAD NICOISE"

Arrange **Boston lettuce** on a large, shallow platter or bowl...stems toward the center. In the center, place a selected premium **tuna** broken up into chunks.

In a starlike fashion arrange....1 section of **whole green bean salad**, 1 section of sliced **pimentos**, 1 section of quartered **ripe tomatoes**, 1 section of **French potato salad** made of oil and vinegar dressing (like the German salad), a section of quartered **hard boiled eggs**, garnished with a few **anchovies and capers and onion rings**. Pour vinaigrette over the whole salad and sprinkle with fine chopped **scallions**. Artichokes are an option.

Serve with French bread.

Wine: A nice Rose D'Anjou or a Sauterne

STUFFED EGGS

Boil **eggs** for 15 minutes. Cool, peel and cut in half. Take out the yolks and with a tablespoon, press yolks through a sieve (a few yolks can get lost in the food processor and it omits cleaning). Mix yolks with **mayonnaise, pepper, salt, some mustard and a trace of cayenne**. Fill this in the 'egg boats' using a small spoon or a small pastry bag with a star tip. Garnish with a **parsley leaf, a caper or piece of pimento**.

Francois Boeres, Chef de Cuisine

ASPARAGUS SALAD

Use whole white or green can **asparagus**. Strain asparagus and place in an oval dish laid out with **lettuce leaves**. Top with an oil and vinegar **"vinaigrette"**. Garnish with slices or ribbons of **pimento and chopped parsley**.

—

Cut cubes of **cheddar or similar cheese**. Serve on a tray with toothpicks.

—

Mix **sour cream, cream cheese with dry onion soup mix** and let stand for half an hour before serving with **toasts, crackers or Taco chips**.

—

Mix **cream cheese** with **chopped olives, pimentos and crisp fried chopped up bacon** (some bacon fat can be added).

—

Use leftover **chicken** to make chicken salad. Mix with **spices, minced celery, minced pimentos and mayonnaise**. Also tuna can be made the same.

STUFFED CHERRY TOMATOES
25 - 35 servings

Cut off a small tip (lid) from cherry tomatoes and save. With the smallest measuring spoon, (1/4 size) spoon out and remove 'pulp'. Sprinkle inside of tomatoes with a little **salt**. Fill with the 'stuffing' and cover tomatoes with the 'lid'. Serve on a tray.

The Stuffing:

Use 1-3/4 cups of **real crabmeat**. If imitation crabmeat, chop into little bits. Add 1/3 stalk of **celery**, peeled and chopped fine. 1/2 cup **mayonnaise**, dash of **Dijon mustard**, dash of **hot sauce (Tabasco), pepper and salt** to taste, 2 tsp. of **hamburger relish**.

Now we can prepare a few of these "things" quick and savvy. Your guests will be astonished if you bring them a nice platter out of "nowhere", filled with stuffed eggs, celery, rolled ham, chicken or tuna stuffed tomato, potato salads, sliced cucumber salad, carrot salad, olives, Swedish meatballs and a "carnival" of other goodies.

If they like what you made them, just tell them you bought this book from Francois! O.K.! I will be deeply grateful and love you for it. But remember that the word "love" was the greatest ingredient you added to all the cooking!

I wish you all a

cheerful and healthy

Bon Appetit

Francois Boeres, Chef de Cuisine

APPENDIX

CONSPIRACY AND INCREDULOUS SORCERY: THE GREAT CONSPIRACY AND ASSAULT ON OUR FOOD

O.K., so you try hard to be good parents and are concerned about your health and that of your family. You play golf, go skiing or fishing with the kids. You want them to be good, smart and healthy in body, soul and spirit. You pay attention to what kind of friends they hang out with, you know, look out for drugs and all that. Then you maybe unintentionally give them bad, adulterated, or maybe radiated food that much later can cause big problems and make them so sick that they need drugs by prescription ...then probably too late. In wartime, I had to eat a lot of "ersatz" (substitutes) and other "finagled" concoctions, but we don't have to. There is so much good food around in our country that can be made healthy and wholesome. We don't have to go to the extreme and surpass the stage of food "conversion" so as to accelerate us further into disaster. (There is a thin wall between sanity and insanity). We now have reached dangerous boundaries that had been required to grow food profitably and marketably. But if we reach the outer limits, how much can we take? Can we afford to experiment with so much at stake?

Over the years, many good things had to make room and were replaced with "ersatz" for the sake of convenience, progress and big profits. Newer generations never had seen or experienced the many good things that have been replaced. So, if anyone ever had seen or known otherwise, they probably never know the difference, so on the way, we have thrown out

HIS-STORY of Good Cooking

the baby with the bath water. You know, to a crow, a buzzard looks like an eagle if no eagles are around!

Some people will say that we have no control in this matter, that this is the way of the world. Don't let anyone be intimidated. Be in control! Demand wholesome food and don't settle for less. It's your life, it's your family. Stand up, go to meetings, organize groups, parties, promotions, talk to friends, ask questions, read labels. Is my food safe or is it irradiated? That can eventually lead to low resistance in your body because you are killing all that fights your sicknesses. Was food exposed to harmful gasses in transport? Or chemically threatened with already too many alterations? If it's "junky" don't buy it. Learn to return items that are bad, poor or unacceptable. Please! Don't say...." Oh well, it's not too much, can't bother, have no time for this." By accepting this attitude you have established another low standard for all of us. Persevere, demand your money refunded. By not doing so, all that we believe in may be gone tomorrow and probably get worse.

Quite often I have returned bad cheese, bread with big holes, strawy oranges, caked up flour, cracked eggs and other flim flam. It was not only the money, but a matter of principles. Now I won't hit all these people on the head that bring us our food. I'm amazed how they manage to bring us so much, so fast, for so many people, all year round. This was unimaginable in the old days.

Some identify people who demonstrate as militant activists. These people often fight for your rights. Maybe you should join them, if you have the courage. This courage once was demonstrated in our small community in Central New York, where we all opposed a nuclear dump site to be built on our farmland. In spite of all the odds against us, our commitment and perseverance prevailed and we won!

In old Europe, merchants who fooled around with the merchandise by cheating and diluting were severely punished. The baker got "dipped" (from an iron basket into the water), the butcher was often chased out of town. Presently we have a lot of "hoopla" about salt, fat, high cholesterol and all this. The most important thing is to eat wholesome food with good substance in moderate proportions, thoughtfully prepared and only served for Lunch and Dinnertime. Fooling around all day eating this and that should be avoided. This eventually can lead to an unhealthy, obese and

Francois Boeres, Chef de Cuisine

dangerous life. Also alcohol and other spirits should be respected and served to enhance the "dinner table" without abuse, just like a good companion.

The best food still is the one you cook at home, yourself....from the start with time and love. There also is nothing closer than a family sitting together at the table, getting to know about good food, engaged in close conversation. And if I don't know anything about cooking and eating by now, I sure would like to have all my apprentice and culinary school money reimbursed!

THE GROUNDWORK OF ALL

HAPPINESS IS HEALTH

Hunt

TODAY IS THE LAST TIME

TONIGHT WILL HAPPEN

WHAT ARE YOU WAITING FOR?

DON'T JUST STAND THERE!

GET IN THE KITCHEN
Finis

Many wines are recommended with recipes.

There are about 330 recipes in this book plus many not mentioned in this Index.

The "Supplementary Concoction" is our menu from the last week just to show you what a "Senior Citizen" budget can do. As you see ,there are no Lobsters or Filet Mignon here. The soups we usually had for lunch are included.

GOOD ANY DAY SOUP

On the high slopes, stony barren grounds, painted green with sedges and mat-grass, sporadically caressed by tempered winds from the sea makes the scenery of the Scottish highlands, a land unique, captivating, and remembered. Here, you will find Alpine pastures dotted with sheep feeding on young tender grass shoots. This is the land of Sir Walter Scott, Robert Burns, and Bonnie Prince Charlie, fine barley to make good beer and soups that stick to your ribs.

SCOTCH BARLEY SOUP

Have at hand one pound of lamb shoulder or neck cuts from beef.
In a big heavy pot, boil one cup of round barley in sufficient water with a pinch of salt. Add; crushed peppercorns, bay leaf, thyme, and a cut up carrot.
Cook for ten minutes.
Add all the meats, a cut up turnip, 2 cut up potatoes, one diced celery stalk, and a few small onions.
Simmer slowly for one hour, or till done. If necessary, add water. Traditionally this is served from the pot with bread on the side.

Francois Boeres, Chef de Cuisine

MONDAY DINNER
QUICK CELERY SOUP

In butter, sauté lightly one cut up onion, 4 cut up celery stalks, 2 medium potatoes, cut up. Cover with bouillon or chicken broth, add little salt, pepper, marjoram, dash of soy sauce. Cook slowly for one hour. Blend in a mixer, adding cream or butter.

CHICKEN BONNE FEMME for 2

In a heavy shallow casserole, sauté 4 medium size thighs (from smaller fryers) in a 2 tbs. cooking oil and 2 tbs. butter until light brown, adding

    2 pieces of bacon, cut up
    2 small quartered onions
    2 crushed garlic cloves,
    pinch salt
    one bay leaf
    1/4 tsp. sage
    1/4 tsp. rosemary

Sprinkle chicken with flour and paprika, saute golden ,cover with a light chicken stock, adding a whole carrot cut into sticks, 4 small onions, 2 medium size potatoes cut lengthwise into 4 pieces. Cover and cook for one hour until done, stirring occasionally. Reduce the sauce and serve in a terrine.

FLUMMERY DESSERT

Boil 1 and 3/4 cup water mixed with 1 and 3/4 cup milk 3/4 cup sugar, add one cup wheat farina. Stir constantly for four minutes adding one cup blanched raisins, almond extract and 3 egg yolks. Pour into a bowl and refrigerate. After cooling, turn the flummery over into a shallow dish. Garnish with sliced apricots, pineapple. Optional: drizzle with raspberry syrup.

HIS-STORY of Good Cooking

TUESDAY DINNER

DUTCH CONSOMME

To clarify broth quickly: On a low fire, boil lean beef bones with 1/2 cup lean ground beef in 2 quarts of water, salt, and one bay leaf. Set aside. Cool and skim off all the fat. Mix three egg whites with the shells. Add one fine chopped onion and two celery stalks. Mix this into the broth and slowly let it come to a boil. As the froth floats to the top, strain carefully through a clean, damp towel or cheesecloth.

To make the veal balls: take 1/2 pound veal shoulder steaks and cut in small cubes. Chop these fine in a mixer or a meat grinder. Add: one slice of bread soaked in milk, two beaten egg whites, 1/4 teaspoon onion powder, 1/4 teaspoon salt, pepper to taste, 1/2 teaspoon thyme, basil, and chopped parsley. Add a little flour. (To test, drop a veal ball into the simmering consommé. If it is too soft, add more flour.) Mix the veal mixture well, dip your hands in flour and shape the veal into one-inch balls. Simmer them in the consommé until done. Serve in a soup bowl with chopped scallions for garnish.

WHOLE MACARONIES or BUCATINIES MILANAISE

In plenty of water, with a pinch of salt and a teaspoon of oil added, boil pasta until soft, strain and rinse. In a casserole, sauté two fine crushed garlic cloves in olive oil and butter, with salt and pepper. Pour in the pasta, adding sour cream and grated Parmesan. Stir well. Top with Italian parsley. For a vegetable side dish, serve blanched broccoli and roasted red peppers.

DESSERT

Raspberry sherbet with round gaufrettes

WEDNESDAY DINNER
BAR HARBOR FISH CHOWDER

Have at hand: 3/4 pound of fresh haddock and six ounces small shrimp. In a large saucepan: render 3 oz. diced salt pork. Add, all cut into small cubes: 2 onions, one small green pepper, one stalk celery, diced Idaho

Francois Boeres, Chef de Cuisine

potato, one bay leaf, 1/4 tsp. thyme. Pour in; 1 pint water mixed with 1 pint milk, a pinch of salt, a pinch of pepper, and 2 garlic cloves. Cook for 3/4 an hour, then drop in the haddock, cover and cook slowly till done. Before serving, break up the fish into small pieces, add all the shrimps and a cup of cream, let it come to a boil and add just enough dissolved cornstarch to thicken slightly.

ALPINE PORK SCHNITZELS WITH LEMONS

Take close to a pound of selected rib or nice shoulder steaks. Pound them flat, sprinkle with salt, pepper, and trace of celery weed. Now, dip in flour, egg wash and fresh ground bread-crumbs, tap and shake them well. Fry schnitzels lightly in oil until done and golden. Last, add butter, lemon juice, and parsley. Dress on a platter and pour the butter sauce over the schnitzels. Garnish with lemon wheels.

Serve with whole green beans, fresh mushrooms and English style boiled potatoes topped with crisp bacon bits.

DESSERT

Strawberry shortcake with whipped cream or baked cinnamon apples in white wine.

THURSDAY DINNER
CHINESE EGG DROP SOUP

Make a strong chicken broth using one chicken breast with a few necks in one quart and a half of water. Boil this for one hour, strain and remove all the fat. This makes about one quart. In this broth, cook a few Chinese noodles. Add the chicken breast cut into small strips, chopped up scallions, salt to taste, a dash of soy sauce and some sherry. Last, slowly stir in 2 shirred eggs so they look like big flakes.

SIRLOIN TERIYAKI for two

Make a marinade of fresh ground pepper, ground ginger, fine chopped garlic, cooking oil, a dash of sugar, dry sherry wine, and soy sauce. Tenderize a big sirloin steak in the marinade for one hour. Remove and dry the steak from the marinade. Broil on high temperature in a frying pan or on the BBQ Grill to your preference. Deglaze pan with a little beef stock and add to the marinade. On a board, cut sirloin steak diagonally into slices (London Broil style) Try to save all the drippings. Arrange neatly on a warm platter. Last, pour over the marinade.

Serve with steamed short grain rice and snow peas with fried peppers.

DESSERT

A fresh fruit medley of steamed pears, apricots, sections of pineapple, dark cherries, mandarin orange sections, sugar, chopped crystallized ginger and walnuts.

FRIDAY DINNER

As a boy I got very ill staying in a parochial school in "Remich", Luxembourg. Here a "Sister" fed me one of the best tomato soup ever. (I soon recovered) They still make this soup today. Thanks "Sister"!

A GREAT TOMATO SOUP

In a pot with butter or margarine, glaze one medium chopped onion, one crushed garlic clove. Add 3 crushed ripe tomatoes (or a 14 oz can of Italian tomatoes) One 8 oz can tomato puree, two cups of bouillon, cut carrot, celery salt, marjoram, pepper. Cook for one hour and blend trough a mixer. Last, add ½ can of tomato paste, few drops of Tabasco, some "Maggi" (soy sauce) and a cup of cream.

Optional: cilantro, butter and croutons.

OVEN BAKED SCROD OR HADDOCK

Pour some oil into a fireproof serving dish and lay in the fish marked into portions (about ½ pound per serving). Add some white wine and two

Francois Boeres, Chef de Cuisine

lemon wheels. Sprinkle with a mixture of breadcrumbs, marjoram, paprika, savory, dill seeds and fresh parsley. Cover with melted butter or olive oil. Oven broil at 300 or till done. Don't over cook! Garnish with lemon wheels dipped in parsley. Optional: medium size shrimps.

Serve with mashed potatoes and Boston lettuce with artichokes

DESSERT
SOUTHERN LEMON PIE

Have at hand one 8-inch graham cracker pie shell, home made or from the store.

Mix: one can of sweet condensed milk,
    2 tbs sugar
    ½ cup lemon juice
    grated rind of a lemon
    2 eggs separated

Mix and beat well: the milk, juice, rinds, sugar, egg yolks, and one tsp of dissolved cornstarch.

Beat egg white until it forms peaks. Add some sugar and a pinch of cream of tartar. Pour the "filling" into the Graham pie shell and cover with the meringue (egg white). Bake in 300 preheated oven for ten minutes or until done. Cool in the refrigerator.

SATURDAY DINNER
CARROT BISQUE

In a pot, with butter or bacon fat, sauté one cup up onion and ½ celery stalk, chopped fine. Pour in 4 cups of light chicken broth, ½ cup tomato or V-8 juice, 4 big carrots cut into small wheels.

Add: salt, pepper, trace of ginger. Simmer for one hour and blend fine in a mixer. It should be thick, If not, reduce by slowly cooking a bit more. Serve with heavy cream or butter.

OVEN BROILED CORNISH HENS

A smaller hen per person is a good portion.
A slightly heavier hen can serve two.

Take out innards if any, clean and bend wings backwards. Sprinkle in the cavity a mixture of coriander, cardamom, turmeric, celery seeds, 2 orange wheels, (save the rest for garnish).

Place hens in a roasting pan, sprinkle with salt and pepper. Top with melted margarine and a slice of bacon. Surround the hens with cut up onions, carrot and two crushed garlic cloves. Oven broil hens at 350 for 1 and 3/4 hours or till they have a crisp skin. Baste often, adding some water or wine if needed. Dress on a serving platter and keep warm. Deglaze pan to make the sauce, adding a little broth or water, boil and thicken slightly with corn starch, strain and serve sauce on the side. Use a poultry shear to portion hens on the table. Serve with Parisian potatoes (inquire within). Acorn squash cut in half, seeds removed and filled with brown sugar and butter are suitable to this dish. The squash takes over an hour to cook so place them in the oven a half hour later with the hens.

DESSERT

CREME CARAMEL

Have at hand about 8 custard cups
Place cups in a pan (like a small roasting pan) in 1 inch hot water.
In a heavy saucepan pour 3/4 cup of sugar and water to make it "runny." Over a good fire, swirl pan around until sugar is caramelized and brown. Divide caramel into the cups (Please, do this carefully.)

In a mixer, beat four large eggs and four yolks with 3/4 cup sugar, vanilla, a little salt. Then, in a stream, beat in 3 and ½ cups of preheated milk. Divide into all the cups, place pan with the custards in the preheated 350 oven, takes about 40 minutes. Test by inserting a knife into the custard, it should come out "clean."

Take the custards from the pan, cool and refrigerate. Loosen custards around the edge with a knife and serve caramel side up. Top with rum or whipped cream.

Francois Boeres, Chef de Cuisine

SUNDAY DINNER

NOVA SCOTIA CHEDDAR SOUP

Make enough thin white sauce (Béchamel) for your soup, adding a little salt, white pepper, bay leaf, mace and a pinch of mustard. Slowly cook for a while, then stir in the grated cheddar. Top with rendered pieces of bacon and sour cream.

Serve with small buttered croutons and parsley. Sherry wine may be added.

Choose:

GIGOT (LEG OF LAMB) SADDLE or CROWN ROAST

Ask the butcher to prepare the Crown Roast to shape the crown (16 plus.. chops per crown) by tying and sawing it firm or using the spring band from a cake form. Insert a few garlic cloves in to the roast, cover the bones with aluminum foil. A crown roast takes about one to one and a quarter hours at 325 for rare.

Cover and rub all roasts with a mixture of salt, crushed pepper, thyme, oregano, rosemary, and basil. Roast Saddle in a preheated 475 oven for 15 minutes, then reduce to 425 basting occasionally for about 45 more minutes or to your preference. The meat should be red at the center. A leg of lamb takes about 1 and ½ hours. Deglaze the pan to make the jus and let the roast rest some before serving.

Serve with **Chateau Potatoes** (blanched potatoes trimmed lengthwise, cut in four pieces and oven roasted),whole green beans sautéed in butter and almonds.

DESSERT

Thin French crepes with fried bananas topped with a hot sauce of butter, fresh orange juice, sugar and whiskey.

BIBLIOGRAPHY

of Notes and References

Le Petit La Rousse and La Rousse Gastronomique
History of the World, Volume 1898 by Ridpath
History of the United States; 1877 by Ridpath
The Outline of History; by H. G. Wells
Frederick the Great and His Court; 1866 by L. Muhlbach
I Knew the Washingtons; 1865 Translated by Radziwill
Scribners Encyclopedia Britannia; 1875
The American Revolution in New York; S.U.N.Y. 1926
The Young Housekeepers Friend; 1859, by Mrs. Cornelius
Wild und Hund; 1937-42 and Das Moselland; 1939-1942
The Harp of Thousand Strings; 1855

Le Portefeuille L'AMERIQUE' Mazure; 1839**Notes**

INDEX

Index

Beef

Carpaccio	162
Chop Suey	208
Curry	242
Gumbo	177
Korean Yuk-whe	165
Marinade	185
Meatballs	253
Meatloaf	200
Mixed Grill	172
Pot au Feu	119, 125, 126
Prime Rib	182
Prime Ribs Deviled	226
Ragout	13, 102, 215
Roasting	183
Salad	138, 145
Salpicon	13, 14, 102, 232
Sauerbraten	185
Steak, Minute	148
steak au Poivre	205
Steak Henry IV	12
Tongue	234

Cheese

Clabber	46
Cottage	117
Creme Fraiche	37
Curds	114
Fondue, Belgian	53
Fondue, Swiss	139
Mozarella	116
Parsi	236
Paska	113
Rarebit	253

Desserts

Brandy Sauce	239
Cafe Diablo	226
Carrots, Indian	243
Chocolate Mousse	86
Coffee Glacee	82, 85
Creme, Caramel	86
Custard, Cream	80
Custard, Pudding	79
Custard, Rum	80
Election Cake	38
Floating Island	79
Flummery	67
Gaufrettes	85
Genoise	83
Indian Pudding	20
Melba Sauce	84
Meringue	81
Pear Helene	85
Pizelles (Gaufres)	85
Plum Pudding	238
Popovers	184
Puff Pastry-Cream	83
Puff Pastry-Light	82
Sally Lunn	74
Syllabub	50
Trifle	79
Whipped Cream	11

Eggs

Mexican Omelet	176
Omelettes	176
Stuffed Omelette	176

Fish

Bass, Papiotte	25
Bouillabaisse	246
Cacciucco	248
Cioppino	247
Clams, Casino	23
Clams, Deviled	227
Coquille St. Jacques	206
Crab Bake Gumbo	177
Crab Cakes	180
Deviled Bass	227
Dumplings	117
Escargots	205
Friture	137
Herrings marinated	150
Herrings Roll Mops	150
Lobster Americaine	188
Lobster Thermidor	186
Lox - Salmon	163
Mussels Mariniere	24

Oysters
- Angels on Horseback ... 27
- Half Shell ... 26
- Hangtown ... 24
- Mediatrice ... 28
- Poulette ... 27
- Rockefeller ... 27

Paella	244
Perch	136
Pike	136
Pompano Papiotte	25
Salmon, Marinated	163
Scallops, Broiled	24
Scallops, Marinated	165
Seviche	162
Shrimp Bisque	99
Shrimp Creole	177
Shrimp Gumbo	177
Sole, Dover	158
Sole, Pirate	28

Hors D' Oeuvres

Asparagus	93, 256
Beef Salad	138
BLT	251
Celery, Stuffed	250
Celery Knob Salad	94
Crab Louis	254
Cucumber Salad	252
Curred Eggs	240
Eggs, Stuffed	255
Guacamole	254
Herring, Marinated	150
Herring, Roll Mops	150
Liver Paté	41
Macaroni Salad	252
Mushrooms, Stuffed	252
Mushrooms a la Greek	251
Potato Salad, German	253
Potato Salad, Mayo	253
Salad Panache	92
Sandwich, Philly	76
Stuffed, Puffballs	229
Stuffed Tomatoes	236, 254
Thousand Island Dressing	254
Tomato Salad	91
Yogurt Salad	94

How to Make

Blanc-Mange	66
Bread	59
Bread Stuffing	73
Brine for Ham	45
Brunoise	188
Buffalo Wings	251
Butchering	214

Cheeses	113
Clarify Stock and Consomme	102
Clean Copper Pots	166
Country Bread	59
Enchiladas	250
Gelatin	46
Ice Cream	68
Indian Pudding	20
Larding	214
Lobster Coulis	99
Marinade	164
Pickle and Cure Ham	45
Preserve in Pressure Cooker	48
Preserve Pickles	48
Preserving Food	47
Profiteroles	84
Smoked Ham	45
Soap	167
Vinaigrette	94
Yeast for Bread	47

Innards

Brain Cervelle	233
Chicken Livers	126
Kidneys, Veal, Beef	232
Liver Dumplings	112
Sweetbreads, Calf	232
Tongue	234
Tripe a la mode	231

Lamb and Mutton

Curried Lamb	239
Madras Stew	244
Mutton	36
Rogen Dschausch	239
Stuffed Tomatoes, Indian	236

Mixed Drinks

Artillery Punch	54
Mint Julep, Kentucky	50
Mint Julep, Quick	50
Mulled Wine	51
Porter	50
Port Wine	50
Rum Fustian	50
Rum Loggerhead	50
Sack Posset	50
Sangria	53
Syllabulb	50
Wassail - Common	51
Wassail - with Tea	52
Wassail - with Wine	52

Pasta

Cannelloni	110
Gnocchi	110
Linguini	191
Noodle Dough	109
Spaetzle	109

Pork

Alentenyana	178
Blood Sausages	44
Brine for Ham	45
Denver Club Sandwich	230
Hacksen, Hot and Cold	137, 138
Head Cheese	46
Nasi Goreng	242
Scrapple	46
Smoked Ham	45
Sweet and Pungent	208
Tenderloin Garcia	179
Tenderloin Omega	178

Potatoes

Baked	184

Croquettes................................89
Duchesse................................191
Dumplings 111
French Fries 148
Kloesse...................................111
Mashed Potatoes 266
Pancakes 149
Parisienne...............................153
Souffle....................................154

Poultry
Bouchee a la Reine 114
Cantonese Duck 209
Chicken Bombay 241
Chow Mein Chicken...............210
Cocks Combs 14
Cornish Hen Bombay 241
Creole Gumbo, Chicken 177
Diablo Grilled Chicken...........228
Duck Salmis.............................15
Goose, Roasted 42
Goose, Stuffed 42
Goram Masala Chicken 241
Nasi Goreng Chicken..............242
Nouhgen Niam Chicken 240
Paella 244
Pheasants, Salmis.....................16
Poultry Seasoning 73
Red Salpicon 14
Turkey Roasted with
   Apple Stuffing 72
   Chestnut Stuffing................. 72
White salpicon 13

Relishes
Chutney..................................239
Mango Relish.........................237
Onion-Red 237

Rice
Cajun......................................180
Risotto Milanaise...................246
Saffron 238
Steamed 179
Wild 219

Sauces
Allemande..............................104
Armoricaine 118
Bechamel 103, 115
Bernaise.................................106
Bordelaise..............................101
Brown Stock 100
Burgundy 140
Chicken Stock........................103
Cumberland 73
Diablo 101
Dijon Honey 93
Duxelle...................................104
Espagnole...............................101
Hollandaise 105
Horseradish............................140
Italian Tomato 192
Lobster Coulis.........................99
Lyonnaise 104
Madeira..................................101
Mornay...................................104
Nantua....................................104
Parisienne...............................104
Romesco Coulis.....................166
Soubise 104
Supreme 104
Veloutee 103
White Sauces 102
Yogurt......................................94

Soups

Bean 116
Clam Chowder 25
Country Campaigne 123
Gulyas 120
Health 156
Macedonia, Cold 102
Onion 204
Pea 118
Potato Leek 98
Shrimp Bisque 99

Veal
Braggioles 17
Cordon Bleu 119
Jeagerschnitzel 189
Ossi Bucchi 190
Paupiettes 17
Salpicon, Red and White 13, 14
Scallopini 191
Wienerschnitzel 189

Vegetables
Asparagus 93
Beans 88
Belgine Endive 91
Brussel Sprouts 96
Cabbage, Rumpledethumps 117
Cabbage Meal 117
Carrots Vichy 97
Cauliflower 96
Celeraic, Cooked 94
Celeraic, Marinated 94
Eggplant, Stuffed 186
Eggplant Rolls 192
Fava Beans 96
Green Beans 96
Kohlrabi 98
Parsnips 95

Peas 88
Ratatouille 95
Squash, Acorn 221, 267
Squash, India 244
Squash, Indian 244
Stuffed Cabbage 97
Tomato Salad 91
Turnips 95, 98

Venison and Wild Game
Canapes, Liver 222
Deer Saddle 222
Deer Stew 220
Duckling, Wild 218
Grouse, Roasted 217
Hassenpfeffer 215
Larding 214
Marinade 215
Partridge, Roasted 217
Pheasants 220
Pigeons 217
Quails 219, 222
Snipes, Roasted 221
Venison Leg 218
Venison Ragout 220
Venison Saddle 223

About the Author

Francois Boeres was born in Luxembourg in a time peoples learned their craft through years of apprenticeship from the ground up to be worthy and proud professionals.

Here, the author not only writes about tantalizing fares, but also about His Life-Story of hard times through war, of good times and times of the past in Cookery.

His experience in 53 years of cooking in fine hotels and restaurants gives testimony how it was done and doing so, will be most enjoyable and good tasting.

Francois had worked in the States as a Chef and Executive Chef in country clubs and resorts, later to open his own 3 Star Continental Restaurant in Central New York. Some years ago, the Boeres family moved from Putnam, NY to their 100 acre 178 year old farm in Cortland, NY. Francois also is a veteran of the NATO Army.

Printed in the United States
22191LVS00003B/208-228